# MIDNIGHT LUNCH

# MIDNIGHT
# LUNCH

## THE 4 PHASES OF TEAM COLLABORATION SUCCESS FROM THOMAS EDISON'S LAB

# SARAH MILLER CALDICOTT

**WILEY**

John Wiley & Sons, Inc.

Published by John Wiley & Sons, Inc., Hoboken, New Jersey.
Published simultaneously in Canada.

For general information on our other products and services or for technical support, please contact our Customer Care Department within the United States at (800) 762-2974, outside the United States at (317) 572-3993 or fax (317) 572-4002.

Wiley publishes in a variety of print and electronic formats and by print-on-demand. Some material included with standard print versions of this book may not be included in e-books or in print-on-demand. If this book refers to media such as a CD or DVD that is not included in the version you purchased, you may download this material at http://booksupport.wiley.com. For more information about Wiley products, visit www.wiley.com.

ISBN: 978-1-118-40786-8 (cloth)
ISBN: 978-1-118-41785-0 (ebk)
ISBN: 978-1-118-42196-3 (ebk)
ISBN: 978-1-118-43447-5 (ebk)

Printed in the United States of America
10  9  8  7  6  5  4  3  2  1

*With deepest love to my husband, Wayne*

*When you honor me, you are also honoring the vast army of workers but for whom my work would have gone for nothing.*

—Thomas Alva Edison

# Contents

# Contents

# Contents

# Foreword

I first met Sarah following a speech she delivered in 2011 at a high-level innovation leadership conference hosted by Kraft. I was immediately struck by the relevance of her teachings. As a cofounder of Brightidea, a company that focuses on tools to harness innovation, I was captivated by Sarah's presentation. Her understanding of innovation practices used by Thomas Edison, and the links between those practices and today's urgent need to continually innovate, sheds light on how some of the world's most revolutionary inventions came to be. And critically, how Edison's practices might be successfully contemporized and translated today.

In *Midnight Lunch*, Sarah brings Edison's timeless collaboration formula to the fore. She advances our understanding of the rapidly changing innovation environment by providing deep insight into Edison's proven collaboration processes. Importantly, her teachings allow innovation practitioners to apply those proven practices in the digital era. Sarah notes that Edison emphasized collaboration as a discovery learning process, which served as the backbone of his innovation efforts. Rather than adopting a classroom-focused or task-focused orientation, collaboration for Edison was highly hands on, experiential, and project-driven. His teams learned through interaction with their colleagues, allowing them to unlock their own innate creativity and enhance ideas through collaborative adaptation. Sarah shows us how to inject Edison's undeniably brilliant insight into the collaborative process.

Sarah's insights could not come at a better time. Those companies that successfully innovate continue to flourish. But companies that fail to innovate risk their very survival. Almost 50 percent of companies that made the 1999 Fortune 500 list (238 companies to be exact) were absent from the 2009 list due to dramatic falls in revenues. Extend that history, and the results become even more onerous: only 71 companies listed as part of the original 1955 Fortune 500 have survived to grace today's 500. The world has become a tougher place, and the corporate playing field is littered with companies that failed to make the grade through successful innovation. I think of Blockbuster, Eastman Kodak Company, Borders, and Hostess Brands as recent examples. To survive, companies can no longer rely on past successes. Rather, surviving in an ever-changing global economy requires continual, effective, culturally embedded innovation and collaboration approaches.

Sarah describes Edison's collaboration process as being composed of four interlocking phases: capacity, context, coherence, and complexity. One thread running through the phases is an intriguing discussion of metalogue, a method of inquiry for exploring diverse conversations and the context around those conversations. Sarah speaks to the emerging role of technological advancements and digital links among teams around the world as a component of metalogue, allowing companies to activate innovation and collaboration in rapid and scalable ways. Sarah's comments about this process align with our own experience developing the Innovation Grid, a concept championed at Brightidea. A platform now touching almost every part of the world, the grid creates online channels of deep communication and collaboration, resulting in a marketplace of new ideas. The grid also provides methods to predictably repeat the innovation process by allowing companies to focus collaborators in many different geographies, from start-ups like Kickstarter and 99Designs, to established companies such as GE and P&G, which are fostering open innovation.

But where does collaboration come from? How do companies develop collaborative structures that help drive future brand loyalty, market share, and profitability? The innovation process is a creative activity. What Edison seems to have realized is that, first, everyone is creative and, second, that if properly nurtured, the most important assets of a company—its employees and customers—can generate a constant stream of good ideas that connect to needs. To do so, companies must develop a culture that nurtures creativity, addresses customer needs, and strives to apply the good ideas that percolate upward like so many diamonds. People can be taught to innovate. They can be taught to recognize the creative gifts that they have been given and to apply those gifts. As Edison shows us, what they need is leadership, a collegial environment, and inspired direction.

In recent years, the infrastructure to frame, nurture, and positively motivate innovation has significantly improved. Companies no longer need just a factory floor, a research and development (R&D) department, or a physical data center to innovate. Instead, as Sarah reveals in *Midnight Lunch*, we are finding new ways to link internal resources like these to external networks, jointly creating new context for solutions and new smart networks. In essence, we are innovating ways in which we all innovate. Online collaboration, social media innovation processes, and cloud-based capabilities allow companies to reach out to employees, customers, and other stakeholders to encourage creativity, explore needs, and foster idea generation within a focused framework. Using the smart layers that Sarah describes in the complexity phase, for example, it's now possible to track a variety of innovation metrics from idea generation to social interactions to implementation rates and a host of other insights, all wrapped around a particular product, service, or challenge-focused topic.

If Edison were alive today, he would be fascinated by the evolution of the innovation process. Using new combinations of human capital and technology, we enjoy higher levels of innovation predictability—outcomes Edison would have applauded. Edison would revel in the Internet as a method of encouraging collaboration in ways never before possible, approaches that allow tens of thousands of collaborators to connect to a single live team. But despite the opportunities that the Internet offers, Edison would still insist that collaboration must have a human core. Focused conversations, leadership, and human interaction are necessary to produce great, successful, market-changing ideas.

Sarah understands the deep, inner workings of this process. She deftly delves into Edison's true collaboration formula, empowering companies to better use collaboration as a disruptive tool. *Midnight Lunch* offers a fitting and timely message that sets the stage for individuals and companies to incorporate collaboration into an innovation framework, delivering powerful results that drive competitive advantage, disruptive business models and technologies, and long-term success in challenging times.

—**Matthew Greeley**
Chief executive officer and cofounder, Brightidea

# Acknowledgments

An entire constellation of people contributed to the thinking behind *Midnight Lunch*.

My deep thanks to the innovators who prompted me to delve more deeply into Edison's collaboration methods, seeking to trace applications between his genius and the pressing needs of the twenty-first century: Harun Asad, Kevin Bennet, Buckley Brinkman, Dr. Jacqueline Byrd, Dr. Curt Carlson, Dr. Jean Egmon, Pia Erkinheimo, Art Fry, Ted Grabau, Matthew Greeley, Richard Guha, Anthony Gyursanszky, Verne Harnish, Larry Keeley, Braden Kelley, Renu Kulkarni, Ray Kurzweil, Dr. Robert Langer, Wayne Lindholm, Robert Lowe, Moises Norena, Richard Perrin, Chuck Peters, Carol Phillips, Robert W. Schmidt, Maria Thompson, and Rishad Tobaccowala.

I'm also grateful to the many business leaders who offered their insights into key specialty areas that directly link to collaboration and shared their thoughts on how teams affect the role of leadership in a collaborative setting: Tom Barwin, Guy Blissett, Vincent Carbone, John Copenhaver, Greg Cox, Emily DeRocco, Dr. Ashok Patel, Jay Scherer, Jason Sherman, Daryl Travis, Craig Wortmann, and Jim Ziganto.

## ACKNOWLEDGMENTS

In addition, of huge importance were the individuals who served as resources for historical references to Edison's life and legacy and the power of his ideas, which endure undiminished even now. A big thank-you to Michele Wehrwein Albion, whose seminal book *The Quotable Edison* served as a font of historically verified quotes from Edison. I also wish to deeply acknowledge the contributions of Leonard DeGraaf, Dr. Paul Israel, Rachel Weissenburger, *The Thomas A. Edison Papers* staff at Rutgers University, and The Thomas Edison National Historic Park staff.

My thanks to all those who assisted in compiling the manuscript for *Midnight Lunch*, both in its early and its later forms: Nina Fazio, Matt Holt, Adrianna Johnson, Linda Kooper, Elizabeth Londo, Stanton B. Miller III, Susan Moran, and Janelle Noble. I would also like to specially acknowledge Michael J. Gelb, coauthor of my first book, *Innovate Like Edison*, who encouraged me to keep writing.

And a final word of gratitude to my children, Nicholas and Connor, for spurring me on in the quest to keep the Edison legacy alive in our family, bringing his thinking to a new generation of innovative and collaborative leaders.

# Introduction

When we call Thomas Edison to mind, our first thought is of a brilliant inventor and innovator whose creations transformed modern life. We often think of him toiling away in a laboratory all by himself, long into the wee hours of the morning.

And yet, we rarely consider the role that collaboration played in Edison's world-changing success. Tangled in the lore of the lone American inventor, our mind's eye conjures up Edison's spray of white hair and his signature bow tie, quickly ascribing his 1,093 US patents to innate genius.

Tempting as it is to sustain this image of Edison, it is inaccurate. In an age when many speak of Thomas Edison and Steve Jobs in the same breath, it's important to refresh our understanding of the pivotal role collaboration played in Edison's innovation prowess. He viewed collaboration as the beating heart of his laboratories, a sustaining resource that fueled the knowledge assets of his sprawling innovation empire.

Rising from humble beginnings, Edison was largely self-educated, pursuing his relentless passion for learning well into his seventies, when he taught himself botany. Deeply skilled in chemistry, telegraphy, acoustics, materials science, and electromechanics, Edison's thirst for discovery began in his early teens and never ceased. Like a magnetic force all its own, Edison's brainy leanings drew others to his quests, attracting bright colleagues with a huge diversity of skills.

From his earliest years renting space in workshops and small laboratories, Edison collaborated with others. Realizing the value of sharing his inspirations with people who held different skills than he did, Edison felt a unique bond with those who labored with him. After establishing his famed Menlo Park Laboratory at the age of 29, Edison journeyed from the failure of his first patented invention at age 22 to becoming a world-renowned inventor in just nine years, establishing collaboration practices that came to be a signature of his campus-style operations.

But this book is not intended to be a historic regurgitation of Edison's accomplishments. Rather, it aims to remind us of what is possible when we strive toward a purpose that unites us with others, providing a roadmap for how twenty-first century teams can become more collaborative. Edison's dedication to collaboration crystallizes what we are capable of at our best. His astonishing contributions inspire us to achieve more, to embrace more, to explore the richness of our mental capacities. Edison's achievements consistently defied the boundaries of what the scientific community believed was possible—indeed, what was believed to be humanly possible. *Midnight Lunch* challenges each reader to examine their professional or personal ambitions, reimagining what one person is capable of producing when working in true collaboration.

*Midnight Lunch* also offers a deeper view of the collaboration competency identified in my first book, *Innovate Like Edison: The Five-Step System for Breakthrough Business Success. Innovate Like Edison* explores what I call Edison's Five Competencies of Innovation, laying out the mindset, creative processes, work culture, value creation practices, and team engagement approaches Edison consistently applied. *Midnight Lunch* takes a step-by-step look at how collaboration served as the connective tissue binding Edison's masterful innovation process together, becoming its sinews, its tendons, and its very muscle fiber. Without the culture of collaboration he created, it is unlikely Edison could have achieved the breakthrough innovation success whose impact we still feel today.

The linkage between innovation and collaboration underscores why Edison's collaborative approach becomes such a relevant subject for us now. Given the increased scrutiny placed on the role of innovation as a driver of growth for every economy, whether emerging or developed, we must ask whether collaboration is also engaged. Like a symbiotic organism that can thrive only when its host is present, innovation can gain sustainable traction only when true collaboration also exists.

As you will read, we are living in what has been described as the third economic revolution in human history, dubbed by many as the Innovation Age. This massively transformational era is projected to last just 30 years, a period 10 times shorter than the Industrial Age, which preceded it. Perhaps even more challenging, 10 of those 30 years have already expired. At a time when inexpensive yet hugely powerful digital technologies rest at our fingertips, the Edisonian spirit calls us to maximize the brilliance and innate creativity that lies within each of us to tackle the major problems we face worldwide. Edison's timeless innovation and collaboration processes remind us that we can look at the next two decades as an era in which true collaboration can thrive, allowing us to mirror his passion for discovery learning and the thrill of conquering new frontiers.

The kinship I hold with the Edison legacy is a unique one. My great-great-aunt, Mina Miller, married Thomas Edison in 1886, when she was 20 years old and he was 39. As the daughter of an inventor, my great-great-grandfather,

Lewis Miller, Mina had glimmerings of the quirks and eccentricities that often accompany a brilliant mind. Her faithful love and companionship served as fuel for Edison's seemingly inexhaustible energy for work. My aim in *Midnight Lunch* is to propel this unique legacy into the Innovation Age, contemporizing methods that placed Edison ahead of his time even during the most fruitful era of US innovation. By delving into the collaboration practices of one of the world's foremost thinkers, we can all find new fuel for grappling with today's daunting global challenges.

If Edison were alive now, he would be harnessing the power of digital networks and smart devices to collaborate on a new scale. He would evangelize the notion of flat teams and flat organizations, philosophies he instituted in his own laboratories. Edison would remind us to find the value creation opportunities that emerge from asking new, probing questions and sending small, dedicated collaboration teams in search of the answers. As well, he would drive us forward—relentlessy.

This book endeavors to reveal the spirit and the collaboration practices Edison would bring us in the Innovation Age. His inventions touched more than half the people on the planet during his lifetime—and virtually every single person today. I hope you will use *Midnight Lunch* as a spur to transform your own beliefs about what is possible through collaboration and newly engage them in your daily endeavors.

—**Sarah Miller Caldicott**
Great-grandniece of Thomas Edison

**CHAPTER 1**

## What Is True Collaboration?

**G**ravity is one of the most pervasive forces in the universe. Physicists classify it among the most unique phenomena ever discovered, essential to shaping planets, stars, and solar systems. We recognize the impact of gravity everywhere—its pull on water coursing through riverbeds, its mastery of the wind whistling across sheer mountain slopes, and its ability to hold buildings, cars, and people on Earth's surface.

Gravity's more subtle properties, however, have caused it to be less studied. Gravity is relatively less understood by the scientific community than other forces.[1] When compared with the awesome power of fission, vividly demonstrated in an atomic bomb or an exploding star, gravity works softly, and with a more velvet hand.

Collaboration has shared a similar fate. Like gravity, collaboration is a pervasive force. It lies at the heart of what uniquely shapes teams and organizations. It connects people

1

to the vast power of their own knowledge and shines a light on the purpose of their work and their lives. Collaboration holds the power to link teams with diverse skills and traits, urging them to come together in an aligned way and yielding breakthroughs that can impact hundreds—even millions—of people.

Yet collaboration as a business force remains less visible than others dominating today's headlines. It feels less tangible than gyrations in stock or bond prices, less sexy than deals hammered out in a corporate merger. It doesn't rivet our attention like the jaw-dropping price tag of a hot Internet start-up.

But that is about to change.

In the next decade, as the planet absorbs the impact of a population topping 8 billion, we will see the entry on the global stage of a new, young workforce totaling in the hundreds of millions.[2] As cellular phones and smart technologies come within reach of more young minds in Brazil, Russia, India, Indonesia, China, and Africa, as well as the United States and other developed economies, unprecedented levels of connectivity will exist across the planet.[3] Like a giant pulsing brain, a new kind of collective intelligence will become possible by the end of the decade, redefining how knowledge networks operate and how microcosms of people drive value-creating activity across vast geographies as well as entire organizations. Rather than being an afterthought, *collaboration will underpin virtually every business practice that exists today.*

Rishad Tobaccowala, vice president (VP) of innovation at global media group VivaKi, puts it this way: "Among the top three things organizations must focus on right now are (1) staying relevant, (2) innovating, and (3) attracting and retaining talent. Collaboration is crucial to all three."[4] Greg Cox, president of the third largest network for Dale

Carnegie's vast global leadership training operations, echoes this view, emphasizing that collaboration is a surging phenomenon that will newly balance the skills of the individual with the power of collective action. "The future will not be based on individuals, but on extraordinary combinations of people."[5]

Are *you* ready to collaborate? Do the teams within your organization understand what it means to collaborate? Can you describe how you would harness collaboration to tap the emerging power of what has been termed the "next billion workers," or how you would position collaboration as a driver of value creation in your business? What structures are required to accelerate collaboration and link it to other practices? What barriers to collaboration exist that beg your attention?

This book addresses these questions, revealing the core skills and strategies you can begin using to master "true collaboration." *True collaboration*, a new term that embraces the research revealed throughout *Midnight Lunch*, can unlock the potential that lies not only within yourself but within every team in your organization. True collaboration can revolutionize the culture of your workplace or your community, connecting people through new types of team experiences that create collective knowledge and a commitment to shared purpose.

> Almost all important decisions are now made in teams, either directly or through the need for teams to translate individual decisions into action.
>
> **—*Peter Senge*, The Fifth Discipline**

True collaboration can transform the way you grow as an individual, the way teams in your organization innovate, the way teams connect with customers, and the way value is delivered in your operation both now and for the long term.

# IS IT TRUE COLLABORATION, OR IS IT A TEAM?

Part of where we go astray in our basic understanding of collaboration itself lies in our diverse definitions for *team*. At the most basic level, we recognize teams as groups of two or more people, working toward a shared outcome or common goal. But teams seem to be everywhere today. They pervade the world of sports. We see teams operating in local clubs, urban communities, and professional associations. Are they all really functioning the same way?

Part of our confusion surrounding teams also traces to an expanding ability for groups of people to operate remotely from one another. Today, people who don't live or work in the same geographic area can operate as a team by connecting online. Virtual team members can be 3, 30, 300, or even 3,000 miles apart from one another. In fact, a major 2011 study conducted by Forrester Consulting revealed that more than one-third of US companies are using virtual teams, with 40 percent of employees involved in some type of virtual team structure—a percentage expected to rise to 56 percent in the next three years.[6] However, many organizations are finding that distance becomes a relevant—and limiting—factor when team members are separated by more than three time zones, after which extensive use of smart technologies and social networks is needed to mitigate the gap.[7]

With team members operating in so many different environments, *are people actually collaborating?* Are they connecting in ways that magnify their individual skills? By having a Skype conference with colleagues halfway around the world, is true collaboration being engaged? If I'm using social media, am I collaborating?

And what about committees or task forces? What about new product development teams or accounting groups?

Or the fluid relationships between people in social networks? Do these teams represent true collaboration—or could they?

This book addresses these diverse questions and seeks to create a distinction between what we commonly understand as teamwork and the broader role of true collaboration as a core practice within an organization. It also lays out step by step how you can begin recalibrating your approach to collaboration itself, designing powerful teams that deliver deeper levels of creativity and productivity for the long term.

## TEAM A VERSUS TEAM B

To illustrate some of the key differences between teamwork and true collaboration, consider the example of a pair of two-person teams: Team A and Team B. Imagine they each have one member who is 5 feet tall and another who is 6 feet tall. Team A has been tasked with traveling together from one end of a football field to the other in less than 10 minutes. Team A's members respond by simply clasping hands and running side by side from one end zone to the other, easily achieving their goal of reaching the opposite end zone within the allotted time.

Now, imagine that Team B is given the same assignment. But Team B elects to travel the length of the field side by side in what is called a three-legged race. The left leg of one person must be bound to the right leg of the other person. Suddenly, unlike Team A, the members of Team B face a different context for running the length of the field. They must grasp each other's shoulders just to keep their balance. They must determine the best place to bind their legs together so that they can move in unison. Simply making a left-right-left-right running motion doesn't make sense any more. Even the height of the two individuals now becomes a factor in traversing the football field without falling down.

The members of Team B must actively talk, strategize, and use trial-and-error methods to move a mere 15 yards.

However, by the time Team B reaches the 50-yard line, they've discovered how to move more efficiently. They've learned how to leverage the resources of both the taller and the shorter team member. Picking up speed with each three-legged stride, Team B streaks to the finish line within the 10-minute time allotment.

What are the differences between how Team A and Team B operated in these two races? The teams each had identical goals—traveling 100 yards in 10 minutes—but they accomplished their objectives in completely different ways.

In Team A, the pair handled their assignment as a task. Each person's role was relatively uncomplicated and straightforward. Team A realized they could complete the challenge of running down the field with little additional thought or strategizing.

But Team B had to engage, to deeply connect, and verbally motivate each other just to make it to the 50-yard line. Although the goal of reaching the opposite end zone was spelled out just as it was for Team A, the specific steps needed to navigate their way to the opposite end zone weren't crystal clear. Team B had to discover the steps, learning as they progressed.

Although Team A indeed functioned as a team, each member "did his or her part" and no more. But Team B truly collaborated. Team B engaged in a discovery learning process that united them in a common, shared experience. Their efforts required motivation and determination. Team B encountered unexpected complexity in shifting the context of their thinking about what it meant to run or walk in a coordinated way, especially when two people of differing heights were bound together. Keeping their common goal in mind as they struggled to determine the best course of action, they created a unique coherence in their efforts, a kind of alignment that could actually be repeated the next time they had to run a three-legged race or coach someone else on how to do it.

> Collaboration is not the same thing as teamwork. Teamwork is simply doing your part. Collaboration involves leveraging the power of every individual to bring out each other's strengths and differences.
>
> —*Greg Cox, president and chief operating officer at Dale Carnegie, Chicago*

How can we harness the deeper learning generated by the shared experiences we see in Team B? Can this type of learning be developed on a larger scale? How can we engage a handful of people—or even scores of teams working together—in running their own form of the three-legged race? What would be the impact on an entire group of employees equipped with the skill sets to drive true collaboration, all working shoulder to shoulder?

Collaboration has been a tricky beast for organizations to tame. Operating as the "invisible glue" that brings together *discovery learning and performance in an environment of shared experience*, collaboration as a core practice has proved challenging to embrace. More than just "doing your part," Greg Cox, president of Chicago's robust Dale Carnegie training operation, comments that "collaboration involves leveraging each other's strengths and differences" when team members come together.[8]

In a world now absorbing the next billion workers, true collaboration will not be optional. Going forward, understanding how to capture the essence of the exchanges we saw in Team B rather than Team A will serve as the bedrock for the way people come together to innovate, develop new products and services, or design new business models or manufacturing capabilities. On a crowded planet, the collaboration skills of Team B will also be essential for governments and communities to function effectively.

A unique "superskill," true collaboration pairs the power of discovery learning with diverse relationship-building and leadership skills now gaining new prominence in today's business environment. As you will read further in Chapter 2, following the "global reset" that took place during the Great Recession of 2008, huge forces that operated within discrete domains we once described simply as research and development (R&D), marketing, and strategy are rapidly merging. They are taking new shape in the form of open innovation, customer-led development processes, and "smart" networked feedback mechanisms that move faster than typical annual planning cycles or cumbersome product design cycles. In a global business environment that increasingly values speed and nimble thinking to deliver breakthroughs, true collaboration now represents a superskill that will be fundamental for you and a high percentage of the individuals in your organization to possess. Less visible, and traditionally less valued, skills that marry the talents of the individual with interlocking webs of capability, such as data synthesis, leading and inspiring others, perceiving and communicating progress, and facilitating debate, will surge to the fore. No longer the province of nice to have, the superskill combinations present in true collaboration offer a new backbone for organizations to achieve high-impact results in the digital era.

This book offers insights into how you can inject true collaboration superskills into your operations and your own thinking. In the coming chapters you will learn about a process that leverages the innate creative capacities of the brain for developing context as well as for addressing complexity. You will learn how to leverage qualities that distinguish true collaboration from the more task-driven approaches that often

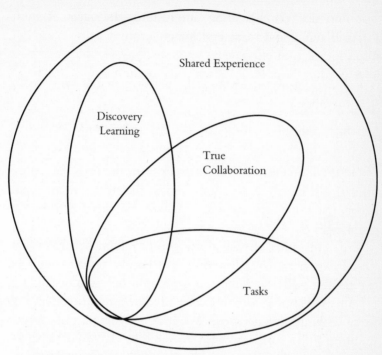

**Figure 1.1 True Collaboration Is the Nexus between Discovery Learning and Performance**

*Note:* True collaboration embraces a broad array of skills that leverage discovery learning and doing within a context of shared experience.

dominate team efforts. Figure 1.1 offers a visual illustration of how collaboration relates to discovery learning and shared experience, moving beyond the mere performance of tasks. In essence, rather than continuing to function like the members of Team A, you'll learn how to function like the members of Team B. True collaboration embraces:

- A discovery learning mindset versus a pure task orientation
- A belief in anticipating and creating rather merely reacting and responding

- Presence of inspiration across multiple facets of both individual and team endeavors
- Coherence of purpose
- A dedication to elevating the performance of every team member
- Connections to human and social networks of influence

Do these qualities sound different from the ones valued by your team? Do they draw upon ideas that feel new or seem broader than your current concept of what teamwork embraces?

True collaboration will allow you to reframe qualities that may have characterized many teams you've worked with in the past. It will also help you develop a new understanding for how collaborative groups can become a unique operating force within your enterprise. Whether you are part of a large, tradition-rich company with hierarchical layers or a small entrepreneurial endeavor, whether your organization is public or nonprofit, whether you are serving in an aging governmental body or an entrepreneurial operation still in its formative stages, *Midnight Lunch* offers a step-by-step guide for bringing true collaboration to the center of your efforts.

Collaboration allows us as individuals to understand something we didn't have the background knowledge to grasp before.

*—Art Fry, 3M Fellow and Technical Scientist,*
*Inventor of Post-it Notes*

The uniqueness underlying the backbone for true collaboration stems from its source: the world-changing teams of Thomas Alva Edison (1847–1931), one of history's foremost inventors and innovators. The recipient of an astounding 1,093 US patents and 1,293 international patents, Edison's vast innovation empire commanded an estimated $6.7 billion in market value by 1910, or roughly $100 billion today. Pioneering iconic products and services that we now view as central to the infrastructure of modern life—such as lighting, power, recorded sound, and storage batteries— the value of the markets and industries built on the shoulders of Edison's contributions exceeds an estimated $1 trillion globally.[9]

Consider the value-creation engines within your organization right now. From a standing start, could it drive billions of dollars in revenue annually . . . and continue to do so for 40 years? Does it have a backbone like Edison's true collaboration process to sustain it?

While Sergey Brin and Larry Page of Google along with leaders of Global 50 companies such as Apple would no doubt answer "yes" to this question, consider that Edison managed to drive billions of dollars in market value with fewer people and fewer resources than a Global 50 operation. A flat organization with an employee base that, at its height, numbered a few thousand rather than tens of thousands or hundreds of thousands, Edison's ability to deliver value has much to teach us about collaboration and value creation in an era when resource constraints represent the norm for many organizations, both public and nonprofit.

Like the connective tissue in the human body, Edison's true collaboration methods gave backbone, sinews, muscles, and tendons to his world-changing innovation process. Today, we can examine this connective tissue for timeless, value-driving approaches that bring new perspective to the growth and innovation efforts we seek in our digital world. With true collaboration as a force within your enterprise, you can build new capacity for capturing productivity growth from the next billion workers as well as achieve many other goals you envision for your organization.

## THOMAS EDISON MASTERED COLLABORATION AS A FORCE FOR SUCCESS

When you call Thomas Edison to mind, what mental image do you see? A man in a lab coat? An inventor toiling away, surrounded by disassembled machine parts and half-read books? An entrepreneurial guy who worked by himself? *Mindset* author and psychologist Dr. Carol Dweck, an expert on the role of images and their impact on our thought patterns, comments on the reaction she frequently gets when asking audiences this question: "What comes to mind when you think about Thomas Edison? What is he doing?" The standard response Dweck receives is revealing:[10]

> He's in New Jersey. He's standing in a white coat in a lab-type room. He's leaning over a light bulb. Suddenly, it works! . . . He's kind of a reclusive guy who likes to tinker on his own.

And yet, contrary to the perceptions we commonly hold of Thomas Edison, he was not a lone wolf inventor. Dr. Paul Israel, the world's leading expert on Thomas Edison today and director of *The Thomas A. Edison Papers* archives at Rutgers University, comments, "From the earliest days of his inventing endeavors, Edison worked collaboratively with others. Even before he became a world famous inventor through his achievements at the Menlo Park laboratory, Edison sought out like-minded colleagues who could aid him with materials, prototyping, and the invention process itself."[11] Edison fostered a spirit of true collaboration among the prototypers and machinists he sought out in his young adult years as a budding telegrapher and inventor. Throughout his career, he carried the belief that working in teams magnified the skills of each member, yielding results that exceeded the individual capabilities of any single contributor.

Edison held wide-ranging passions that surfaced early in life, and remained with him for decades. Following a few frustrating months of traditional schooling, young Thomas's mother, Nancy—a retired schoolteacher—allowed Edison to indulge his passions by homeschooling him for several years. His love for chemistry, mathematics, physics, telegraphy, the building of small motors, and the design of motorized equipment were fostered at a young age, ultimately spurring Edison to construct a large, independent laboratory—the storied Menlo Park, New Jersey, facility—in 1876. Israel notes that, via this world-changing facility, Edison "grafts an electrical and chemical laboratory onto a machine shop . . . creating a new kind of invention institution."[12] What Edison dubbed an invention factory, today we know as the world's first managed research and development facility.

During a brief stint as a Western Union employee, various managers created hurdles for Edison in regard to his telegraph inventing efforts. Seeking a freer environment for developing his ideas, Edison's Menlo Park lab enabled him to bring teams of skilled workers together in a collegial environment with few hierarchies and restrictions, encouraging small groups of employees to move freely from area to area devising products and prototypes spawned by Edison and his teammates. Figure 1.2 shows Edison surrounded by several of his Menlo Park colleagues. Although Edison generally served as the catalyst and primary driver of these inventing efforts, his small teams at Menlo Park yielded dozens of individuals who rose to become masters of the collaboration and innovation philosophies Edison modeled. A networked community where communication

**Figure 1.2 Edison, Seated at Center Holding a Hat,
Developed a Highly Collaborative Culture at His
Menlo Park Laboratory**

*Source:* National Park Service, Edison National Historic Site.

flowed with great regularity through frequent verbal exchanges
as well as notebook sharing across teams, *Menlo Park operated as
a collaborative ecosystem with few equals.*

The collegial environment of the Menlo Park lab ultimately
became a petri dish for an even larger-scale vision Edison held
for the scope of research and development itself. In 1887, Edison
designed a three-story laboratory at West Orange, New Jersey,
but also added extensive manufacturing capabilities clustered
on a multiacre campus. At West Orange, Edison also built
specialized outbuildings dedicated to specific forms of research,
each within walking distance of the large, primary laboratory.
The three-story laboratory combined machine-making equipment alongside small, no-frills offices where employees could

gather to work in solitude or to meet jointly for experimentation. Edison also dedicated portions of this larger central facility to a massive library that housed 10,000 volumes, making Edison's West Orange collection one of the top five largest libraries in the world at the turn of the century. Edison's vision for true collaboration at West Orange uniquely combined a discovery learning environment with the resources needed for prototyping, scale testing, and then launching new products and services. Embracing a workforce drawn from diverse disciplines, "Edison recognized the importance of placing Ph.D. chemists and trained engineers alongside machinists and fellow inventors to realize his creations" inside this huge industrial laboratory complex.[13]

Importantly, not only did Edison demonstrate a penchant for collaborative engagement of teams within his laboratories, he brought true collaboration principles to many of the new companies he founded. A global thinker and businessman, one of Edison's most famous collaborative endeavors—the formation of the Edison General Electric Company—remains a thriving organization more than 125 years later. Now known simply as GE, the company ranks as one of the top 50 largest public companies in the world. Edison ultimately founded more than 200 domestic and international companies during his lifetime, many specifically designed to manufacture his inventions. His collaborative efforts in research and development yielded dozens of commercially successful products for businesses and consumers.

> The Edison laboratory worked as a collaborative organization. Laboratory employees were assigned to work on many projects while Edison supervised and involved himself, sometimes intensively, sometimes at arm's length. Ultimately, Edison was the guiding force for the fruits of his laboratory.
>
> —*Mary Bellis, science writer and historian*

Decades ahead of his time, in an age when most Industrial era companies were creating layers of supervisors and clerks, Edison instead built flat organizations and flat teams. Eschewing layers of management titles or fancy corner offices, Edison valued a combination of discovery learning and hands-on engagement as a means to train workers in a broad array of skills and disciplines. As you will read in more detail in Chapters 3 through 6, the depth and diversity of the collaborative project work he offered enabled Edison to attract, and cross-train, a rich talent pool. In a very real way, the underpinnings of Edison's true collaboration approach served as the backbone to sustaining his innovation success.

Offering insights that can inform our modern notions of talent deployment, team design, employee engagement, and approaches to project complexity, Edison's collaboration practices offer a framework for how organizations today can drive value through flatter, more streamlined structures now gaining traction in the digital age.

In addition to its reliance on flat team structure, another distinguishing feature of Edison's true collaboration approach lies in its emphasis on discovery learning, an approach that galvanizes common goals and shared purpose. Decades later, we recognize Edison's zest for discovery learning in the passion of leaders like Bill Gates, who created software that could unlock the vast potential of computers, and Steve Jobs, who sought to discover new ways for people to relate to technology. Like these modern-day innovators, Edison, in his time, unleashed in his workers the power of discovery learning to yield new knowledge and new processes. Tackling meaty challenges that held potential to touch the lives of millions, Edison awakened in his teams a thirst to dare something bold, the fruits of which still resonate in our world today.

**Edison's Legacy: The Fruits of True Collaboration**

The world's first document duplication technology

The world's first phonograph and record

The first practical incandescent electric light

The world's first central power station

The world's first comprehensive system for distributing electrical power

The world's first movie studio

The world's first motion picture camera

The world's first motion picture projector

The world's first films

The first commercially viable fluoroscope

The world's first alkaline storage battery

As the next billion workers transform our understanding of the nature of organizations themselves, we can draw upon Edison's bold collaboration methods in modern times, contemporizing his approaches for the twenty-first century.

# TRACING EDISON'S COLLABORATION BELIEFS AND PRACTICES

Although we do not have specific statements or individual documents describing Edison's collaboration philosophies, his views on collaboration are widely evidenced in rich archives tracking Edison's personal, scientific, and business activities. A treasure trove of information about Edison's life and work is publicly available through the Edison National Historic

Park at West Orange, as well as *The Thomas A. Edison Papers* archives at Rutgers University. Through these records, it's possible to view thousands of Edison's notebooks, his business correspondence, patent documents, court testimonies, personal letters, and other historical papers, together exceeding 5 million pages—enough to afford a lifetime of reading. Detailed records of Edison's invention efforts log the extensive experiments he undertook with colleagues in his laboratories over more than 50 years. It is even possible to trace the royalty payments Edison shared with colleagues appearing on dozens of his patents, as well as profit sharing with laboratory employees, a practice well ahead of its time in the late 1800s. Frequent shoulder-to-shoulder gatherings between Edison and his employees reveal a unique and uncommon commitment to collaboration that can refresh our modern view.

## EDISON'S FOUR PHASES OF TRUE COLLABORATION

Unlike what Doblin Group chief executive officer (CEO) Larry Keeley calls the *bumper sticker practice* of collaboration— simply sharing facts or making task assignments within a team—Edison viewed true collaboration as a value creation continuum. He saw it as an ongoing, holistic practice rather than a linear, stop-start process. It embraced both the uniqueness of the people who engaged in Edison's team efforts as well as their deeper, shared experience in laboring toward a common purpose. True collaboration was nourished by the presence of diverse physical environments— some open and flexible, such as bare-bones offices with no equipment, and some highly structured and sophisticated, such as Edison's machine shops. Whether operating on a massive scale by joining teams together or simply working with small clustered cadres of workers, *Edison organized his true collaboration endeavors with the recognition that complexity was a norm that all employees needed to understand and nimbly address.* This held true for interaction between Edison's workers with partners operating beyond the walls of the laboratory as well, such as supplier teams and other external parties.

If one were to find a single notebook entry capturing Edison's definition of true collaboration, I believe it would read something like this:

> Applying discovery learning within a context of complexity, inspired by a common goal or a shared purpose.

Vastly different from Webster's rather bland definition of collaboration, which reads simply, "The act or process of collaborating," Edison's definition colors collaboration with a much brighter palette. Operating within a framework that recognized collaboration as a continuous force operating within an environment of complex interactions, Edison created a fluid yet phased process that combined discovery learning with hands-on, practical applications. True collaboration for Edison operated like an invisible glue that fused learning, insight, purpose, complexity, and results together in one continuous effort. This fusion offers a unique mélange we can leverage in establishing true collaboration in teams today.

Edison's true collaboration process is composed of four phases:

Phase 1: Capacity

Phase 2: Context

Phase 3: Coherence

Phase 4: Complexity

These four facets of true collaboration are structured as successive and overlapping building blocks, with Phase 1 feeding into Phase 2, Phase 2 feeding into Phase 3, and Phase 3 feeding into Phase 4. All the processes within each phase are designed to link together, becoming an intertwined and self-referencing system. Unique to Edison's belief that individuals served as core linchpins for collaboration success, emphasis is placed on the contributions of each team member as a point of magnification and multiplication of the team's joint efforts. Designed to activate the innate creativity Edison believed was hardwired into the human brain, an individual's capacities for breakthrough problem solving and "out of the box thinking" expanded through the very act of true collaboration itself.

The four phases within Edison's collaborative approach also allowed teams to iterate back and forth between steps, reworking any parts that required more intense focus as progress was made. When Phase 4 was reached, initiatives either advanced forward to completion, connected with related initiatives under way in other teams, or served as the seeds for an entirely new project. Some, if they were unable to deliver short- or long-term value, were shelved.

Explored in depth in Chapters 3 through 6, each of Edison's four phases of true collaboration have two parts. The phases and their components can be summarized as follows, with a core question serving as the launching point for the exploration of each phase:

**Capacity:** How do we create the foundation for true collaboration to flourish?

*Phase 1—Capacity:* Select small, diverse teams of two to eight people who will thrive in an environment of discovery learning and collegiality.

*Part i, Engage diversity:* Formulate a team representing a meaningful cross-section of expertise, thought styles, and backgrounds, maximizing the depth of perspective available to the team as a whole and expanding the range of discovery learning experiences for each member.

*Part ii, Assemble small teams:* Build teams ranging from two to eight people, fostering a small-group experience characterized by nimble communication and genuine collegiality.

**Context:** How can our collaboration team reframe the problem at hand, driving the greatest range of creativity and breakthrough solutions?

***Phase 2—Context:*** Focus the outlook of the team toward development of new context that broadly frames the problem or challenge under consideration. Use a combination of individual learning plus hands-on activities to drive perspectives for potential solutions.

*Part i, Solo meld:* Each individual prepares for true collaboration outside of team meetings by engaging in a discovery learning process which includes questioning existing assumptions, reading broadly, and using analogies to spur new connections. Individuals prepare insights without locking down on any specific idea or direction.

*Part ii, Group meld:* The team comes together as a group, discussing insights on the problem at hand based on their Solo meld efforts, then reframing and morphing ideas within a broader, expansive context as team sessions progress. The team experiments with a range of solutions, developing rough prototypes, including stories as a form of narrative prototype. Group meld yields new insights that multiply results beyond the mere sum of each individual's efforts.

**Coherence:** Can the collaboration team stay the course and continue forward despite disagreements?

*Phase 3—Coherence:* Maintain collaboration momentum, creating frameworks for progress through inspiration and inspirational leadership even though disagreements may exist. Newly discover, or reemphasize, the shared purpose that binds the team together.

*Part i, Presence of inspirational and emergent leaders:* Members collectively inspire one another when gnawing feelings of negativity or doubt arise. The team creates coherence by engaging in a common, positive purpose, elevating the performance of each member. An inspirational leader may already be present, but others can emerge.

*Part ii, Communication of progress toward shared goals and purpose:* Team members must feel that progress toward shared goals is taking place, even if this comes in the form of small wins. Shared goals must be realized for internal team members as well as external partners to align around project-related efforts. All team members and partners must develop an ability to handle conflict.

**Complexity:** How can our collaboration team leverage internal and external networked resources nimbly and with speed?

*Phase 4—Complexity:* Equip and reskill teams to implement new ideas or new solutions using internally and externally networked resources, rapidly accessing or managing complex data streams the team must navigate.

Leave a footprint that contributes to a broader collective intelligence.

*Part i, Organize for complexity through development of smart layers:* Identify what types of internal and external complexity have greatest impact on your team, organizing in fluid patterns that allow you to adapt to rapidly shifting conditions. Reduce dependence on hierarchies by building "smart layers" that expand the reach of your decisions, creating virtual and social networks of influence pushing beyond the boundaries of your team.

*Part ii, Footprint your team's collective intelligence:* Consider the work of your team a knowledge asset, a kind of collective intelligence that links to a broader realm of meaning and purpose. Create a unique footprint for your endeavors that other teams can follow using notebooks, videos, sound recordings, prototypes, stories, and other media to capture the heart and soul of your project.

Within the four phases of capacity, context, coherence, and complexity lies the invisible glue that linked Edison's true collaboration practices to the success of his innovation empire. Without the coherence and alignment created through true collaboration, it's likely that Edison's innovation efforts would have been scattered like beautiful bones that lacked a skeletal frame. Figure 1.3 reveals a visual framework for the interconnection between the four phases.

Regardless of how your own true collaboration effort may originate, it's crucial that as many facets as possible within each of the four phases are engaged to prevent costly project breakdowns. Dr. Jean Egmon, executive director of the Ford Center for Global Citizenship at Northwestern University, and past director of the Complexity in Action Network, notes the

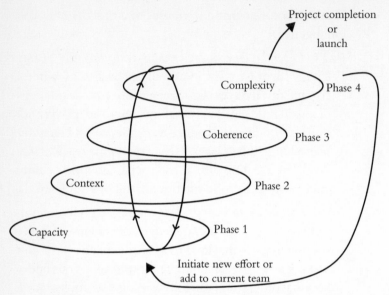

**Figure 1.3 Thomas Edison's Four Phases of True Collaboration**

*Note:* Thomas Edison's comprehensive approach to collaboration embraced four interlocking phases.

seduction of fast-tracking true collaboration by shortcutting steps. Egmon warns, "Skipping steps can come back and blindside you. If you have a group tasked with complex challenges, the temptation can be to just start in Phase 4 and proceed without a deeper understanding of the problem itself. That can be a recipe for failure. Ensure that the entire team has developed a thorough grasp of the context for the challenge while also setting out its goals. Engaging in all four phases is crucial."[14]

Chapters 3 through 6 reveal the nature and structure of each true collaboration phase, using historical examples from Edison's era as well as modern-day illustrations from leading companies such as Apple, Intel, Amazon, Facebook, Procter & Gamble, W. L. Gore, Ford, Emerson, Whirlpool, and 3M. You'll read how true collaboration efforts within these organizations are driving inspirational and emergent leadership, shifting workplace structures, driving value creation, and embracing social networks as well as other unique forms of Metalogue. The applications you find will accelerate your own collaboration success.

*Midnight Lunch* also offers examples of how nonprofit and government operations can increase the power of their value creation efforts through true collaboration, with applications from the Mayo Clinic and the pioneering Village of Oak Park, Illinois. Harnessing the power of true collaboration in resource-constrained environments offers a range of insights for your team efforts.

Hands-on exercises are included for each of Edison's four phases, offering you a chance to begin practicing many of the skills you'll read about in the coming chapters. Creative ideas for gaining experience with each phase are included at the end of Chapters 3, 4, and 5 and are embedded directly in the body of Chapter 6. As Edison would desire, the structural design of each phase is also depicted visually through illustrations at the end of these same chapters.

## TRUE COLLABORATION FOSTERS A GROWTH MINDSET: BALANCING LEARNING AND PERFORMANCE

Importantly, the discovery learning and value creation continuum that Edison envisioned in his four-phase collaboration process is not applicable to every single endeavor a team undertakes. As noted by Herminia Ibarra and Morten T. Hansen in their recent research on collaboration, "Once leaders start getting employees to collaborate, they face a different problem: overdoing it. Too often people try to collaborate on everything and wind up in endless meetings, debating ideas and struggling to find consensus. They can't reach decisions and execute quickly. Collaboration becomes not the oil greasing the wheel but the sand grinding it to a halt."[15]

It's a reality that some projects require raw implementation. Sometimes all the steps for completing a process have been fully laid out. Roles for individual team members have been pre-defined, and the process for achieving an outcome is already well delineated. In such instances, true collaboration may not offer the best approach. In Edison's operations, for example, task-driven functions such as shipping or distribution typically were not engaged in true collaboration efforts the way that laboratory and manufacturing operations were. Here are a few examples of task-based efforts where a discovery learning approach may not prove valuable to the results desired:

- Developing monthly or quarterly reports for your group or division

- Assisting customers with service requests that must be handled immediately

- Coordinating distribution of information packets for a sales conference

- Conducting annual contract negotiations with current suppliers

- Monitoring results from digital campaigns supporting a new product launch

- Identifying the products or services released by competitors in the past year

Initiatives like these often rely on performance-driven objectives, where individuals or teams are assessed on how quickly and effectively they complete a set of tasks. Much as

Team A simply joined hands and ran across the finish line without feeling a need to give the assignment a lot of extra thought, task-based efforts generally place low emphasis on broader learning objectives. The rapid and effective fulfillment of the task remains primary.

However, as Dr. Carol Dweck notes in *Mindset, sometimes organizations can become too reliant on task-driven efforts.* They forget that employee engagement today is increasingly driven by new learning employees can leverage to expand expertise both within their current position and within future positions, even ones that may entail working for other employers years down the road.

The danger in relying too heavily on task-driven structures is that *most people make trade-offs between performance goals and learning goals.* Dweck indicates that "when performance goals dominate an environment, people are motivated to show others that they have a valued attribute, such as intelligence or leadership. When learning goals dominate, they are motivated to *develop* the attribute they learn. Performance goals . . . induce people to favor tasks that will make them look good over tasks that will help them learn."[16]

If your team efforts consistently skew toward task-driven activities, you may be engendering what Dweck calls a fixed mindset, a collection of beliefs that holds your focus on the status quo. Dangerous for employers and employees alike, the fixed mindset fails to see the world as a continuum of changes. Instead, the processes around us are viewed as linear, stop-start functions. The fixed mindset is often unable to respond to fluid situations, where data may be incomplete and no clear direction is provided. The bearers of a fixed mindset are considerably hobbled in a fast-moving environment like the one we are living in today, where change occurs constantly—and new learning must flow along with it.

Thomas Edison not only had a growth mindset, he could think divergently. He could put together unusual combinations of things, creating patterns that others frequently didn't recognize. Often, individuals who excel at collaboration are not only able to see modifications or improvements in something that already exists, they can generate ideas that are unique and unusual, developing breakthrough concepts which have never existed before.

—*Dr. Jacqueline Byrd, codeveloper, Creatrix; author of* **The Innovation Equation**

In contrast, embracing a learning-based approach to your work, as Edison did, yields what Dweck describes as a growth mindset. Aligned with Edison's practice of true collaboration, a growth mindset fosters an ability to shift the context of your thinking and adapt to new sequences or patterns. The growth mindset embraces an attitude of "I don't know every step in advance," recognizing that discovery learning is essential to mastering complexity and challenge—while also delivering results. By embracing a growth mindset, you can most fully realize the fruits of true collaboration.

Here is a brief illustration of how you can begin making the shift from what may be a fixed mindset toward a growth mindset, using collaboration as a propelling force. This quick exercise helps frame what it means to move from a pure task-driven, performance-based orientation to one that also embraces discovery learning in your project results.

If we were to reexamine the same six task-driven activities listed earlier but place them in a context that includes discovery, we could begin expanding the range of options available to fulfill the tasks themselves while also driving new learning. Like Team B did in running a three-legged race to fulfill its assignment earlier in the chapter, we could look at the six tasks listed in the previous list from a different angle, *newly reframing each item to engage learning and a growth mindset that actually delivers not only a desired result but knowledge to the team*. Here is one way to reframe the six performance-based tasks, placing them in a true collaboration framework:

1. Identify a distribution mechanism for releasing quarterly results, allowing more rapid access to data by internal and external stakeholders.

2. Identify an approach that allows more service representatives to knowledgeably assist customers with urgent requests.

3. Create a method for delivering sales conference content both live as well as digitally.

4. Determine what factors may be causing delays in annual contract negotiations.

5. Identify how a particular target audience prefers to receive digital communications for new products or services.

6. Identify factors that could vault a new product or service from your organization ahead of the competitive field.

Can you see the difference? The task orientation of the first list has been shifted to engage a discovery learning orientation. This second list of actions broadens the scope of collaborative activity compared with the first one, allowing for the *development of new knowledge versus mere completion of tasks*. Just as Team B fulfilled its objective of crossing the finish line in less than 10 minutes, it also learned a new web of skills. When thinking about how you can build learning-related activity into your efforts, performance-driven activity does not have to be excluded. As you think about how and where to engage true collaboration in your team's endeavors using the four-phase process described in *Midnight Lunch*, consider how your project work can begin cultivating a growth mindset rather than a task-driven, fixed mindset.

Chapters 4, 5, and 6 shed light on the interlocking lattice of benefits that flow from bringing a learning orientation to individuals and teams through Edison's true collaboration approach. Jay Scherer, managing partner for global executive development firm BPI Group North America, recommends these initial questions for examining how discovery learning can be balanced with performance requirements in a collaboration effort:

- Why is it valuable to bring a discovery learning approach alongside a task or performance-based approach for this initiative?

- What benefits will my group derive from undertaking a discovery learning effort that engages true collaboration?

- How does discovery learning improve the ability of the team overall, or individuals on the team, to also think strategically about their challenge?

- What expanded roles can individuals who participate in true collaboration efforts play in our organization over time?

- How can results of the team's learning efforts help deliver revenue or profit goals?

- Does this true collaboration endeavor transform our ability to compete?

In considering these questions, Scherer notes, "Leaders need to recognize that learning objectives can provide a straight line between the individual's goals and the performance goals of the organization. Learning goals and performance goals are symbiotic, and need to be set up that way. One set of goals does not have to operate at the expense of the other."[17]

Here's what an individual can ask when thinking about true collaboration and its contribution to a growth mindset as well as learning objectives:

1. What new skill sets will engaging in a true collaboration effort offer me?

2. Will discovery learning lead to new knowledge that can positively impact my team's results?

3. How can a true collaboration endeavor impact my own current knowledge or open pathways to an entirely new mode of operating or thinking?

4. What is the contribution of a learning-driven effort to my sense of purpose?

5. Do I see a connection between the learning efforts I'd like to pursue and my performance objectives?

As you read further in *Midnight Lunch*, begin jotting down similar questions you can ask to reframe your own thinking— or your team's thinking—regarding learning versus performance. Think about whether you currently operate with a growth mindset, or if you may be locked into a fixed mindset. Consider teams you've been part of in the past, perhaps task forces, committees, or community projects, where the team did not fulfill its full potential. Was discovery learning absent? Did the members of the team line up around tasks rather than collaborating? If you are undertaking a new effort, use the five questions noted above as well as insights from the upcoming chapters to sew discovery learning into your approach. Part of the power Edison recognized in collaboration was its ability to balance experiential forms of learning with tangible performance outcomes.

## TRUE COLLABORATION IS A SUPERSKILL THAT BUILDS A NEW TYPE OF KNOWLEDGE ASSET

For Edison, not only did true collaboration create a unique connection between learning and practical results, it served as a superskill—a networked mechanism linking webs of crucial capabilities we often describe as soft skills. Collaboration as a superskill became equally as important in Edison's operations as areas of functional expertise, like proficiency in mathematics, chemistry, or a deep understanding of the scientific method. Edison's teams, valued the underlying web of soft skills that collaboration embraced, including intangible, tough-to-measure capacities such as seeing problems from the vantage point of a different discipline, being willing to question facts, inspiring others to go beyond their known capabilities, and navigating conflict productively. Almost impossible to teach in a classroom setting, these superskills became embedded in Edison's workforce through the hands-on, experiential nature of true collaboration itself. Explored in more depth in Chapters 3 through 6, Table 1.1 shows a few examples of how diverse soft skills will emerge through Edison's process of shared team learning and group experience.

The interlocking network of soft skills yielded by the four phases of collaboration became a signature unique to Edison's laboratory. Positioning collaboration as a superskill allowed Edison to adaptively combine and recombine an agile workforce that had a common denominator in its ability to drive inspiration across teams, ask new questions, and approach challenges from diverse angles. *Edison viewed the presence of*

### Table 1.1 Interlocking Web of Soft Skills in True Collaboration

| | |
|---|---|
| **Phase 1: Capacity** | • Seeing a challenge through the eyes of another discipline |
| | • Creating collegiality |
| **Phase 2: Context** | • Developing new context for framing a problem |
| | • Being willing to question facts and test creative hypotheses |
| **Phase 3: Coherence** | • Inspiring others to go beyond their perceived limitations |
| | • Navigating conflict productively |
| **Phase 4: Complexity** | • Recognizing how complexity impacts team effectiveness |
| | • Capturing the collective intelligence of a team |

*these superskills as a unique type of knowledge asset that could be regenerated over and over again with each team combination he created.* Through his true collaboration process, he could drive the presence of these soft skills, whose value no amount of functional expertise could replace.

"Knowledge assets don't show up on balance sheets or financial statements," says Kent Barnett, CEO at KnowledgeAdvisors, whose research estimates that knowledge assets held within the human capital of an organization represent 1.5 times to 2.0 times the value of the fixed assets it owns. "Knowledge assets are intangible, but they are crucial to driving growth."[18] Edison recognized that the knowledge assets of his organization flowed from the support his true collaboration process provided to his innovation efforts.

Leaders who have scratched their heads over how to bring a deep yet relevant array of soft skills to their workers can now, finally, turn to the superskills of true collaboration as a foundation. By establishing a collaborative work environment within his culture, Edison intuitively devised a mechanism that gave rise to a skill-embedding process that enhanced the competitiveness of his workforce—one that is translatable to employees today.

> We see the world of work moving from control to collaboration. An orientation to collaboration will in the future mark the difference between successful and unsuccessful companies. This "mega-change" is driven by shifts in generational attitudes and a rise in workforce diversity, as well as technology like smart devices and social media. Everyone's got a global playing field now.
>
> *—Jay Scherer, managing partner,*
> *BPI Group North America*

As Rishad Tobaccowala of VivaKi noted earlier, thriving in the global economy means that collaboration must be present in everything from innovation, to hiring and retaining skilled employees, to staying relevant. Workers and leaders alike need to cultivate a growth mindset, recognizing how new learning can be applied to the constantly shifting environment characterizing today's business climate. With the impending arrival of the next billion workers, the magnitude of the shift organizations as well as individuals, represents a "megachange"—a total recalibration of thinking that steps away from the control-based structures spawned by the Industrial Revolution toward collaborative structures that can ensure speed and competitiveness in the digital era. Edison's four phases of true collaboration offer unique insights into how we can begin the recalibration process crucial to the success of every organization and employee today.[19]

# CHAPTER 2

## Why Is True Collaboration So Crucial Now?

*The years from 1985 to 2005 were a time of incredible change. . . . It is hard to find another 20-year period in the history of humanity when our world changed as much as during this time.*

—David Houle, *The Shift Age*

**F**iling into the Nokia Theatre in New York City grasping large coffee cups and the last remnants of morning bagels, hundreds of executives wearing badges that read "May 2009 World Innovation Forum" began taking their seats. I hurriedly found an open spot in the fifth row as the lights dimmed, a hush falling over the crowd as everyone awaited word of what lay ahead for the global economy just months after the Great Recession had sunk its grizzly teeth into markets across the world.

Stepping onto the stage in a dark blue suit was Dr. C. K. Prahalad, twice voted the number one thinker in the world by Thinkers50 and a decorated professor at the University of Michigan Ross School of Business. Standing beneath a glaring spotlight, Prahalad began gesturing broadly. "We're in the midst of a true global reset," he said. "The basic industries which underpin most economies—housing, construction, utilities, banking, and automotive—are all being fundamentally restructured. The business landscape created during the Industrial Age will never return."[1]

The crowd gulped, motionless. Prahalad continued. "This reset will restructure how organizations compete, what industries they compete in, who we hire, how we hire, how companies connect with customers, and how products and services are designed. This reset will be permanent. . . . Going forward, value creation, innovation, and strategy will all become one and the same. Organizations will now simply have a mandate to grow through innovation and coherently integrate all organizational activities to support this effort."

Over low muttering that now rippled through the audience, Prahalad offered that leaders and employees alike needed to shake off decades-old "wait and react" habits, moving to an "anticipate and create" approach instead. Emphasizing the need to "build collaboration as an ecosystem that creates value for both employees and customers," Prahalad stressed that new, collaborative structures would be needed to embrace networks of digital technologies rather than more lumbering annual planning cycles that operate too slowly to meet rapidly shifting customer demands. Prahalad declared that we must reduce dependence on "what a lone vice president would sanction rather than what a collaborative team could devise," and position collaboration as a central part of what makes each organization's culture tick. By connecting more employees directly to the value creation process itself, he prophesied that customer insights could be generated more rapidly and more effectively than ever before. In turn, by newly focusing workers toward value creation and collaboration, a full reshaping of their skill sets would be essential. Organizations would now need to begin seeking new combinations of skills in their employees, valuing most those people who could "anticipate and create" rather than those requiring constant direction or oversight.

> Plan-driven development doesn't work now. The environment is too changeable for a plan developed in January to apply even nine months later.
>
> *—Richard Perrin, author,*
> **Real World Project Management**

Buzzing with discontent, many in the crowd received Prahalad's words as heresy. It seemed almost unimaginable in 2009 that discrete departments and practice areas within organizations could somehow merge—that innovation would actually come to overlap with strategy or other value-driving disciplines, as illustrated in Figure 2.1. It felt unfathomable that annual planning processes would need to shift, that they had become too slow in the face of other nimbler, more continuous value creation concepts like open innovation, design thinking, or customer-led development. Bringing new collaboration skills to bastions of experts in engineering, marketing, or manufacturing could mean a loss of power for these independent, high-flying groups. How could people retain their power, their titles, or their long-coveted positions if they suddenly had to rub elbows with other disciplines?

Rather than ruffling his feathers, had Edison been in the audience at the Nokia Theatre that morning, he would have been nodding in robust agreement. The notion of a collaboration ecosystem linking innovation, strategy, and value creation stood at the heart of Edison's laboratories as well as

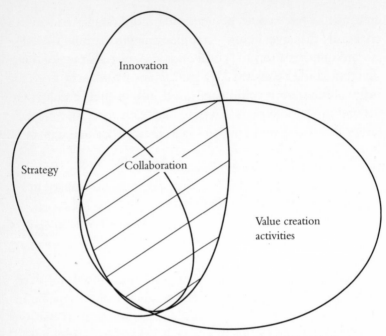

**Figure 2.1 Collaboration Ecosystem: Post-Reset
Merging of Once Separate Organizational
Practice Areas**
*Note:* As innovation, strategy, and value creation merge, collaboration
serves as their common linkage.

his manufacturing empire. He was already on board with the
notion of flat team structures and the value of flat organizations that focused on addressing customer needs. True collaboration already lay positioned as a superskill that his
employees were required to master. Decades earlier, Edison
had created an approach that sketched in many of the same
lines Prahalad had asked his audience to draw in May 2009.

No organization is immune to the shifts set in motion
by the global reset. Its ripple effects have shaken the very
foundations of how business is being conducted today,

continually reshaping our view of how leaders, teams, and customers interact. Our core challenge is to acknowledge where and how to embrace collaboration as the centerpiece for this new ecosystem. If our goal is to build the best true collaboration teams possible, we must anticipate and create how successful teams will look in the wake of the reset Prahalad describes. What else will we need to be aware of in designing an effective approach to collaboration? I believe Edison would direct us to look at three major forces: complexity, metalogue, and reskilling. Each of these forces is either already in play or will increasingly come into play in your organization:

1. *Complexity:* The accelerated pace of technological change has erased familiar industry boundaries, opening the way for rapid formation of new markets. A tsunami of data can now be consumed—and generated—by individuals armed with mobile phones as well as smart devices.

2. *Metalogue:* Feelings of fragmentation yielded by economic and technological shifts have deepened the need for connection and common purpose across large groups of people. Communities, organizations, and governments face an imperative to hear the opinions of diverse constituencies that now can generate influence outside of traditionally recognized channels of decision making or authority.

3. *Reskilling:* The broad availability of smart devices places new emphasis on what people can potentially create rather than what they already know. Skills linked to knowledge sharing, such as effective communication, adaptive thinking, and cross-generational leadership, are gaining new prominence in realms where functional expertise formerly dominated.

Examining how complexity, metalogue, and reskilling are operating in the post-reset environment offers us a backdrop for their importance in Edison's true collaboration framework. By understanding the impact that this trifecta of forces is wielding, we can begin incorporating them into new collaboration ecosystems in the twenty-first century, recalibrating our thinking about ways each shift impacts our own individual capabilities.

## SHIFT #1: THE RISE IN COMPLEXITY DUE TO MASSIVE GENERATION OF DATA AND REAL-TIME DATA SYNTHESIS

"Today, for only a few hundred dollars, we can hold in the palm of our hands smart devices with computing power that 10 years ago would have cost more than $1 million. With gigabytes of storage capacity, anyone with a smart phone, a laptop, or a tablet computer can generate and analyze huge streams of data—data that would have cost billions of dollars in the 1970s. Smart devices today are a million times cheaper and a thousand times faster than anything available 30 years ago."[2] Crystallizing the mind-numbing advances in digital technology driven by Moore's Law over the past three decades, Ray Kurzweil, scientist, futurist, and author of *The Singularity Is Near*, puts into perspective a new form of complexity impacting today's business environment: the ability to inexpensively generate and store massive amounts of data. Looming largest as a force within this arsenal is a growing army of 5 billion mobile phones, all operating on a planet teeming with 7 billion people. Mobile connections link virtually every country in the world with streams of users communicating around the clock, providing an immediacy of information and data access that has never before been possible.

> Data is increasingly at the heart of just about anything we do. Now, almost every interaction is quantified. We have to be comfortable with data and technology. For a lot of people, that isn't their normal state of being. We're seeing increasing challenges and opportunities around this new combination.
>
> —*Guy Blissett, IBM Wholesale Distribution lead*

In the process of simple daily activities, individual users within this army of 5 billion mobile phones not only can connect verbally but actually can become walking *data generators*, collectively snapping millions of pictures, sending billions of text messages, and casually typing out volumes of tweets. If an individual mobile phone user also happens to have a smart device, he or she can readily access the World Wide Web, click on an item to purchase with a credit card, or send megabytes of videos uploaded from yet another digital source. This same user can scan checks in seconds, sending the captured images to his or her bank for immediate deposit rather than physically visiting a branch or ATM. He or she can buy an e-book or like and unlike products on Amazon or Facebook. Just a glimmer in the eye of Harvard student Mark Zuckerberg in 2004, Facebook alone now boasts more than one billion users globally, making it a huge, collaborative magnet for any mobile user with a penchant for viewing or sharing images, videos, downloadable apps, and even virtual games.

What is the impact of all these digital interactions, and all these data? Collectively, per Steve Teig, president and chief technology officer (CTO) of Tabula, the quantity of data generated in a single day across all sources exceeds several zettabytes, with one zettabyte roughly equivalent to "every movie ever made, generated every five minutes."[3] That would make even Edison's head spin.

Harnessing the information—and the collaborative power—inherent in these massive streams of digital output offers a new form of complexity for every organization in the modern era. As Guy Blissett, team lead for IBM's Wholesale Distribution group notes, "Now, almost every interaction is quantified. Need something from a store? You can check online to see if it's in stock, then purchase it virtually. While you're on the store's website, you can even rate its customer service, or connect to other fans on Facebook. Want to evaluate which car insurance to buy? Go to YouTube and see if there's a video for the brand you have in mind."[4] According to Forrester, a respected research firm, everyday decisions like these can now require up to 13 traceable interaction points if the processes of searching, purchasing, liking, and then evangelizing the final choice through social networks are counted. That's more than double the number of interactions possible in a single purchase decision less than 10 years ago.[5]

Interpreting the output from this 24/7 hum of digital activity requires new levels of data synthesis and an ability to detect emerging patterns in huge arrays of numbers. Most organizations are not staffed to tackle this type of complexity, nor are employees trained in how to navigate it. Commenting on the difficulty of creating meaning from millions of data points collected from digital banking transactions each month, in a recent speech at Research Triangle Park, Bill Rogers, chief executive officer (CEO) of SunTrust, said, "We find ourselves requiring new collaborative tools just to analyze what the data means."[6] For organizations, complexity stems not only from the sheer volume of data generated by the users of its products or services, but from actual analysis of the data as well. It can even flow from the challenge of finding employees with the skill sets to synthesize all this output in ways that are practical and insightful.

A second related area of complexity for organizations today lies in the blurring of industry boundaries, and along with it, the disappearance of familiar business models. One example making daily headlines is publishing, an industry where the once unchallenged popularity of corner bookstores, such as the now-defunct Borders, has been upended by popular digital tools, including e-books, e-readers, and online newspapers. Banking has felt a similar seismic shift. Bill Rogers comments, "The traditional boundaries of the banking industry have been muddied. Customers no longer have to come into a physical banking location to deposit funds or get cash. Roughly two-thirds of all bank transactions today are electronic. One of the fastest growing trends—scanning checks for remote deposit—has grown faster than any other service in banking today. We now compete not just with the bank down the street, but with Facebook and PayPal." Lacking familiar signposts, employees face complexity in simply identifying who their competitors are and what offerings will be perceived as relevant to a constantly morphing user base six months, nine months, or even one year into the future. Anticipating what lies ahead even 18 months from now often feels impossible.

> We find ourselves requiring new collaborative tools just to analyze what the data means, and to determine who our competitors—or potential competitors—are.
>
> —*William H. Rogers, CEO of SunTrust*

A third type of complexity that flows both from the explosive popularity of digital technology as well as a blurring of industry boundaries is a shift in familiar value creation processes, with product development experiencing a particularly deep transformation. A muddying of boundaries between innovation, strategy, and value creation has arisen much the way Prahalad predicted it would. No longer solely the province of research and development (R&D), engineering, or marketing, the complex and often deeply time-consuming process of developing new products is being transformed by collaborations between external customers and internal teams. Intel, for example, armed with huge digital pools of user data, no longer has to rely solely on groups of leading-edge engineers in its R&D labs to develop a new microchip. Working with prescreened user audiences, Intel now can quantify user experiences to more rapidly navigate the product development process. Desiring to observe nuances in customer behavior firsthand, Intel has begun assembling live audiences to respond to various themed concepts it seeks to explore. Recently sponsoring live mashup events with Grammy award winning musician will.i.am of the Black Eyed Peas, Intel developed customized music videos and lifestyle content for its targeted Generation Y audience. The live event featured streaming links to this online content, allowing Intel to discover out how audience members were using their laptops, smartphones, and tablets during the event itself. A novel example of pairing *data generators* with *data analyzers*, Intel engineers, product designers, system specia-lists, and marketers all work collaboratively to analyze the complex data streams generated by this type of product development effort. Holding similar product development aims, Google has partnered with rock band Arcade Fire to feature the company's cloud computing software tools, gaining data in real time during its own live events with key target audiences.[7,8] A far cry from the strict, department-driven thrusts of the late Industrial era, both these unique product development approaches illustrate the

44

newly overlapping nature of innovation, value creation, and strategy within the collaboration process. Rather than stumbling on the complexity inherent in bringing multiple disciplines together for these efforts, Intel and Google have embraced new methods for deriving insight from complex data streams and created industry-spanning ecosystems that can harness emergent insights about customers.

Even the US government is interested in understanding how ready access to zettabytes of data is impacting business processes. Eager to put its arms around the potential economic development opportunities inherent within digital networks and armies of smart devices, the Center for Economic Development recently commissioned a study to delve further into the implications of these tools as forces for value creation. Conducted by the McKinsey Global Institute (MGI), the study's sobering findings suggest that we are now living in "the third economic revolution" in world history.[9]

A phenomenon debated over the past several years by experts in Silicon Valley and Washington, DC, alike, the third economic revolution spotlights an accelerating sequence of technological shifts that started somewhere between 2001 and 2003, predating the global reset. Per the MGI study, the progression of these shifts is outlined in Table 2.1.

Projected to be a mere 30 years in duration, the third economic revolution, dubbed the Innovation Age in the MGI report, follows on the heels of much longer economic cycles that lasted hundreds, even thousands, of years. *Our ability to thrive in such a compressed era of transition will depend significantly on our ability to anticipate and create new structures for collaboration, bringing people and technology together in meaningful ways.* The success of our adjustments will also depend on how rapidly we can reshape our thinking and how deeply we can

### Table 2.1 Timeline of Global Economic Shifts by Era

| Name | Length Dates | Theme |
|---|---|---|
| First economic revolution | 3,000 years: 1300 BC–AD 1700 | Agricultural Age |
| Second economic revolution | 300 years: 1701–2000 | Industrial Age |
| Third economic revolution | 30 years: 2001–2030 | Innovation Age |

*Source:* "Jobs and US Economic Recovery: A Panel Discussion," August 2011. (Adapted from *McKinsey Quarterly*, August 2011, by McKinsey Global Institute.)

embed more fluid, collaborative structures in the environments that have an impact on us every day.

Although operating in a different technological era, Edison embraced complexity as a fundamental component of collaboration itself. Recognizing that complexity is best addressed by the presence of diverse perspectives, Edison basked in the ability to handle complexity at the very start of Phase 1, drawing his teams from multiple disciplines. Each successive phase accounts for the presence of complexity through the context in which problems are evaluated, the range of options considered in the solution set, as well as the unique tools that can be wielded to pare back unnecessary layers or steps in the value creation continuum. Embracing complexity rather than sidestepping it represents a hallmark of Edison's true collaboration process. The collaborative culture Edison launched at Menlo Park in 1876 was extended and expanded to embrace even more complex, large-scale projects at his West Orange laboratory, shown in Figure. 2.2

**Figure 2.2  Photo of Edison and West Orange Team**
*Note:* Edison, at center in front row, embraced increasingly complex
collaborative projects at his West Orange laboratory, built in 1887.
*Source:* National Park Service, Edison National Historical Site.

## SHIFT #2: THE RISE OF THE METALOGUE AS A TOOL FOR CREATING PURPOSE AND CONNECTION

With the availability of all these zettabytes of data, and with
billions of mobile phones and smart device users who have
a seemingly endless thirst for ever newer, faster devices, a
transformation is occurring both around the *kinds* of conversations these users are having and the *scale* at which these

conversations are occurring. Whether in organizations, in communities, or across entire nations, dialogue engaging thousands, even millions, of individuals now stands as a reality through the use of social networks and smart devices. Social networks have become a tool for citizens in developed economies, as well as in emerging ones, to explore common purpose and renew a sense of what binds them together. In preparing for the arrival of the next billion, it's crucial to form new collaborative forums of expression that allow people to find their voice amidst the growing complexity they perceive around them.

To engage constituents in big, meaningful conversations, an increasing number of organizations are turning to a solution I describe as metalogue, a term I first heard used by Wayne Lindholm, a former 3M R&D executive and president of the Scanlon Leadership Network. Lindholm describes *metalogue* as "a method of inquiry for exploring diverse conversations and the context around those conversations."[10] Metalogue can take place as either an open-forum conversation that runs top to bottom in an organization or one that runs horizontally across peer groups or user communities. Designed to serve as a means of probing and responding to one or two key themes of interest to the community engaging in the metalogue, the resulting network of conversations surfaces new collaborative solutions to challenges the community is experiencing.[11]

Edison used metalogue as a tool in times of competitive crisis, rallying his entire workforce around a key need or a key challenge. In May 1888, stung by news of Alexander Graham Bell's impending launch of a phonograph and cylindrical record that would best his own, Edison developed the notion of a lock-in, a multiday period during which dozens of employees turned their sole focus toward devising new technology capable of leapfrogging a competitive entry. These lock-ins allowed Edison to access the knowledge residing in every single worker across his entire employee base, creating a unique form of metalogue. Making the full scope of his organizational resources available to any employee working during the lock-in, Edison galvanized the best thinking about how to address an unexpected competitive shock. Here is one account of the first phonograph lock-in:

> That May, Edison, who for the past 11 years had tinkered with the phonograph, resolved to best Bell's "graphophone." In what newspapers soon called the "phonograph vigil," Edison locked his team into his West Orange laboratory, not to emerge until the group could boast of the "perfect" phonograph. Three sleepless days (or what some newspapers exaggerated to a "sleepless, five-day orgy of toil") later, Edison's team burst forth from the labs not only with a better phonograph, but with America's imagination soon to be regained.[12]

By using lock-ins as a means to engage in metalogue with his workers, Edison's search for a superior technology that would push back Bell's competitive thrust proved victorious. Although over the years Edison's lock-ins did not always yield success, they demonstrate how metalogue unleashes the thinking of individuals passionately interested in solving a problem via large-scale, mass collaboration.

Ironically, Lindholm first began working with the notion of metalogue while exploring how innovation percolates most effectively through organizations. Mirroring the collaborative culture Edison fostered in his laboratories, Lindholm observed that the most powerful conversations took place when leaders and employees engaged in purpose-inspired dialogue themed around specific projects or endeavors. Rather than a forum for debating facts, metalogue served as a means to transmit a climate for breakthrough thinking.

Today, social networks and smart technologies facilitate metalogue in ways Edison might have portrayed as a wonder of science fiction. Now, every input and every exchange, can be captured electronically. The purpose of a metalogue is typically to drill down on a single core question—or related group of questions—of broad interest to the community engaging in the metalogue itself. Responses to each question can be viewed by the entire community, allowing participants to agree or disagree with any comment or to challenge what they perceive to be underlying assumptions within the responses. Sometimes people even disagree with the underlying questions. Breakthroughs often derive from this challenging of assumptions, and the probing and responding that bounces between participants as the metalogue progresses.

Less structured forms of metalogue also occur on a daily basis today, themed around broad topics of interest to an entire community. Twitter communities, for example, run regular 60-minute #hashtag chats themed around #innovation, #leadership, #collaboration, #blogging, and dozens of other topics. Often led by subject matter experts, transcripts from Twitter metalogue sessions are typically available within minutes, and often get read—and searched—weeks after the metalogue is complete. The value of these exchanges lies in an ability to galvanize a core community of interest that remains loyal to the process of dialogue itself, surfacing key voices with specific opinions. Participants gain insight from these casual metalogue sessions that would not have been available via any other means, providing a sense of shared purpose for members within the metalogue community itself. Were he alive today, Edison would view these as valuable "practice sessions" for larger, more complex metalogue sessions like the ones he facilitated during his lock-ins.

In the modern era, multiday metalogue exchanges were probably first explored by IBM in what it dubbed its Values

Jam in 2003. Asking the question, "What are our core values?" across IBM's entire global employee base, then-CEO Sam Palmisano challenged the organization to reexamine its core values for the first time in nearly 100 years. Through Values Jam, IBM held an unprecedented 72-hour metalogue hosted on its own global intranet. Tens of thousands of IBMers came together to redefine the essence of their company, using IBM's own prodigious network of internal servers as a platform to capture each exchange. The result? A new set of core values, defined by IBMers for IBMers, that reshaped the way individuals within the company offered leadership, the way they made decisions, and the way they served clients.[13] Inspired by the sense of shared purpose yielded by this first metalogue, Palmisano repeated the effort in 2006, this time themed around key innovation questions. Lasting several days, that metalogue resulted in 10 new business concepts, each receiving $100,000 in funding, and a deeply renewed belief in the power of collaborative dialogue to yield breakthrough thinking.

But what happens when full-blown metalogue is not present, or even forbidden? Consider the contagious impact of the Arab Spring uprising of 2011, with discontent rippling from nation to nation in the Middle East fueled by under-the-radar communication via social networks. Or, recall the headlines in the late summer of 2011, when thousands of angry teens and young adults looted neighborhoods in London. Venting their anger in response to increased costs for education, the BBC reported that these young people "lacked hope" and "felt let down by society."[14] The disruption and destruction yielded in these two sweeping events reveal, in different ways, the steep challenges posed to society when real metalogue is absent. Being "left out" of conversations that lie at the heart of what makes people feel valued and purposeful can lead to a sense of disempowerment that can turn violent if not addressed.

Considerations for how collaboration can serve as a propellant for creating constructive community metalogue and greater social engagement served as a central theme at the 2012 World Economic Forum (WEF) in Davos, Switzerland. Klaus Schwab, founder and executive chairman of WEF, comments that creating "collaborative power" requires the focused attention of the entire world, emphasizing that decision-making processes must shift away from old hierarchies to embrace new, more responsive structures:

> We have lost sight of the fundamental transformation that the world is undergoing and of where conventional modes of decision-making have become outdated. What we clearly need are new models for global, regional, national and business decision-making which truly reflect that the context for decision-making has been altered—in unprecedented ways. . . . [A] new model is needed to account for the fundamental power shifts that have already and are continuing to take place. . . . Power has become much more distributed. Thus, we need new models where governance processes on all levels integrate newcomers in the most collaborative way. In the old world, it was hard power—hierarchical power—that was decisive. Then came soft power—the capability to have a convincing message. But today, we need to integrate empowered newcomers in what I call "collaborative power"—the capability to exercise collaborative power will determine the future on the business, national, regional and global levels.[15]

Part of our success in devising *collaboration ecosystems* today will flow from an ability to engage metalogue as a key form of collaborative power. Edison's true collaboration process recognizes the central role of collegiality and team discussion as crucial components that lay the groundwork for dialogue—and ultimately, metalogue. Grounding his teams with an understanding of how debate and conflict could be constructively harnessed, Edison maintained a high level of team coherence even when pressures mounted. Given access to the smart technologies and servers available today, Edison would no doubt advocate the use of metalogue and other smart layers you'll read about in Chapter 6 to drive collaboration across diverse communities of participants.

## SHIFT #3: THE NEED FOR RESKILLING WORKERS IN THE INNOVATION AGE

Generation Y, a cadre of workers born in America from roughly 1980 to 2000, is projected to comprise up to 75 percent of the US workforce by 2025.[16] Exhibiting a love for the latest digital gadgets and the hottest Internet trends, Gen Yers share a penchant for creativity and thirst for collaborative work and collaborative work environments. Internet native, this generation of workers grew up in the early days of MTV and saw the rise of YouTube, cell phones, Apple, laptops, Facebook, Amazon, and all things Wi-Fi. Their context for problem solving and connecting with the world consistently revolves around the use of digital tools. Any organization seeking to generate a collaborative culture in the Innovation Age must capture the interest of Gen Y.

But few Gen Y workers are finding collaboration happiness in traditionally structured organizations, especially the Fortune 500 companies. A 2012 study by Millennial Branding that surveyed 4 million Gen Y Facebook users—the social network that defines this generation—revealed that only 7 percent of respondents reported working for a Fortune 500 company. If this low percentage holds, "40 percent of the

Fortune 500 will no longer exist 10 years from now."[17] Unless this powerful young cohort views your organization as possessing the ability to create flat teams, and to work on collaboration projects that allow them to learn as well as connect to a sense of purpose, your company may be unsuccessful in attracting the Gen Y workers it needs to thrive. Millennium Branding founder Dan Schawbel notes, "Companies need to allow Gen Yers to operate entrepreneurially within the corporation by giving them control over their time, activities and budgets as much as possible." If we heed Rishad Tobaccowala's comments about attracting and retaining talent, your organization's recruitment efforts must be driven by the question, "What new combination of skills and collaborative team structures will allow us to compete?"

The process of rethinking which skill sets *are* most needed for a collaborative workplace served as the subject of a 2010 address by Emily DeRocco to the Iowa Association of Business and Industry. DeRocco, then president of the Manufacturing Institute in Washington, DC, described the ideal employee for the Innovation Age as offering a combination of technical or functional expertise plus soft skills that allowed them to communicate effectively with partners inside and outside their workplace. In her comments, DeRocco called the creation of this nexus between expertise and soft skills a "reskilling" process.[18] Ill-prepared by traditional education systems to deliver the desired combination of hard and soft skills, DeRocco indicated that a majority of the US workforce, regardless of industry thrust, would require some form of reskilling over the coming decade. Within the manufacturing realm, DeRocco has pushed for the development of advanced manufacturing skills targeting a new generation of workers, including a massive certification program based in community colleges. These reskilling efforts go beyond learning a specific trade and include broader concepts embracing computer-aided design as well as the ability to reconceptualize the context of a problem. Rather than just focusing on manuals and procedures, DeRocco emphasized that reskilling must drive creativity and collaboration into the manufacturing workplace.

An oddly provocative term, the notion of *reskilling* actually began surfacing in 2010 in Europe.[19] At its core, reskilling integrates a focus on hard skills, such as embracing the use of digital technology or learning how to access virtual networks, with soft skills, like one-on-one communication and rapport building. Among the key elements reskilling embraces are:

- Strengthening a belief in the creative power of the individual
- Mentoring and receiving mentorship
- Understanding how to use virtual networks and smart devices
- Synthesizing information from diverse sources
- Generating insights from data
- Working collaboratively to solve problems
- Establishing rapport

In a recent white paper themed around shifts in the global talent pool, Braden Kelley, author of *Stoking Your Innovation Bonfire* and cofounder of the highly respected *InnovationExcellence* web site, emphasizes another key reskilling requirement: the need for employees to understand *how to link learning from external teams to the work of internal teams*. The rise of open innovation and codevelopment projects operating beyond the walls of an organization requires workers to synthesize information in new ways. Kelley notes that most of our Industrial era training and acculturation focuses on managing flows of internal data, then pushing information outwardly to other parties. But now, Kelley notes that "to foster a collaborative approach," organizations will increasingly require employees to develop skills that enable them to "focus on the integration of external projects" as well, handling incoming flows of information from teams outside the organization.[20]

> Today, it's not so much about the specific expertise of each worker, but what they can create. It's less about the facts they already know and more about the new knowledge they can generate.
>
> *—Buckley Brinkman, executive director,*
> *Wisconsin Manufacturing Extension Partnership*

Whether you are in a service-based enterprise, a technology-driven organization, or a manufacturing concern, reskilling employees in ways that bring hard and soft skills together in an environment of collaboration will be crucial to staying competitive and attracting Gen Y workers. In addition, keeping Gen Y employees engaged in reskilling efforts that also involve older generations of workers will place a premium on methods that are both creative and highly experiential.

Edison's four phases of true collaboration offer a unique platform for embedding collaboration as a superskill in your organization using discovery learning and hands-on engagement rather than tired classroom-style approaches. Instead of pushing lectures to teach creativity and problem solving, Edison's experiential approach engages the reskilling process by activating creative centers of the brain and thereby developing large neural networks that drive learning more deeply than task-based or fact-based approaches.

# CHAPTER 3

## Phase 1

*Capacity—Creating the Foundations for*
*Collaboration to Thrive*

*Diversity helps drive discovery learning at different levels. It allows*
*you to see things from different angles and ask new questions.*

—Moises Norena, Global Director of Innovation,
Whirlpool Corporation

As you begin your true collaboration endeavor in Phase 1, examine your willingness to bring a discovery learning orientation to the project you're undertaking. Are you intending to operate more like Team B or Team A? Are you willing to run the three-legged race and deeply contribute to the success of your group rather than merely playing a pre-defined role? Regardless of whether you are already on a team that has initiated a project or whether you are beginning Phase 1 from scratch, start by answering these questions:

- Is there an opportunity to create new knowledge through our team's efforts?

- Could sharing the learning we generate benefit others beyond our team?

- Could our efforts result in an expansion in market value, customer value, product value, or service-related value?

- Can we balance both tasks and learning in our team project?

- Does each individual anticipate receiving new skills that will be valuable to him or her both in the short and long term?

If you're able to answer "yes" to a majority of these questions, you're starting out on the right foot. By being willing at the outset to engage in a discovery learning perspective rather than a sheer task-driven perspective, you are activating the power of your own innate creativity. Engaging your willingness to learn becomes a trigger not only for generating new ideas but harnessing true collaboration as a superskill. It enables you to see collaboration as the melding point for innovation-driving skills, value creation skills, and strategic thinking capabilities that Prahalad described as crucial in the post-reset environment (see Chapter 2).

Innovation author Steven Johnson, in *Where Good Ideas Come From*, writes about the impact of discovery learning versus task-driven activities on the neural networks of the brain. He describes discovery learning as stemming from "the creating brain," saying, "The creating brain behaves differently from the brain that is performing a repetitive task. The neurons communicate in different ways. The networks take on distinct shapes."[1] Brain patterns registered during discovery learning have a different neural signature. The signals extend more deeply into the brain itself, lighting up more regions, and accelerating connections that propel the observation of new patterns.

For Edison, activating his creating brain at the start of a collaboration effort allowed him to either reshape concepts he was already familiar with or build new knowledge around something that took him into entirely unknown territory. In Phase 1, Edison opened himself to the notion that although he may have initial glimmerings of the outcome to a project, he would allow new solutions to emerge as his discovery learning process took root. Rather than vaulting ahead thinking that he or his team members already knew the outcome of their quest, Edison used Phase 1 to engage his creating brain to guide him in new directions right from the start.

Like a young boy starting a new game, Edison described this discovery learning process as a hunt. By hunting, Edison allowed his creating brain to probe for new answers, including the questioning of existing facts. Edison reveals his relish for the discovery learning process in a conversation with Mr. R. H. Beach, head of the street-railway department of the General Electric Company in 1900. Setting out to create a battery made without liquid chemicals or lead, Edison said, "Beach, I don't think Nature would be so unkind as to withhold the secret of a good storage battery if a real earnest hunt for it is made. I'm going to hunt."[2]

The core mission for your true collaboration effort is to hunt for possible solutions. By shaping your endeavors using the components Edison incorporated into Phase 1, you will maximize the power of your hunt and yield the most creative array of potential outcomes. Edison began Phase 1 this way:

- *Part i, Engage Diversity:* Formulate a team representing a meaningful cross-section of expertise, thought styles, and backgrounds, maximizing the depth of perspective available to the team as a whole and expanding the range of discovery learning experiences for each member.

- *Part ii, Assemble small teams:* Build teams of two to eight people, fostering a small-is-mighty mindset and a group experience reflecting nimble communication and genuine collegiality.

Let's begin by examining the importance of diversity to the activation of the creating brain and the hunt.

# PART I, PHASE 1—CAPACITY

When we endeavor something new, oftentimes we lean on an unhelpful myth held by many: "I'm not creative enough to do this." We convince ourselves in the early going that we don't have what it takes to succeed in a project requiring novel thinking. Importantly, Edison did not allow this mindset to operate in his laboratory, or in his manufacturing, sales, marketing, or functional groups.

## Discovery and Diversity Are Key Ingredients for Collaboration Soup

Like a master chef, Edison viewed each employee as representing a different yet essential ingredient for the fabulous concoctions he desired to create. Each team he assembled yielded a kind of "collaboration soup," blending different combinations of employees together and giving the soup unique flavors and nuance.

When selecting people for true collaboration teams, Edison focused less on résumés and educational attainment than the innate, untapped knowledge and creative potential possessed by each individual. Edison believed that all people possessed deep creativity—they simply needed a spur to fully demonstrate it. He said, "The brain can be developed just the same as the muscles can be developed, if one will only take the pains to train the mind to think."[3]

Believing that a diverse group of individuals offered the best spark for *training the mind to think*, Edison consistently launched his true collaboration efforts by assembling talent from multiple disciplines. Seeking unique capabilities that complemented one another in concocting his collaboration soup, Edison drew upon experts as well as generalists, even including individuals who served as apprentices to the team. By intentionally colliding different disciplines and thinking styles together, not only did Edison's diverse teams engender discovery learning within the team itself, they yielded more robust solutions than would be possible by simply choosing representatives from one specialty.

> We can only really know about 70% of anything. There's always 30% that's emergent. But what we discover and learn as we go, we discover together.
>
> **—Dr. Jean Egmon, past director, Complexity In Action Network, Northwestern University**

In assembling a combination of generalists and specialists to tackle incandescence, for example, Edison linked the realms of chemistry, mathematics, and physics with hands-on capabilities ranging from glassblowing to instrument making. The unique melding of these skills led to breakthrough insights into how incandescence could be harnessed. In the hunt for ways to develop a long-burning filament, Edison and his team tested more than 100 compounds, including odd choices like bark, feathers, and boar bristles, ultimately discovering that bamboo fiber impregnated with carbon could burn evenly for hours.

It is not always necessary, perhaps not always desirable, to be a specialist in a subject in order to make suggestions related to it which start useful angles of research. We specialists are likely to get into ruts of our specialties out of which it is difficult to progress.

—*Thomas Edison*

While at first glance it would be hard to see Edison's logic for assembling the people shown in the table that follows, the diverse skills and expertise of each person meshed to yield not only a scientific breakthrough but a commercial breakthrough. Table 3.1 lists the individulas Edison called upon to aid him in conquering incandescence.

Edison viewed the creation of diverse teams as a powerful vehicle for *magnifying the innate creative capacities of each team member*. Instead of groups capable of linear thought processes randomly strung together, Edison saw diverse teams as interweaving and blending multiple thought styles. This intermingling served as the fundamental spur that activated the team's innate creative abilities. Building a

## Table 3.1 Edison Assembled Diverse Expertise for His Work on Incandescence

| Employee Name | Background and Expertise |
| --- | --- |
| Charles Batchelor | Textile worker, master experimenter |
| John Ott | Instrument maker |
| Ludwig Boehm | Glassblower |
| Francis Jehl | Apprentice |
| John Kruesi | Machinist, prototyper |
| Francis Upton | Mathematician, physicist |
| John Lawson | Chemical assay expert |
| Martin Force | Laboratory assistant |

diversity of expertise into each team allowed Edison to continually pull the best from the creating brains of his employees. Being drawn into new conversations that prompted many team members to go beyond their existing skill set, each member had to not only absorb but further contribute to the master pool of ideas being generated. Rather than functioning as a linear, stop-start process, *diverse teams allowed true collaboration to operate as a value creation continuum.*

Although bringing together generalists and specialists may seem like an obvious path for creating a collaboration team, today we often have to be prodded to consider diverse resources for such efforts. In his work at the Columbia Business School in New York, financial services expert and business author Michael J. Mauboussin emphasizes that diversity in how people think, as well as their life experiences, play a role in helping teams tackle complex issues and identify deeply novel solutions. Mauboussin emphasizes that creating diverse teams is not an easy process, and "we have to be mindful of it every day, because our natural inclination is to hang out with people who are mostly like us."[4] As Edison did in his era, Mauboussin believes it's essential for today's leaders to drive intellectual curiosity and discovery learning through the diversity of expertise they assemble for true collaboration efforts.

> I never have to worry about "creativity." Because we work using diverse teams, creativity takes care of itself.
>
> —*Dr. Curt Carlson, President,*
> *Stanford Research Institute*

Recognizing that today's collaboration teams will increasingly reflect the melding of innovation, value creation, and strategy, Herminia Ibarra and Morten T. Hansen recently published in the *Harvard Business Review* their research on collaboration and leadership, which further confirms the importance of team diversity. The authors note, "Left to their own devices, people will choose to collaborate with others they know well or who have similar backgrounds. Static groups breed insularity, which can be deadly for innovation."[5] Just as Edison brought together mathematicians, chemists, engineers, mechanics, prototypers, and scientists in his collaboration soup, today's teams must be "intentionally putting together different points of view that will challenge one another."[6]

> By building in diversity at the very start of an effort, you are improving your odds of dealing with complexity down the road. Complex systems are made up of diverse agents acting together. So by recognizing the role of diversity on a project team, you are increasing your chances for success.
>
> —*Dr. Jean Egmon, past director,*
> *Complexity in Action Network, Northwestern University*

## Diverse Teams Nurture Talent Density and Embed Reskilling

In addition to deepening the ongoing creative drive of his employees, Edison, through his insistence on having diverse teams, created a unique outcome: a vastly cross-trained and adaptive workforce. One foundation for his true collaboration success became the "talent density" he developed within his employee base. Serving as an ongoing mechanism for reskilling his workers, the breadth of learning experienced through Edison's project endeavors led to a broadening of skill sets within each team member over time, creating cadres of talent that could be formed and reformed into new teams over and over again. Exposing individual team members to skill sets held by other members also created a deep awareness within each participant of the breadth of knowledge required to solve problems.

True collaboration in Phase 1 thus became a mechanism not only for placing skilled people onto teams with a mix of talent but for cross-training them. *Diverse teams played a role not only in advancing the results of an individual within a team but in driving a long-term reskilling process within Edison's broader operations.*

Decades ahead of other business leaders in the Industrial Age who preferred to assign one worker to one task repeated many times, Edison viewed his workforce as a dynamic pool of talent that could tackle a broad array of problems. By offering diverse experiences to his employees, Edison continually expanded employee skills in a way that deepened the broader talent pool from which Edison could draw. In essence, true collaboration became a foundation for ongoing reskilling experiences that continually replenished diversity both within the lab and in his manufacturing operations.

Edison's intentional placement of Reginald Fessenden on a team assigned to create new technology for the world's first central power station in lower Manhattan—the Pearl Street station—offers one example of how Edison used true collaboration to reskill his employees. In the early 1880s, Fessenden approached Edison for employment, introducing himself as "an electrician by training." Despite Fessenden's protests, Edison hired Fessenden as a chemist, deploying him to develop insulation material for conduit wire at Pearl Street. At first somewhat confused and annoyed with Edison's decision, Fessenden went on to develop breakthroughs for an entirely new insulation material, making crucial contributions to the patents filed for wire insulation. By placing him on the Pearl Street team, Edison leveraged Fessenden's understanding of electricity while also challenging him to understand how electricity behaved when contacting other substances.

Years later, Edison appointed Fessenden as the head of his chemical laboratory at West Orange, New Jersey, replacing the PhD chemist whom Edison had previously hired. Initially believing that having a PhD head his chemistry lab would open doors to the latest thinking on new chemical compounds required by emerging industries of the 1890s, Edison came to realize that a different balance of skill sets was needed. Edison saw in Fessenden an ability to engage in what we today might call directed search—that is, asking questions within a general framework and then probing for new patterns and insights. Fessenden was creative, yet he did not cast his net so widely that he unduly wasted resources. Fessenden struck a balance between the hard skills of chemistry and electrical systems with the soft skills of experimentation and questioning.

> The privilege which I had being with this great man for six years was the greatest inspiration of my life.
>
> *—Arthur Kennelly, Edison employee, electrician*

In his new role heading the chemical laboratory, Fessenden's focus shifted from true collaboration participant to collaboration facilitator. He combined a deep understanding of the hands-on applications needed by Edison's project teams with a tolerance for the ambiguities associated with forward-looking research efforts. Edison recognized that Fessenden not only could continue the cycle of discovery learning at the lab but possessed the skills to mentor and cross-train others.

An even more dramatic transformation in capability is witnessed in Edison's reskilling of textile worker Charles Batchelor. One of Edison's first collaborators, Batchelor's connection to Edison predated the establishment of the

Menlo Park lab in 1876. Becoming a skilled experimenter under Edison's tutelage, Batchelor was later cross-trained in chemistry, electromechanics, and motor design. After contributing to the development of the phonograph, the record, and the incandescent electric light, Edison pushed Batchelor even further, sending him overseas to set up a massive display of Edison's electrical power technology for the Paris Exposition of 1881. Suddenly coming into the role of general manager, Batchelor had to scramble to learn the business side of Edison's operations rather than just the research and development side. Batchelor's diverse skills ultimately proved so valuable to Edison that he gave Batchelor a percentage of the total proceeds of the laboratory.

> Give me a boy with a willingness to work and learn and I'll do something with him.
>
> —*Thomas Edison*

In personally witnessing the skill expansion of workers like Fessenden and Batchelor, Edison's employees realized the depth of capability that resided in the lab. Like scores of Rocky Balboa fighters in training, the lab operated with a "we can conquer anything" mindset. Edison's employees realized they could consistently pool their capabilities and adapt their learning to yield winning results in a wide variety of competitive settings.

## Diverse Teams Power Success in Organizations Today

We can see echoes of Edison's belief in the power of diverse teams in many organizations today. Business maverick Ricardo Semler, head of Semco's diverse operations in Brazil, writes in *The Seven-Day Weekend* about the power of viewing his employees as a massively diverse group of individuals who can be shaped and reshaped into diverse project teams, creating collaboration soup much the way Edison did. Leader of a business empire with a portfolio ranging from real estate services to the manufacture of marine products and heavy-duty machinery for the oil and gas industry, Semco is a private company with leading positions in highly competitive industry segments. Growing more than 40 percent per year without public investment, the company now employs more than 3,000 employees. Speaking of the diversity represented in Semco's project teams, Semler says he uses discovery learning as a vehicle to maintain high employee engagement levels while also generating more adaptive thinking within its teams. Semler notes, "'Discovery' is one of those splendid words that radiates power, like balance and exhilaration, passion and calling, satisfaction and fulfillment."[7] Semler believes discovery learning within a diverse team setting aids employees in developing broader thinking styles and expertise. Dedicated to cross-training in engineering, customer service, project management, and quality control, Semco's diverse teams have yielded competitive advantage for the company through its talent-dense and flexible workforce.

> Then again a lot of people think I have done things because of some "genius" that I've got. That too is not true. Any other bright-minded fellow can accomplish just as much if he will stick like hell and remember that nothing that's any good works by itself.
>
> —*Thomas Edison*

Transformations in the increasingly complex realm of information technology (IT) offer another view of why diverse, multidisciplinary teams are increasingly valued today.

"IT projects are now so big, and they touch so many aspects of an organization, that they pose a singular new risk."[8] IT experts Bent Flyvbjerg and Alexander Budzier, in recently published research, emphasize the power of diverse teams to address increasingly complex linkages between customer needs and an ever-expanding menu of computing platforms they can access. The interconnection of smart devices with Internet-based systems and secure in-house networks mean IT design teams have to work harder to see the big picture. The authors note, "Software is now an integral part of numerous products—think of the complex software systems in cars and computer appliances—but the engineers and managers who are in charge of product development too often have limited understanding of how to implement the technology component."[9] Once the provenance of hardware geeks and computer scientists, IT teams now require the presence of industrial designers alongside generalists and specialists from service-driven industries. This is especially crucial to ensuring that broad perspectives about how the system will function and who will use it are considered.[10]

### Diversity Drives Creativity, Deeper Thinking

Our modern understanding of diversity embraces not only multiple thinking styles and life experiences but ethnic and gender diversity as well.

From the perspective of ethnic diversity, in his labs, Edison employed skilled workers hailing from England, Ireland, Scotland, Sweden, Germany, France, Switzerland, Italy, Hungary, Poland, and several other

*(continued)*

*(continued)*

nations. Edison's roster of foreign-born employees constituted more than 25 percent of his total workforce by 1914.[11]

Although no women were employed in Edison's laboratory, notebook logs reveal that his second wife, Mina Miller Edison (Figure 3.1), conducted electrical experiments at West Orange. Women also worked in the West Orange manufacturing operations during World War I. Although it was extremely rare to find women in professional roles during the early Industrial Revolution in America, were he alive today, Edison would readily embrace the participation of women in every facet of his operations. A proponent of women's rights and a believer in "equal partnership" between men and women,[12] Edison would cheer the recent findings of a 2011 study conducted by Anita Woolley of Carnegie Mellon University and Thomas Malone of the MIT Sloan School of Management, revealing that teams that included women scored higher on group intelligence dimensions versus teams solely composed of men.[13]

Rather than slavishly ticking off columns on a diversity checklist, Edison was most interested in creating *meaningful diversity* on his teams. Today, he would urge us to view diversity with a wide lens, consciously considering the types of diversity that are valuable on a given team and striving to develop collegiality across a broad spectrum of expertise, thought styles, life experiences, gender, ethnic acculturation, and work styles.

**Figure 3.1 Mina Miller Edison**
*Source:* National Park Service, Edison National Historic Site.

What does the collaboration soup look like on your team? Are diverse types of expertise represented? Have you considered different technical skills and functional capabilities? Does your team include members who are willing to question and probe existing facts and conventions? What kinds of life experiences are present? Take time to consider these questions as we begin looking at the second facet of Phase 1: the importance of small teams.

# PART II, PHASE 1—CAPACITY

A second component of Edison's true collaboration process in Phase 1 entailed the leveraging of small teams. Edison particularly favored nimble groups ranging from two to eight people. The emphasis on small team size allowed Edison to fulfill two key objectives: (1) speedy team communication and (2) nurturing of deep collegiality.

In this segment of Phase 1, we'll explore the benefits Edison derived from small teams and how his philosophies are being used by organizations operating in the Innovation Age. We'll also look at the pros and cons of virtual teams—a digital wrinkle that Edison did not have to navigate during the Industrial Revolution.

## Edison Preferred Small Teams for Nimble Communication

A man who preferred streamlined structures over unnecessarily convoluted ones, Edison relished the speed and high impact that communication within a small team afforded. Edison believed in making decisions rapidly and having at hand all the resources needed to keep projects running smoothly. He found small teams of two to eight people ideal for the rapid and dynamic exchange of thinking among team members. Edison relished frequent, pithy communications, creating a culture that valued intense information sharing that was focused and direct. Whether Edison was personally leading a true collaboration team or simply advising it at intervals, all team members knew they needed to be at their best when communicating with him—and with one another.

At Menlo Park, as well as at West Orange, individual teams could operate in a single room for live meetings without undue logistical complications. In Edison's time, it was common for teams to be situated in the same location, or at most, two hours away by horse and carriage. Edison stayed in close contact with teams via liberal use of telephone and telegraph communications, frequently using these tools along with handwritten letters. Giving team leaders autonomy for making certain decisions while he provided others, Edison streamlined the communication process within his collaborations, allowing for rapid decision making and quick response times. Often impatient when he was required to wait for results, his authorized biographers, Thomas Commerford Martin and Frank Lewis Dyer, refer to Edison as "the living embodiment of the song, 'I Want What I Want When I Want It.'"[14]

In his true collaboration efforts, Edison found small teams operated as a multiplicative rather than an additive force. Like a band of Delta Rangers who could take on a fighting unit many times its size, the interweaving of skills and intensive communication that characterized Edison's nimble teams enabled them to create a kind of collective group intelligence. This collective intelligence put big projects within Edison's reach—projects that other organizations operating in a more task-driven team structure would have deemed impossible.

In instances where extensive manpower was clearly required, Edison banded several small teams together to form a larger pool of resources. When this occurred, his small teams unified rapidly into a bigger mélange, all drawing upon their common denominator of training within Edison's true collaboration framework. One remarkable example of the seamless orchestration made possible using clusters of small teams is offered through Edison's design and development of the world's first central power station in lower Manhattan from 1880–1882. Edison's "need for speed" in innovation, creativity, data analysis, and pithy team communication reached an extreme in his deployment of resources scattered across New York City during the construction of the Pearl Street station. An undertaking that ranked the first of its kind in the world, Edison focused nearly 20 small teams on innovating the solutions needed for diverse types of equipment to be housed in the station itself, ranging from voltage meters, switches, wiring, and insulation to the production of lightbulbs and dynamos—even coordinating the construction of the station itself.

> Small teams? It depends on what you're trying to do. If you're setting about to change something but the ways to do it are well known, it's not a creation—it's a construction. You can assign that to a whole bunch of people and it gets done. But, if you're assigning something that's creative, not everybody will get it. The "slow molecules" will stop you and slow you down. If you select the team members based on their passion for doing something new, you will make more progress.
>
> *—Art Fry, 3M Fellow and Technical Scientist,*
> *Inventor of Post-it Notes*

Often operating around the clock for weeks during the summer of 1882 as the September launch date neared, bands of chemists, engineers, machinists, and mechanics invented new equipment for the plant, with each design moving into manufacturing almost as quickly as it was drawn up and tested. Edison physically traveled by horse and carriage between the Pearl Street construction site and various small laboratory sites he'd leased uptown, using notebooks as well as telephone calls and what became known as "bug reports" to receive continual progress updates. Although Edison would no doubt have given his eyeteeth for a smartphone in 1882, the true collaboration culture favoring rapid communication between teams enabled Edison's organization to bring the Pearl Street station online within less than 24 months. Using small teams as the bedrock for his Herculean efforts, Edison delivered new-to-the-world technology in virtually every component installed at Pearl Street. True collaboration enabled his small teams to yield hugely productive output across their innovation, design, and production efforts.

> Eight people can do the work of 20. Give them a problem to solve, and they'll just go at it relentlessly.
>
> —*Robert W. Schmidt, President,*
> *Systems Engineering & Manufacturing Inc.*

Mark Zuckerberg, wunderkind chief executive officer (CEO) of Facebook, grasps the notion of multiplicative versus additive impact when small teams operate collaboratively. Mirroring Edison's true collaboration philosophy, Zuckerberg assembles legions of small, dynamic software teams to write code that keeps Facebook at the leading edge. In a barbed exchange with (then) Yahoo! CEO Carol Bartz in mid-2011, Zuckerberg actually claimed Facebook was 100 times more productive than Yahoo! Why? Facebook's small teams operate like Team B, multiplying their learning and efficiency with each undertaking, whereas Yahoo!'s operate like Team A, getting the basics done but little more. Michael Schrage, a research fellow at MIT Sloan School's Center for Digital Business and author of *Shared Minds*, commented that Zuckerberg's software design teams focus on higher-order functions such as robustness, scalability, ease of use, and maintainability—qualities that drive leading-edge software performance in the Innovation Age. Yahoo!'s teams, however, are still using linear metrics from the Industrial Age, such as "lines of code written per day."[15]

---

**Illustration of Software Team Productivity at Yahoo! versus at Facebook**

At Yahoo!, team productivity is additive:

$$5 + 5 + 5 = 15.$$

At Facebook, team productivity is multiplicative:

$$5 \times 5 \times 5 = 125.$$

Net result for three teams:

Facebook = 8 $\times$ more productive.

The preceding calculations illustrate the differences between the multiplicative versus additive power of small teams like Edison's and Zuckerberg's. Offering a hypothetical example comparing three teams of five programmers from Facebook with five programmers from Yahoo!, Facebook's teams would be eight times more productive than Yahoo!'s. Facebook's collaborative structure leverages eight times more knowledge resources and ultimately yields more value. In commenting that his organization is 100 times more productive than Yahoo!'s, Zuckerberg, is emphasizing the multiplier value of true collaboration.

---

Amazon CEO Jeff Bezos also embraces Edison's love of small teams as a multiplier of creativity and productivity. Coining a now-famous phrase—*two-pizza teams*—during a 2004 interview with *Fast Company*, Bezos remarked: "If it takes more than two pizzas to feed them, the team is too big."[16] Symbolizing the company's desire to keep its thinking nimble and fresh, members of Amazon's two-pizza teams contribute to several projects simultaneously, cross-pollinating their skills and consistently yielding new business ideas.

Ricardo Semler of Semco offers a slightly different take on the force-multiplying capacity of small teams, considering them what he describes as a collection of tribes:[17]

> At Semco, our units are always a size that permits people to know each other, understand the whole . . . We usually organize along the lines of a half dozen to ten people who directly interact. . . . Groups of between six and ten people who know all about each other do not need outside control. Better to have six teams of six people each rather than an unwieldy thirty-six member unit.

Bold to a degree that would make Edison smile, Semco's tribes operate on what Semler describes as a *minimum common denominator*—passion, talent, and trust. A signature of Semco's small tribes lies in targeting major opportunities in markets characterized by high complexity. Although small in size, these teams pride themselves on carving out market-dominating positions that larger teams in competitive firms can't move fast enough to capture.

## Small Teams Reduce Social Distance and Augment Trust

In addition to creating speed of communication and multiplicative power, small teams fulfilled a second crucial objective for Edison's collaborations: creating collegiality. *The depth to which team members created collegiality and trust represented a distinguishing feature of Edison's labs.* In a departure from the strict separation of owner versus worker or supervisor versus employee typical of Edison's era, Edison viewed the lab as a workplace of colleagues. Edison wanted team members to trust one another and feel comfortable sharing information that could prove vital to a project.

To encourage collegiality, Edison created unique opportunities for social connections between his lab employees, forming an invisible glue that fostered dynamic conversations. In creating a close-knit, collegial environment, Edison intuitively used what today we would describe as employee rituals. The most notable of these—*midnight lunch*—inspired the title of this book. *Midnight lunch* references the affectionate slang Edison's Menlo Park crew gave to after-hours gatherings Edison sponsored for workers who were staying well into the night to complete their project efforts. Never shy about rolling up his sleeves and laboring with his employees, Edison created a shoulder-to-shoulder connection with team members during these late night sessions, which bonded them in a way few other processes could.

One vivid midnight lunch episode was recounted by apprentice Francis Jehl in his book *Menlo Park Reminiscences*, documenting the perspective of an actual midnight lunch session through the eyes of a reporter from the *New York Herald* who visited Edison's Menlo Park lab late one night. After arriving by train to Menlo Park, the reporter heads to the second floor of the lab, spying the famed pipe organ housed there. The "horseshoes" referenced are the uniquely shaped carbonized filaments Edison was testing in his lightbulb experiments:[18]

> The last visitors had departed and . . . Edison had gone to his house . . . an hour before; the boys up at the laboratory had told me that he would scarcely come back before morning. . . . Then I heard the notes of an organ. . . . The notes that came were those of (HMS) Pinafore. The little outer office where they test the telephones was tenantless. In the distance a solitary, aproned figure stood before the small furnace

where they bake the little carbon horseshoes, so I ascended the stairs. At the far end . . . were scattered about eight or nine of the assistants, lounging on stools and benches, and at the extreme end, seated before the organ, was one of them rolling out the too familiar melody. [Mr. Batchelor] said: "We're having a little music. Sit down and join us."

The visitor joined master experimenter Charles Batchelor along with glassblower Ludwig Boehm and several other employees for a raucous round of out-of-tune singing with the organ. The reporter then recounts:

But during the playing a man with a crumpled felt hat, a white silk handkerchief at his throat, his coat hanging carelessly and his vest half buttoned, came silently in, and, with his hand to his ear, sat close by the glassblower. . . . "That's nice," said he, looking round. It was Edison. [The throng continued by singing and whistling a variety of tunes. As the merriment proceeded,] Edison took a writing pad from his pocket and scratched rapidly with a pencil on it for some minutes. He beckoned to Boehm. "Can you blow that?" Edison handed him a rough drawing. "Yes," said Boehm.

[By 10:30 PM,] the conversation turned on scientific topics, roaming over wide fields. . . . "I'm hungry," blurted out Francis. "Where's the lunch?" said Edison. "There was none ordered," said Francis. . . . "We didn't think you were coming back to work all night."

Hearing that no food had been brought in, Edison quickly proceeded to order a midnight lunch of meat, bread, cheese, and beverages for the entire crew, with the discussions of carbonized filaments, voltaic arc lights, and glass bulbs continuing far into the night.

Often peppered with raucous stories and cigars, as well as singing, these midnight lunch sessions became social occasions mixed with scientific conversation and the sharing of insights. But most important, they offered an opportunity for workers to get to know one another in a new way. They could cut loose and be themselves, without feeling like they were being watched or evaluated. By rubbing elbows with Edison himself, employees felt they were receiving special attention, and they valued the pithy insights Edison often let fly during these spontaneous midnight lunch chats. In later years, as shown in Figure 3.2, midnight lunch crews working to develop new technology during World War I became known as the Insomnia Squad.

During midnight lunch, as well as other casual gatherings Edison sponsored—fishing excursions being a favorite—Edison reduced the social distance between workers in his laboratory. *Rather than functioning merely as teammates, employees became true colleagues.*

In her extensive study of team dynamics, associate Babson professor and cross-functional teamwork expert Anne Donnellon describes social distance as a gauging mechanism we use to determine whether we will offer our trust to someone. Her insightful book, *Team Talk: The Power of Language in Team Dynamics*, illustrates that teams operate best when members are not constantly "sizing each other up" as they work. Social distance relates to the feeling of equality, connection, collegiality, and relatedness in a team setting. Donnellon's studies also show that by reducing social distance, team members can truly collaborate, trust one another, and become willing to share their deepest insights. Teams holding high trust for its members can be described as having low social distance. Teams with low trust exhibit high social distance.[19] Using small teams and shared social rituals as key bonding mechanisms, Edison was successful in creating collegiality in his labs, reducing the social distance between his employees so they felt free to collaborate and share information fully among the group.

**Figure 3.2 Edison's Midnight Lunch Gatherings
Became Known as the *Insomnia Squad* During
World War I**

*Source:* National Park Service, Edison National Historic Site.

Mauboussin comments that one key to successful collaboration is the willingness to share what today is termed private information, that is, data, experiences, or insights that might reside only in one person.[20] Like a trump card being held in reserve, team members sometimes withhold their private information to ensure they can wield power or control over others. Employees often "reserve their unique information" so they can use it as backup if something goes awry. According to Mauboussin's studies, without the presence of openness and a feeling of collegiality, individuals will hoard their private information, choosing instead to focus on details that represent shared information within the team—information already common to everyone. By holding back private information, team members gain a sense of power. Without a level of trust that encourages each employee to put their unique information out for use in a collaboration effort, the group's project can fail.

I have friends in overalls whose friendship I would not swap for the favor of the kings of the world.

—*Thomas Edison*

Through employee rituals such as midnight lunches and fishing excursions to underscore major celebrations and accomplishments, Edison encouraged shoulder-to-shoulder social connections among his employees, building pathways to trust.

Today, a myriad of factors can inhibit the creation of trust among team members, particularly when groups are operating virtually. High social distance can be created by a wide range of considerations, such as job title, pay grade, gender, cultural norms, and educational attainment. Leaders and team members alike must grapple with an expansive list of potential stumbling blocks, including many listed in Table 3.2.

**Table 3.2  Factors That Can Lead to High Social Distance on Teams**

| | |
|---|---|
| Gender | Differences in pay grade |
| Job title | Generational affiliation |
| Religion | Communication skills |
| Educational attainment | Ethnicity or cultural affiliation |
| Ability to speak the local language | Length of tenure with the organization |

By failing to recognize the existence of these factors in a collaboration effort, communication and trust can break down. Bridging social distance is particularly important for organizations that—like Edison's—foster diversity in work teams spanning technical skills, cultural background, and age, among many others. Donnellon's findings reveal that creating trust through reducing social distance is central to creating a level playing field for any highly functioning collaboration endeavor, helping individuals address issues of identity, interdependence, and power differences.[21]

## Leaders Must Personally Model Collegiality

The collegiality that typified Edison's laboratory teams also flowed from personal qualities modeled by Edison himself. He exemplified what it meant to be a colleague rather than merely a teammate. Uncomfortable with being called a genius by reporters or associates, Edison insisted on simply being called an inventor. Minimizing the use of titles in his organization, employees advanced through their abilities to experiment, display creative problem-solving skills, and contribute key insights to projects.

Even Edison's clothing signaled a down-to-earth, collegial style. At Menlo Park, he often donned an artisan's hat and work apron, allowing him to get his hands into all manner of compounds and chemicals without mussing his clothes. Later, even when arriving at his West Orange lab in a suit and bow tie—ready

*(continued)*

*(continued)*

for frequent photo ops and visits by distinguished scientists or overseas guests—he sometimes dispensed with the work apron and would spend the day walking around the lab with chemical residues, grease, or metal shavings on his finery. Although not popularized to the degree that Steve Jobs's signature black turtleneck and jeans came to be, Edison was the first to don dungarees and a work shirt when assembling new equipment for a manufacturing line or troubleshooting a technical problem.

In scenes that could appear today in episodes of the TV show *Undercover Boss*, Edison sometimes pulled pranks on employees in his company's legal department by applying for a job as an inventor. "The embarrassment junior clerks felt at having failed to recognize their boss immediately turned to an acknowledgement of the great man as easygoing and approachable."[22] Edison was often the first to crack a joke or lead a conversation with a humorous story, and his use of humor added to his "common touch." He was one of the guys. Edison modeled what it meant to be a true colleague.

Donnellon emphasizes that the type of language used by team members while they work together reveals volumes about the social distance between them, indicating how comfortable—or uncomfortable—they feel toward one another. Recognizing three categories of language—high power, low power, and collaborative power—Donnellon notes that the more closely the group's predominant type of language resembles collaborative power, the more closely knit the group is. The three categories can be summarized this way:[23]

1. *High Power:* Language is characterized by corrections, interruptions, direct orders, sudden topic shifts, or verbal aggression toward another member.

2. *Low Power:* Conversations include frequent apologies, disclaimers, hedging, or excessive politeness.

3. *Collaborative Power:* Discussion is more casual and free-flowing and includes the respectful use of nicknames for team members, authentic expressions of liking or admiration, expressions of cooperation, emphasis on common viewpoints, or frequent identification of common efforts.

Although not intended to provide a full diagnosis of social distance in your true collaboration efforts, tracking these three categories of language usage can attune you to listen for ways you are personally using words, as well as how others around you may be using language that either discourages or nurtures collaboration.

> He conversed, argued and disputed with us all as though he were a colleague on the same footing.
>
> —*Frank Dyer and Thomas Martin*

Modeling many facets of Edison's Phase 1 practices, W. L. Gore founder Bill Gore facilitates collaborative power by discouraging the use of titles.[24] Recognizing work titles as a potential barrier that separates people, the company creates low social distance among its employees, who are known as associates, and creates a level playing field that contributes to healthy risk taking. With only 10 percent of the company's associates bearing the word *leader* on their business cards, those who receive this designation have been consistently rated at the highest levels of performance by their peers, taking both team and solo efforts into account. In his book

*The Future of Management*, strategy guru Gary Hamel concurs with the viewpoints taken by Edison and Gore, emphasizing that fewer titles mean greater adaptability, more engagement, and more innovation.[25]

## Virtual Teams, Colocated Teams, and Selection of Team Members

Although Edison's true collaboration efforts operated on a face-to-face basis—or FTF as the acronym reads today—not every team in the Innovation Age can be run this way. A 2008 *BusinessWeek* study of white-collar professionals in the United States revealed that 82 percent of respondents reported they needed to partner "live" with others on a daily basis to get their work done.[26] However, a major study conducted in 2011 by Forrester Consulting revealed that emergent within this huge FTF percentage is a growing trend toward virtual teaming, with 40 percent of US companies reporting that their employees participated on virtual teams, a figure projected to grow to 56 percent in the next three years.[27]

Although arguments can be made for the merits of both live and virtual teams, *the crucial factor in driving collaboration success lies in creating connective tissue between each team member*. Bonding through shared experiences forms an invisible glue when people meet FTF, a factor that so far has not been replicated by any digital methods. As VivaKi's vice president of innovation, Rishad Tobaccowala lamented in a blog post following the 2012 Consumer Electronics Show, "I am a carbon life form with analog feelings living in a silicon world."[28] In other words, "treat me like a human being and not a computer."

Although the value of virtual teams to global organizations that share resources and knowledge across borders remains compelling, crucial factors are required to make these structures function effectively. Research suggests that having virtual teams meet online first rather than FTF accelerates the bonding process once they do actually connect live. "Having some initial virtual interactions before a first FTF meeting can actually enhance the benefits of that first FTF meeting" by allowing team members to understand key areas of expertise.[29] In addition, by planning specific timetables for FTF interactions, especially those involving international travel, teams can create a "predictable rhythm of meetings" rather than conducting them on an ad hoc basis. Research by Mark Mortenson and Michael O'Leary indicates that teams which connect FTF soon after their formation, and then continue to connect live at regular intervals, outperform virtual teams that choose to meet live only "as needed."

Jason Sherman, president of SHERMAN Communications and Marketing, participates on a virtual team that operates this way at Geodis Wilson, an international freight forwarding company with nine divisions. Serving on a virtual team with a half dozen members from London, Singapore, Hamburg, and Amsterdam, Sherman notes, "We met live for three days in Germany to help create the content for a new and innovative iPad-based sales tool. Making time to break bread together and share stories during our downtime really helped to establish trust and good chemistry."[30]

Still, regardless of how effectively a virtual team is managed in a true collaboration effort, research indicates that "as teams become more virtual, collaboration declines."[31] Often lacking a deeper sense of shared purpose—a subject to be discussed in Phases 2 and 3—as well as a shared understanding of how the virtual team will operate, many virtual collaborations can lead to frustration. Social distance proves to be a challenging obstacle to overcome.

Believing that live teams are better on all counts, design consultancy IDEO structures each one of its collaborative projects using colocated teams. Sharing a common geography and common office quarters, teams literally camp out in one of IDEO's global office locations. For IDEO, the benefits of decreasing social distance through the more subtle exchanges that take place via water cooler interactions outweigh any other advantages a virtual structure may offer.

Regardless of whether you elect to structure your true collaboration effort as live or virtual, Larry Keeley of the Doblin Group emphasizes a key Edisonian principle: "Choose your teams with intention. Having a sense of the strengths each person brings to your collaboration helps you through the breakdowns that will inevitably occur."[32] Keeley also notes that Edison's team size of two to eight people often proves optimal. "After that, you start to see threshold points at 12 people and 20 people, and then 50 and 300 people. Keeping teams small is the best way to start."[33]

As a final note, Art Fry—3M fellow and famed inventor of the Post-it Note—comments that not every person who starts out as a true collaboration team member will remain one. "If you're assigning something that's creative, not everybody will get it. The 'slow molecules' will stop you and slow you down. If you select the team members based on their passion for doing something new, you will make more progress."[34]

In choosing your true collaboration team, consider how the members will run the three-legged race together. Use the visual illustration of the components in Phase 1, shown in Figure 3.3, to guide you. Are you concocting collaboration soup by building in diversity through expertise, life experiences, gender, or acculturation? Can you structure your group as a two-pizza team? How can you use employee rituals such as midnight lunches to increase collegiality? Whether you are to serve as the team's leader or as a team member, recognize that your group will likely undergo changes and transformations as it progresses through Phases 2, 3, and 4—with some of the slow molecules dropping away over time. Don't be afraid to

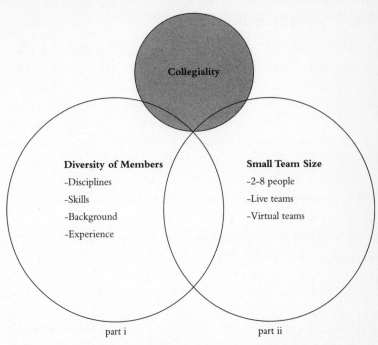

**Figure 3.3 Phase 1: Capacity—from Thomas Edison's Four Phases of True Collaboration**

*Note*: In Phase 1, small, diverse teams encourage collegiality and expanded perspective.

reshape your team if the chemistry between members does not develop as you intend.

## TRUE COLLABORATION TOOLKIT: HANDS-ON EXERCISES—PHASE 1

Here are several exercises you and your team can use to practice the true collaboration principles in Phase 1. Consider starting a notebook to record your observations about each exercise you try.

## Use Improv to Spur Collegiality

Improvisation offers a terrific opportunity to develop connections with people on your true collaboration team whom you don't know well. One unique outcome in any improvisational exercise is a deepened sense of equality and collegiality shared by the participants. No one individual is better or more important than any other. Each person participating in an improv is equally dedicated to supporting his or her colleagues. Improv offers your team an excellent way to begin reducing social distance, creating a humorous and unique experience.

Based on a popular exercise from the Second City comedy club, try this exercise. Sit in a circle with 6 to 10 colleagues. Choose one person—we'll call this person the captain—to begin and then proceed clockwise around the circle. The captain makes a statement on any subject. In response, the person sitting to the right of the captain begins his or her reply with, "Yes, and . . ." and then proceeds to make another statement that in some way supports the captain's sentence. Continue around the circle twice so that everyone has shared two "Yes, and . . ." statements.

What did you discover? Did the group gain a sense of closeness? Why, or why not? Run through the exercise again, this time theming your comments around a specific subject such as coffee or the Super Bowl. Choose a new captain and begin. What did you observe? Repeat the exercise as many times as you desire, selecting a new theme each time. Do you sense new bonds beginning to form?

## Create Your Own Midnight Lunch Experience

Have you ever had a midnight lunch experience with coworkers? If not, create a ritual your collaboration team can share when you need to relax and blow off some steam.

Consider ordering takeout pizza from your favorite local pizzeria or having Chinese food delivered from a nearby restaurant. Pick a special place in your work environment to hold your midnight lunch session—or plan it for an offsite location. Whatever you choose, create a relaxed atmosphere where you and your colleagues can simply talk and not feel like you have to be "on." Open yourself up to hearing conversations about things that interest your colleagues outside of work. Listen for bits of information you can use to connect at a deeper human level with each person.

## Create a Wormhole to Another Location That Helps Maintain Team Connections

Established in 1991 by innovation and design guru David Kelley, IDEO is now a globally recognized firm that has pioneered breakthrough products, including Apple's first mouse and the Steelcase Leap Chair. An advocate for deeply connecting people and ideas, IDEO has developed a unique concept to link its offices together, called wormholes. Wormholes feature live cameras that stream images from one individual global office to another. Rotating the locations periodically, IDEO employees use wormholes to peek in on what's happening in other IDEO work spaces, allowing people to feel connected even though they may be thousands of miles apart.

How could you develop a wormhole to connect with colleagues who cannot operate live on your team? Use the wormhole as a means to learn about projects that relate to new ideas that interest your group and help members create a shared experience around discovery learning.

## CHAPTER 4

## Phase 2

*Context—How Context Accelerates Collaboration and Innovation*

In the late 1860s and early 1870s, scientists in Europe and America began intensively researching human physiology. Particularly keen to unlock the most complex systems of the body, considerable attention focused on how massive networks of veins and arteries served the heart in circulating blood and how the lungs functioned in respiration. Curiously, scientists also "recognized the ear as one of the most complicated parts of the human body,"[1] desiring to probe its mysteriously fashioned bones and membranes for the secrets of registering sound.

In 1876, shortly after this intense interest in human anatomy unfolded, Alexander Graham Bell received a patent for the telephone, creating the world's first technology for transmitting sound using the human voice. Exposed for years to detailed three-dimensional models of the human ear commissioned by his father, phonetics expert Professor Alexander Melville Bell,

Alexander Graham had long been fascinated with how the ear processed sound. As a young child, Alexander had watched his mother, Eliza Grace, grow progressively deaf, ultimately losing her hearing entirely when he was only 12 years old. Eager to understand mechanisms that could aid the deaf to communicate through speech and other means, Alexander gained access to scholarly research on acoustics as well as the mechanics of human speech through a school for the deaf owned by his father. Developing a passionate interest in sound transmission and its connection to how the ear "hears," Alexander conducted experiments that ultimately yielded his breakthrough invention of the telephone. In the eyes of historians and technologists alike, the telephone stands as one of the most important inventions in human history.

Thomas Edison, deaf in his left ear since the age of 16, was also fascinated by sound and communication. Mastering telegraphy in his early 20s, Edison received training in sending and receiving telegraph messages as a teenager, fervently exploring the inner mechanisms of telegraph systems, the world of Morse code, and even methods for producing dots and dashes on diverse surfaces. Linking his gifts for making small motors with a passion for exploring new materials and substrates, in 1877 Edison began developing a telephone transmitter that improved upon Bell's first transmitter, which could propel sound for only about 1 mile.

That same year, Edison also began devising a mechanism for recording and playing back telephone messages. Drawing upon his knowledge of telegraphy and machine making, Edison experimented with a rotating metal drum covered with a sheet of tinfoil, using a stylus to create grooves in its thin surface. By securing a funnel-shaped metal cone to the stylus, the stylus transformed sound waves from words spoken into the cone into kinetic energy, embedding sound waves in slender grooves in the foil as the drum rotated. This unique yet simple design yielded the world's first phonograph and record—disruptive technologies allowing the human voice to be captured and replayed over and over again. Today, we recognize both these groundbreaking inventions as the beginning of musical entertainment, now a multibillion dollar global industry that continues to yield new ways for people to connect through technology, and sound.

> There's no doubt that I shall be able to store up & reproduce automatically at any future time the human voice perfectly.
>
> —*Thomas Edison*

Thomas Edison was born just 20 days before Alexander Graham Bell. The two men were contemporaries as well as competitors, sharing a common passion for acoustics. They both operated laboratories. And yet, coming just one year apart, their pioneering sound innovations took different paths: Bell's in the one-time transmission of sound, with a product whose design was heavily influenced by his under-standing of human physiology, and Edison's in the capturing and replaying of sound, heavily influenced by his expertise in telegraphy, machine making, and materials science.

What created these differences? *Context.*

Bell viewed sound from the context of the human body and its inner workings. He asked questions relating to how the ear processed sound and how words formed by the tongue, lips, and teeth could be propelled so others far away could hear them. But Edison viewed sound in a different context. He saw it as a natural phenomenon that could be captured mechanically and replayed. Viewing sound from this perspective prompted Edison to ask questions about the types of mechanisms that could store sound, reproducing it over and over again with the same pristine quality each time.

Both of these extraordinary men created breakthroughs associated with the same phenomenon—sound—while operating from different contexts. Both Bell and Edison created "new facts" and new realities about what was possible in human communication, one harnessing sound via the telephone and the other via the phonograph and record. In turn, these new facts yielded a completely different threshold of understanding—an entirely new context—for how scientists as well as everyday consumers came to think about sound itself.

The notion of context played a particularly pivotal role in Edison's innovation and collaboration success. *Context served as a bridge between the hypotheses and experiments Edison conducted and the innovative prototypes that flowed from them.* Rather than viewing context as an absolute or fixed construct, context for Edison was like a living vessel that contained robust nuggets of insights that he could recombine to yield new knowledge and new solutions. As you will learn in Phase 2, Edison developed a unique approach to shaping context in a way that drew upon his many areas of expertise, while also joining this expertise with the breakthrough findings from his experiments. Just as Edison came to discover "recorded sound" as a new context that yielded revolutionary ways that the human voice and music could be captured, Edison discovered "moving pictures" as a context that ultimately yielded motion picture entertainment, and "portable power" as a context for what became the alkaline storage battery. Edison masterminded these new contexts and was able to translate them into entire platforms of commercially viable products and services.

*Edison viewed context as dynamic versus static.* Much of what we have learned about context through traditional classroom training positions it as a static phenomenon. If we examine context the way *Webster's Dictionary* defines it, *context* exists at a point in time: "The set of circumstances or facts that surround a particular event or situation."

But Edison viewed context differently. He saw context as *a continuum of knowledge and solution frameworks that shifts over time.* Housed within this core belief—that context is dynamic—we find crucial insights distinguishing Phase 2 of Edison's true collaboration method as a mechanism for sustaining innovative thinking within groups of people. Because Edison did not view the ability to generate novel solutions as a discontinuous "Eureka moment" process, Edison was able to embed the notion of context, and how to develop it, into his true collaboration approach. In viewing context as a kind of breakthrough learning continuum, Edison positioned the development of new context as central to his team efforts at Menlo Park and West Orange. In these environments, new context was continually being created with each project thrust. Edison saw the development of context as a means to move beyond the boundaries of "known thinking" and to free himself and his teams from merely copying what already existed. In adopting Edison's dynamic view of context, Edison's workers became adept at using the same process of questioning and experimenting he did as they sought novel solutions, each worker ultimately learning to rapidly shift his own thinking about what solution frameworks became possible as new context emerged. The ability to work toward the establishment of context at the start of a collaboration initiative, rather than solely thinking about facts or industry boundaries, injected powerful mental depth and creativity into Edison's workforce.

> The man who doesn't make up his mind to cultivate the habit of thinking misses the greatest pleasure in life. He not only misses the greatest pleasure but he cannot make the most of himself.
>
> —*Thomas Edison*

Like a motherboard rich with computer chips sparking diverse connections, Edison leveraged context as a collaborative mechanism to drive new insights in his project efforts. By applying the discovery learning steps Edison introduces in Phase 2, we can begin developing more creative and collaborative work teams—and workers—today. Phase 2 includes the following core components:

- *Part i, Solo meld:* Each member of the small, diverse team selected in Phase 1 begins preparing for true collaboration by participating in discovery learning outside of team sessions. By examining their own assumptions surrounding the problem at hand, reading widely, and employing analogical thinking, each individual develops a broad, yet creative point of view that can later be fed into the team.

- *Part ii, Group meld:* The small team comes together, sharing insights from their individual efforts in Solo meld, morphing and reshaping their ideas collectively through casual discussion. After asking big probing questions, the team experiments with a range of hypotheses as it seeks a resonant new context for its solutions, developing rough prototypes along with narrative stories highlighting its team efforts.

Using the principles of Phase 2, you can either begin refreshing the existing context around a challenge you've already begun grappling with, or establishing entirely new context for a collaboration effort you are about to undertake. The most extensive of Edison's four phases, Phase 2 represents a unique combination of discovery learning driven by individual endeavors coupled with the magnifying power of collaborating with a small, diverse team. In devising this approach, Edison sought to prepare the individual to serve as a ready participant in the team's collaborative efforts, rather than viewing the team as a crutch which allowed individuals to ride on the coattails of others. Let's begin with an examination of how the Solo meld facets of Phase 2 allow you to begin reskilling yourself, driving new levels of creativity, objectivity, and reflection into your frame of thinking.

# PART I, PHASE 2: THE SOLO MELD

In comparing Edison's invention of the phonograph with Alexander Graham Bell's invention of the telephone, we saw how each of these extraordinary innovators shaped a different context for sound. Edison's context was influenced by his deep understanding of machine making, telegraphy, and materials, whereas Bell's was influenced by his unique knowledge of the human ear and the body's sound-generating mechanisms.

As part of the Solo meld step, you will begin to identify how your own skills and knowledge deeply color your individual perspectives and how you can begin reshaping and expanding these perspectives later in Phase 2 to map new context around the problem your team is tasked to solve. In the Solo meld step, you will explore the core assumptions you hold about yourself and your work experiences and how you view the world. You will have a chance to explore how quickly you can shift the context of your own thinking, examining factors that may be blocking your ability to see challenges from multiple perspectives.

## Mental Models

A key factor that shapes our ability to effectively generate new context lies in what learning expert Peter Senge calls our mental models. Mental models serve as the primary filter through which we process information; they are the gateway through which everything must pass. Our mental models come to form the bedrock of our worldview.[2] In *The Fifth Discipline*, Senge describes our mental models this way: "What we carry in our heads are images, assumptions, and stories" of how things work. We take in information from the world around us, including what we read, whom we interact with, and how we experience working with others—ultimately sorting all this input into a personalized set of "operating facts" that collectively serve as our mental model. These personalized operating facts in turn affect how we screen incoming information and navigate our environment over time, impacting the scope of our learning, our actions, our operating styles— virtually everything we do. Ideally, if we are seeking to maintain a growth mindset, as Edison did, our mental model must expand and evolve through discovery learning over time. A healthy mental model actively incorporates new influences, new work experiences, and new friendships, ultimately reflecting a huge tapestry of perspectives rather than a fixed, unchanging set of assumptions.

Mental models operate so powerfully as filters of our reality that they often serve as magnets drawing people together. We might say that people who share a similar mental model are like-minded. Mental models can operate not only at the level of the individual but at the level of team, community, and even nation. Teams, for example, may share a mental model about how to best connect with customers who use a particular type of product or service. Communities may hold a shared mental model about how they wish to attract new businesses or new homeowners to drive growth. Nations often hold shared mental models around the kinds of freedoms its citizens can enjoy.

But *danger lurks when mental models harmonize around "images, assumptions and stories" that reflect a distorted view of reality. Flawed mental models can lead teams—even entire industries—astray.* For example, we can look back at the flawed mental model shared by the Big Three automakers in Detroit during the 1970s and 1980s. As part of its shared mental model, the Big Three believed customers primarily purchased cars based on styling rather than quality and reliability.[3] But as Japanese automakers began making concerted efforts to penetrate the US market in the late 1970s, the underlying basis of the Big Three's industry outlook was fundamentally challenged. Customers in the United States began buying cars based on price, quality, and other factors rather than styling alone. Refusing to shift its understanding of the context for how US customers made car buying decisions, the Big Three took years to adjust its shared mental model, ultimately facing the closure of dozens of factories and the loss of considerable market share to Japanese competitors. Lacking an ability to effectively challenge the underlying assumptions of its shared mental model, the US auto industry was unable to respond to complex shifts in its environment and rapidly adopt new thinking.

Edison recognized the dangers of rallying around a false mental model. He saw that, without an ability to question the underlying assumptions of what was driving the thinking within a mental model for either an individual or a group, the odds of creating a new context for solutions was low. As you will read, the failure of Edison's first patented invention caused him to directly experience the downside of a flawed mental model. Edison's inability to catch flaws in his own thinking at the very start of his career led him to *place heavy emphasis on preventing weak assumptions from ricocheting through the true collaboration process.* By questioning assumptions and more rigorously examining his own mental model, Edison was able to drive breakthrough insights such as those that spurred him to tackle development of the incandescent electric light, shown in Figure 4.1. Rather than creating bigger and bigger layers of flawed thinking, Edison geared the Solo meld portion of Phase 2 around unearthing the beliefs

**Figure 4.1 Thomas Edison Holding a Test Version of His Incandescent Electric Light**

*Source:* National Park Service, Edison National Historic Site.

and assumptions underlying the mental model of each team member, opening it for examination as the true collaboration process unfolded, and preventing the team from perpetrating false logic.

## Failure of Edison's Electronic Vote Recorder Shifted His Mental Model

In 1869, at the tender age of 22, Edison achieved a thrilling life milestone: he received a patent for his very first invention, the electronic vote recorder. Edison applied several principles that leveraged his deep knowledge of telegraphy and electromechanics in designing this pioneering product for the Massachusetts legislature. Edison's electronic vote recorder rapidly tabulated individual votes from each legislator, then sent them to the Speaker for immediate analysis. Astonishing to Edison, however, was that this device—which worked perfectly in every respect—flopped with the legislators. It never achieved commercial success.

What happened? Although Edison had indeed attended several sessions of the Massachusetts legislature, he had failed to watch the legislators at work in other contexts outside the voting chamber itself. From the perspective of the legislators, "voting" was a process that embraced discussion, negotiation, and individual jockeying for power. The actual mechanics of voting and tabulation were secondary. To the legislators, *their context for voting positioned it as an administrative component of a much longer, more complex series of activities*. Speed in voting didn't really matter that much. Legislators were more focused on increasing their effectiveness in the steps that preceded the actual mechanics of voting.

In evaluating his failure with the electronic vote recorder, Edison realized he had based his entire approach on his own ideas and viewpoints rather than the context of the legislators' needs. He'd developed a flawed mental model about how voting worked.

> Humans are incredibly good at linking cause and effect—
> sometimes too good.
>
> —*Michael J. Mauboussin, business author,*
> *adjunct professor at Columbia University*

Stung by this experience, Edison realized he had not established an understanding around the context of voting itself. He had relied solely on his own ideas and his own mental model, which focused merely on "how" to vote. Moving forward, Edison vowed to question his own ideas and existing assumptions first, creating a richer, more diverse foundation for his thinking before pushing toward creative solutions. Edison resolved to focus on a process that yielded utility for the end user rather than simply fulfilling his own perceptions about what would work best in a given setting. He thus began putting all his early thinking out for greater scrutiny by his colleagues, laying bare the assumptions he was making, and more readily avoiding the pitfalls of holding onto a flawed thought process.

If we were to construct the new mental model Edison developed following his failure with the electronic vote recorder, it would probably look something like this:

## Conceptual View of Edison's New Mental Model after His First Commercial Failure

- I will broadly prepare my mind for a journey of collaborative discovery rather than strictly adhering to my own ideas and assumptions.

- Experimentation is an efficient way to probe assumptions and discover outcomes that create new learning.

- I desire creative freedom in designing my experiments and my research.

- I seek to develop radical new solutions to big problems.

- The products and services I launch must have utility and fulfill a need.

- I am open to the discovery of new phenomena.

Edison followed through on his promise to incorporate more of his target users' experiences and needs into his invention process. As evidenced by the extensive visits Edison made to the offices of insurance clerks and agents while devising his next patented invention—the Edison electric pen and press—Edison began working within a framework that created a context around the challenge he was facing first rather immediately thinking about solutions in more discrete terms. Rather than solely relying on his own ideas and his own judgments to guide his collaboration teams, Edison realized he needed to experiment and probe more iteratively, considering multiple possible scenarios or options before adopting a single solution. A simple illustration of this process is shown in Figure 4.2. Edison ultimately pioneered an entire industry around document duplication. His success with the electric pen and press reflected his new thinking about challenging assumptions first and

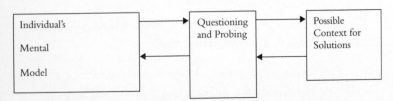

**Figure 4.2 Individuals Must Reach Out with Questions to Probe Underlying Assumptions, Create New Context**

working along with his teams and his customers to expand the context in which a problem was to be solved before seizing upon on any single course of action.

## Creating New Context Is Influenced by Our Mental Model and the Willingness to Question Assumptions

Senge's research suggests that Edison's willingness to reshape his own mental model following the failure of the vote recorder is rare. Most of the time, Senge indicates new mental models "fail to get put into practice because they conflict with deeply held internal images of how the world works."[4] Edison proved willing to step away from "familiar ways of thinking and acting" through questioning and exploring his own mental process and to apply this new learning to his true collaboration efforts. *Edison's new approach placed more focus on creating a broader context for the problem at hand, viewing it from multiple angles.* Edison's ability to create expansive context around each problem he solved fundamentally affected his ability to shape breakthrough solutions and see the world differently than his competitors.

Your first endeavor in Solo meld is thus to unearth your own operating facts, surfacing the set of assumptions you will be bringing into your true collaboration team. What core factors guide your mental model? How do you view the world? Are you willing to hunt for answers rather than seeking a quick resolution? Have you formulated any preliminary assumptions about the challenge posed to your small team or the people who will be working with you? What areas of your own expertise color your thinking? Make a list of the five or six underlying assumptions you see guiding the framework of your mental model at this early stage in Phase 2 and record them for future reference. Be sure to include factors that guide how you process information, how you view the future, and how you connect to others. Then promise yourself, as Edison did, that you will be open to revisit your mental model and make adjustments to it as you progress forward in Phase 2 and beyond. Keep an open mind.

## Reading Spurs Questions That Create New Context

As we begin to drill down into the underlying assumptions that guide our thinking, we also want to practice how to begin questioning the world around us. Developing new context is fundamentally about asking different questions. Edison exercised his ability to formulate challenging questions by reading broadly. Among his first steps when undertaking a new collaborative effort was zeroing in on reading material with themes aligned to the subject matter he was evaluating. This often meant plowing through textbooks and papers spanning diverse scientific topics. But he also read fiction and fantastical works that were completely unrelated to the subject of his endeavors. Edison believed feeding his mind diverse perspectives through the written word was critical to prevent specifically shaping or tainting his perceptions in any one direction as he began his questioning process. Rather than forming a specific point of view that might be false, he preferred to gather a broad array of perspectives that could be shaped into new patterns, and therefore new context, through later meetings with his teams.

> At the time I experimented on the incandescent lamp I did not understand Ohm's law. Moreover, I do not want to understand Ohm's law. It would prevent me from experimenting.
>
> —*Thomas Edison*

An ardent lover of books and newspapers, by 1887, when Edison was 40, his personal collection at the West Orange laboratory exceeded 10,000 volumes, making it one of the top five largest libraries in the world during the late nineteenth century. Drawn from the reaches of acoustics, botany, electricity, mathematics, photography, horticulture, chemistry, materials science, and physics, Edison shared the resources of his library with his employees, encouraging them to continually stimulate their own thinking and questioning skills. Edison viewed the library as a place of refuge, an environment that allowed him to be still and think for hours at a time. His holdings included minutes of the proceedings from the Royal Academy of Science in England, as well as issues of *Scientific American* and numerous industry journals, allowing Edison to stay current on debates afoot in the scientific community. Reflecting his love for storytelling and the deft use of language, Edison's library also embraced extensive works of classical Greek literature plus a vast collection of Shakespeare. He particularly valued science fiction novels by pioneering French writer Jules Verne for the flights of fantasy and freedom from logic they spurred.

We can link Edison's reading to many of the provocative questions he asked. For example, in the late 1870s, Edison poured through extensive accounts of scientific experiments around incandescence that long preceded his own, also consulting the writings of Michael Faraday, a nineteenth century British inventor who experimented with electricity. In the 1880s, Edison followed the work of French physiologist Etienne-Jules Marey, who along with an array of French engineers and scientists, was photographing animals in motion, seeking to record their actions down to the minutest detail.[5] Among the fundamental questions these intensive explorations prompted were:

- Why did previous scientific efforts with incandescence fail?

- What are the properties of incandescence that make it different from other phenomena?

- How does the human eye perceive motion?
- What are the factors that allow the eye to see things in a seamless, uninterrupted way?
- How are light and electricity related?
- Can light and electricity be combined?

Diligently recording his queries and insights in the notebooks that were ever present at his side, Edison returned to these deep, probing questions again and again throughout Phase 2. His intentional gathering of questions became a pivotal spur for experiments and hypotheses that he later introduced when working jointly with his teams.

I didn't read books. I read the library.

—*Thomas Edison*

Many of today's business leaders also use intensive reading to help them formulate powerful questions. Beth Comstock, chief marketing officer (CMO) of GE, says, "I probably spend half of my time immersed in worlds beyond GE."[6] Comstock finds value in reading materials drawn from different industries to bring new perspective to her thinking. Using notebooks and blogs to record key insights, she also shares notes from information she reads at high-level conferences, including global events such as the World Economic Forum in Davos, Switzerland. Comstock notes, "I work hard to curate information that I don't believe many at GE will have heard and to translate information in a way that is relevant to our challenges." Comstock has found particular value in melding her reading about diverse technologies NASA has deployed in space with strategic questions she's developed around GE's medical division, prompting Comstock to begin exploring how space technology and medical technology might connect.

During his tenure as chief executive officer (CEO) of Microsoft, Bill Gates took one or two intensive reading vacations each year, popularly known as Think Week. Spending days in isolation away from family, friends, and Microsoft employees, Gates ploughed through piles of reading material he'd collected for months, drawing from writings as diverse as the timeless work of Leonardo da Vinci to white papers generated by various divisions within Microsoft. (His record was 112 white papers in one week.) Gates used the insights and inspiration from these trips to bring new thinking to the company's strategic efforts, asking questions that would challenge him to think differently about the future of technology itself and directions for Microsoft's labs.

In *Where Good Ideas Come From*, author Steven Johnson frames the value of the intense "deep dive" reading efforts endeavored by Edison, Comstock, and Gates. When immersing ourselves in a topic for a condensed period of time, Johnson explains, the intense flow of information into the brain enhances the probability that we will make interesting connections and combinations among disparate ideas. Johnson calls this forced serendipity.[7] Just as Edison's hours of reading in his library sparked questions to be pursued via new hypotheses and experiments, your own reading endeavors as part of Solo meld can yield serendipitous yet brilliant questions from angles you least expect.

When was the last time you reached for a new hardcover book or bought an e-book? How frequently do you change the types of material you read? Do you follow the same reading routines over and over again? Why not experiment and select three new bloggers to track over the next month? Why not take a reading retreat? If you were to shift your reading list so it looks like something Edison might devise, what would be on it? Get out your notebook with the comments you jotted down as part of your mental model exploration. Write down a half dozen questions that emerged from your reading this past

**Reading Sparks Diverse Connections**

Chuck Peters, CEO of The Gazette Company, reads several books per week. As head of a traditional newspaper that also owns a television station, Chuck's industry domains lie at the epicenter of complex shifts in business models and customer behavior. To ensure he is continually thinking about new structures and new industry mashups rather than accepted, traditional ways of operating, his reading draws from a mélange of topics related to media as well as other themes. His goal is to read quickly, focusing on key points he can apply and share readily with others. Chuck comments, "I'll just pick up the phone and call a colleague to share an idea from what I've read and see if they resonate with it. I love batting around questions with people based on what I'm reading, whether they are reading the same books I am, or different ones."[8]

week. Make a practice of writing down at least one provocative question each day and revisit these at the end of each week. As you progress through your Solo meld reading, what forced serendipities arise? Be sure to record them in your notebook and share them later with your team.

## Use Analogies to Create Connections That Resist Leaps of Abstraction

Every experience we have, every bit of data we encounter, our mind seeks to name and classify. The human brain is wired as an associational colossus, its winding neural pathways simultaneously serving as finely tuned response mechanisms as well as a repository for storing short- and long-term data.

The mind is capable of linking facts with other facts, facts with emotions, and emotions with other emotions.

In *The Tipping Point*, author Malcolm Gladwell writes about the brain's seemingly infinite ability to connect bodies of unrelated information together—to find commonality even when there may be no rational basis for doing so. Gladwell recounts a story about the broken window theory, the brain-child of criminologists James Q. Wilson and George Kelling. "If a window is broken and left unrepaired, people walking by will conclude that no one cares and no one is in charge."[9] If those same passersby then notice a vacant building or a nearby abandoned car covered with graffiti, "an epidemic theory of crime" is created in their minds. Rapidly linking data about the broken window, the vacant building, and the graffiti-covered car together with emotions they may be feeling, the visitors' minds jump to the conclusion that crime is rampant in that neighborhood. The observers have created a "context of crime" around what they've observed, believing that the environment holds danger and menace, even though nothing specifically has transpired to evidence this.

> We are more than just sensitive to changes in context. We're exquisitely sensitive to them.
>
> —*Malcolm Gladwell,* **The Tipping Point**

When we jump to contextual conclusions like the ones Gladwell describes via the broken window theory, we are engaging in "leaps of abstraction."[10] We make rapid mental connections that sometimes are accurate, but other times run the risk of misclassifying phenomena or creating false assumptions.

Edison noticed his own mind's tendency to rapidly classify information. Ever leery of forming false assumptions about what he observed, Edison intentionally sought mental tools that could stream his thinking in ways that would not fall prey to such leaps. He found an ideal tool in analogies, the third component of Solo meld.

Through his own intellectual experimentation and observation, Edison realized that, when using analogies, the brain's logic functions were shifted. The mind slowed down, creating entirely different mental images and thought streams. By employing the use of analogies, Edison found he could link unique concepts and patterns together, but did so in a fresh context that was largely free of prior bias, preconception, or intellectual prejudice.

An analogy is defined as a comparison of two things that are seemingly unlike *with the aim of determining how they are alike*. Analogies, a long-favored tool of authors and literary artists, provide zest and flavor to the written word, prompting readers to make new connections. For example, Shakespeare, in the opening lines of *Richard III*, writes, "Now is the winter of our discontent," pairing *winter* and *discontent* as a means to cast somber emotion upon the first scene of the play. Generally, winter and discontent don't appear in the same context, but Shakespeare connects these words as an analogy, which the mind might associate with sadness, despair, unhappiness, or difficulty.

Edison found that when he paired words or concepts that would otherwise not be logically connected, he generated fruitful new insights. *Through analogies, Edison could actually begin crafting new context from a palette that did not specifically rely on any facts or specific information.* By creating pairings through which the mind at first finds no logical pathway, Edison realized that he could trick the brain into trying to bridge gaps in meaning between the paired ideas. He noticed the mind would still make "leaps of abstraction" by trying to identify likeness between the concepts, yielding a unique, new context that ultimately united them.

Analogies provided an especially fruitful starting point for Edison when he was at the very early stages of thinking about a problem and searching for novel ways to tackle it. In forming analogies, Edison began by using something that was deeply familiar to him and compared it with something that was less familiar. For example, when undertaking his work with motion pictures in the late 1880s, Edison had few specific ideas about where to start. His notions of how to create images that moved seamlessly before the eye were still raw and unshaped.

Edison used an analogy to jump-start his thought process. He compared the seamless flow of sound from a phonograph to what he desired to be an uninterrupted flow of images before the eye, expressing it this way: "[I am] experimenting upon an instrument which does for the Eye what the phonograph does for the Ear, which is the recording and reproduction of things in motion." Edison's initial thinking from this exercise led him to propose "photographing a series of pictures at intervals of eight seconds or more 'in a continuous spiral on a cylinder or plate in the same manner as sound is recorded on a phonograph.' "[11]

The analogy spurred notions of spiraling images the way the phonograph spiraled sound from a cylindrical record, leading Edison to consider the rapid cycling of individual photographs that were very small—perceivable only through a microscope, but propelled mechanically. Although still rough and emergent, these early gleanings prompted Edison to conduct experimental work with a small internal team consisting of photographer William Kennedy Laurie Dickson and machinist Charles A. Brown, ultimately resulting in a new context described as "moving pictures." Through the Group meld process you will read about later in this chapter, Edison and Dickson conducted experiments that resulted in the invention of the kinetoscope, a machine that propelled photosensitive film on sprocketed reels at the rate of 10 images per second.

By anchoring his analogies with one chunk of information that he knew well and comparing it with something he knew much less about, Edison's mind flew rapidly to create options linking the two concepts. Analogies allowed Edison to navigate completely new scientific territory and establish the gleanings of new context that he could take to his teams for further exploration.

### Edison Used Analogies to Spur New Context

Shortly after inventing the first incandescent electric light in 1879, Edison found himself facing a new challenge: how to connect lightbulbs together. Although the great inventor had spent months devising the lightbulb itself, he had no specific notion of how to link one with another. Realizing that the users of his lightbulbs would find it easier to turn on several bulbs at once rather than turning on each one individually, Edison set out to solve this unique challenge.

Not knowing where to begin, Edison formed an analogy between a telegraph system, which he knew a great deal about, and electricity, something he knew far less about (at least at that time). He framed the analogy this way: *How is electricity like telegraphy?* In comparing telegraphy to electricity, Edison was seeking to determine how the flow of information through a telegraph system might look like the flow of electricity through some other kind of system.

Edison made a notebook drawing of seven different configurations that he envisioned by using this analogy, shown in Figure 4.3.

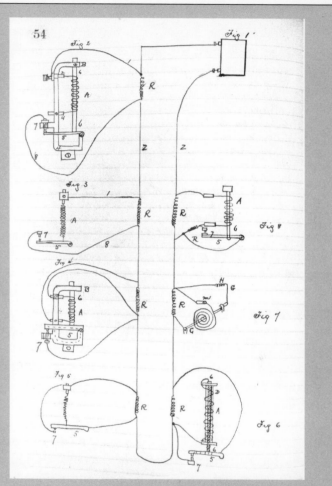

**Figure 4.3  Edison's Notebook Drawing of Possible Electric Circuit Designs, Developed Using an Analogy**

*Source:* Reproduced with permission by *The Thomas A. Edison Papers*, Rutgers University, Piscataway, New Jersey, http://edison.rutgers.edu.

*(continued)*

*(continued)*

Edison later tested the ability of electricity to flow through each of the seven unique configurations he'd drawn. The result? *The world's first electric circuit.* By tricking his mind into bridging the gap between telegraphy and electricity, Edison created new context for how electricity could flow between two or more objects.

Steven Johnson writes about the unique context-creating power of analogies in *Where Good Ideas Come From.*[12] Describing them as doorways to "the adjacent possible," analogies rank among the most fruitful forms of output we can generate as individuals. He says, "The adjacent possible is a kind of shadow future, hovering on the edges of the present state of things, a map of all the ways in which the present can reinvent itself. . . . The strange and beautiful truth about the adjacent possible is that its boundaries grow as you explore those boundaries. Each new combination ushers new combinations."

Analogies offer you the chance to explore the depths of your own creativity, to see what lies in the adjacent possible, by linking the paired ideas you're exploring. Analogies were one of the most powerful tools in Edison's arsenal; use them to prepare your mind for the initial meetings with your collaboration team. Like putting spare parts together in new and unique combinations, use analogical thinking to begin testing ideas related to the challenge your team has been tasked to explore. What analogy could you develop for your true collaboration effort?

Part of coming up with a good idea is discovering what those spare parts are, and ensuring that you're not just recycling the same old ingredients.

**—*Steven Johnson,* Where Good Ideas Come From**

## An Analogy That Made Modern Medical History

*How is a microchip like a drug?* Dr. Robert Langer is the David H. Koch Institute Professor at MIT, 1 of only 14 institute professors within the entire academic program, and head of MIT's famed biotechnology research lab. Winner of the prestigious Lemelson-MIT Prize as well as nearly a dozen other awards from globally recognized institutions, including the Kettering Institute and the Charles Stark Draper Laboratory, Langer has been described as "one of history's most prolific inventors in medicine."[13] Several years ago, Langer was seeking a method for reducing the size of inoperable brain tumors. Protocols that could safely be used inside the brain itself are extremely time-consuming to unearth and often even more difficult to commercially develop.

One day while watching television at home, Langer hit upon an analogy that led him to create an entirely new context for thinking about this challenge:

> One day I was just watching this TV show on PBS. I really wasn't even paying that much attention to it. I just kept seeing how they were making these chips for the computer industry, and I thought to myself "Wouldn't that be a great way to deliver drugs! What if you could create a microchip that could be like a drug delivery device?"[14]

Using an analogy that linked microchips to drug delivery, Langer developed a breakthrough long-chain polymer molecule (US Patent 5,797,898) now

*(continued)*

> *(continued)*
>
> used to safely coat microchips with tumor-reducing medication that can be implanted in the brain.
>
> The spurs that inspire analogical thinking often lie within daily life and do not have to come from complex or highly sophisticated sources. Allow yourself to experiment with analogies.

Here is an analogical thinking exercise you can try as part of your Solo meld process. Select a word that in some way relates to the challenge your small team has been charged to address. Align the word with some facet of the project in which you have actual knowledge or expertise. Then, pair it with a word from nature: sun, planet, ocean, grass, whale—you choose. List the two words on a sheet of paper: one on the left-hand side of the page; the other on the right. Next, create a column down the center with your observations about what is "alike" about the word pair. Try this exercise for 15 minutes today and again later this week. Feel free to also draw images about the connections you find, as Edison did. Don't prejudge your results. Bring the ideas you've generated to your first team session. Later, you can also use analogical thinking as a tool to guide your team during Group meld, when the team is stuck and unsure what the next step should be.

*The Solo meld sequence of examining the assumptions underlying your mental model, forming new questions based on broad reading, and creating analogies that push beyond your usual thought patterns represents a combination you can revisit again and again.* View Solo meld not only as a preparation step for your contributions to your true collaboration team but as a refreshment of your own creativity. Use the steps in Solo meld to reboot your thinking on virtually any subject. Recognize it as a means to get comfortable with the way your brain is wired to receive and process information, allowing the resources of your mind to propel you in exciting new directions.

> We each create our own worlds by what we choose to notice, creating a world of distinctions that makes sense to us.
>
> —*Margaret Wheatley,* **A Simpler Way**

# PART II, PHASE 2: GROUP MELD

In the second segment of Phase 2, we will explore the group-based tools Edison used to form new context. As you and your team progress through each Group meld step, collegiality between members will strengthen. Your team goals will crystallize. Emerging from your shared endeavors of questioning, creating hypotheses, and experimenting will be a powerful new context: a new framework for your thinking and your solutions. You will likely develop an entirely new description of your project, one that differs from the formal "project statement" you may have been handed when your team was selected in Phase 1.

Think back to Team B in Chapter 1. Group meld will be like running the three-legged race. Through this segment of Phase 2, you and your team members will become bound to one another, linked through common experiences that will be challenging to describe in words. Every step—every tool—will create new learning for the entire team, yielding an output that exceeds what could be produced via your own individual abilities.

As you begin this segment, it's crucial that all team members openly share the work they have individually conducted in Solo meld regarding their own mental models, as well as any preconceptions they may hold about the initiative you've been tasked to tackle. Having a rough understanding of the outlook operating within each team member, the group will improve its ability to objectively consider a broad array of viewpoints. This sharing can be conducted either virtually or face to face (FTF), and it may require multiple team sessions to fully absorb.

*Edison valued the contributions of individual team members within his collaborations, but he did not want the team to be viewed as a crutch relieving the ongoing requirement for solo creative thinking outside of team sessions.* Like a canoe that can be placed into a flowing river at any point, Edison wanted individuals to engage their ideas with the team's "stream of thinking," while always having the opportunity to later pull the canoe over to the shore for internal reflection and additional individual inquiry.

## Group Meld Steps Engage System 2

At work in each of the tools in Group meld, we see the engagement of an underlying cognitive process known as System 2, a term developed by Nobel Prize–winning economist Daniel Kahneman in his book *Thinking, Fast and Slow*. *System 2* refers to the mechanisms that slow down the workings of the mind, allowing us to focus intently. System 2 puts us "in the zone." Whenever we are in an engaging conversation, using our hands to construct or physically manipulate something, or combining multiple concepts and ideas into a new pattern, the mind activates System 2.

As a means to minimize the intellectual leaps of abstraction described earlier in Solo meld, Edison intuitively engaged System 2 via the experiential nature of his collaborative process. For Edison, collaboration was an experience of the body, not just the mind. Collaboration was palpable. It meant deeply engaging with his physical environment as well as the mental energies of his colleagues. Edison viewed collaboration as a living continuum of activity that could be felt on multiple levels.

If you can't think a thing out yourself, get as many other people as you can to thinking on the subject. Somebody may find some facts that have eluded you and through them come to find the solution.

—*Thomas Edison*

Let's begin exploring the four primary tools Edison used in Group meld: team discussion, experimentation, prototyping, and proactive use of collaborative space. The insights generated by these four tools will help you devise new context for your project. Figure 4.4 offers a sneak preview of how the process works:

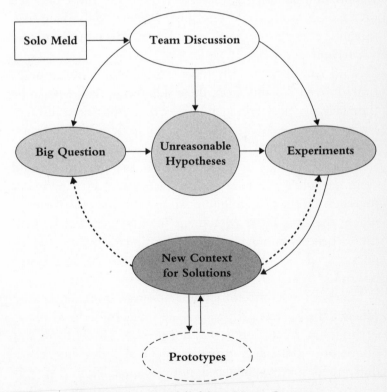

**Figure 4.4 Establishing New Context**

## Engaging in Team Dialogue Advances Insights and Collaborative Thinking

For Edison, the heart and soul of true collaboration began with team dialogue—and the establishment of diverse settings for team conversations to occur. The meat of these dialogues took place in casual exchanges between Edison and his team members in small side rooms at Menlo Park or West Orange, where Edison would gather his colleagues to share thoughts from their notebook entries, readings, or preliminary experiments conducted outside the group setting. As the laboratory's lead facilitator and primary catalyst, Edison himself often spearheaded these meetings. In such instances, Edison would offer his own line of thinking first, soliciting input from the team and using this input to propel what happened next.

With conversations still under way, Edison's teams sometimes moved as a unit from these side rooms to the machine shop, talking and working out bits of their discussions through hands-on engagement with actual equipment. Other times, right in the midst of a session, Edison would have the team assemble chemicals or compounds so that dialogue could continue while the team jointly conducted an experiment together. Or the team might move to a specific area of the lab where the specialized equipment they needed was housed. Like a bellows fanning a flame, Edison's collaborative dialogues served as organic, thriving exchanges yielding sparks nourished by the group.

Edison's model for collaborative dialogue was adopted by others in the lab, especially team leaders responsible for working with groups when Edison was not present. Heavy focus was placed on maintaining an environment of collegiality where outlying ideas were embraced, not cast aside. Team members recognized that if they did not explore unusual themes in their dialogue, Edison would freely step in to inject them. Governed by few rules, team dialogue was intended to test the edges of a problem and begin fleshing out the depth and nature of the issues at hand.

> Hell, there are no rules here—we're trying to accomplish something.
>
> —*Thomas Edison*

Although today we sometimes discount the kinds of casual discussion and fluid dialogue Edison preferred in favor of more formal agenda-based exchanges, Kevin Dunbar, a professor at the University of Toronto, has determined that "talking through a problem" in an informal setting provides a crucial accelerator to developing new insights.[15] Seeking to identify what separated top scientists from average ones, Dunbar set up cameras in four leading molecular biology labs and recorded the exchanges that took place among colleagues. As part of this process, Dunbar conducted extensive interviews in which team members "described the latest developments in their experiments and their shifting hypotheses." He then transcribed all interactions using a classification scheme that allowed him to track patterns in the flow of information through the lab. It turned out that the most important ideas emerged during regular lab meetings, where a dozen or so researchers would gather and informally present and discuss their latest work.

Dunbar's conclusion? Casual discussion prompted a deeper sharing of ideas. In particular, ideas that may have initially been perceived as outliers often became the subject of intense dialogue. An environment of casual exchange helped recontextualize the team's more surprising findings, making unique ideas and findings less likely to be dismissed as "experimental errors."

Edison intuitively recognized what Dunbar's research formally revealed: "The results of one person's reasoning becomes the input to another person's reasoning," resulting in significant changes to the power and momentum of each idea. For Edison, casual team discussion created an environment where new combinations could occur, where information could spill over from one person to another. Through the process of casual team discussion, new context impacting the thinking of the entire team emerged.

Ted Grabau, vice president of global technology at Emerson, a leading provider of industrial process controls, agrees with the value Edison and Dunbar found in team discussions. "When you meet with colleagues to talk and collaborate together, it's a bond. You become very additive rather than competitive."[16]

But in some settings, group dialogue proves to be the very thing team members dread the most. Concerned about looking foolish or inept, some team participants shrink from sharing their thoughts in front of others, even when they consider them colleagues. To address this reluctance, Dr. Curt Carlson, president of the Stanford Research Institute (SRI) and author of *Innovation: The Five Disciplines for Creating What Customers Want*, has given a unique moniker to casual team meetings at SRI. Carlson terms them value creation forums.[17] He believes if people come together, value must be created from the session. "If you don't have something productive to contribute, you shouldn't be at the meeting." Attendees must focus their attention on contributing actively versus being passive and simply showing up in "receive-only" mode. By shifting the context around collaborative team sessions this way, Carlson has encouraged high levels of engagement, as each participant realizes his or her ideas will be heard and valued rather than merely glossed over.

By positioning your team sessions as casual yet dynamic exchanges between colleagues, you will expand the possibility for discovery learning to evolve.

A good idea is a network. . . . You can't have an epiphany with only three neurons firing.

—*Steven Johnson,* **Where Good Ideas Come From**

## Setting Team Goals

As part of your initial Group meld discussions, develop working goals for your team. What are you trying to accomplish as a collaborative unit? Why has the collaboration itself been formed? Larry Keeley, CEO of the Doblin Group, notes that groups who set out their goals in the early stages of team discussion experience significantly greater success than teams who don't. "Consider yourselves passengers in a row boat, all pulling on the oars together."[18] Encouraging teams to make their initial goals as specific as possible while recognizing they are not yet set in stone, Keeley says, "Move beyond bumper sticker language to include specific metrics, like the growth you'd like to target in the category you think you'll be addressing, or the shifts that will happen in the industry segment you're aiming to impact, or how a particular target audience will perceive the fruits of your efforts. If you do this, you set the stage for a twenty-fold improvement in your likelihood of success."

John Copenhaver agrees. Director of disaster response and recovery services at WorleyParsons, Copenhaver serves as an expert in rapidly creating goals across teams that span entire communities, including early responders. Copenhaver agrees that goals need to be specific but adds, "People can sometimes feel like they *need* to collaborate without understanding *why* they should. Each team member also needs to have a clear understanding of why they are participating in the collaboration and what will be gained from it. They need to feel good about coming together to solve something that's meaningful for them as well as the broader organization."[19] However, Copenhaver cautions that if the team develops a task-driven mentality rather than a learning-driven mentality, it can lose its collegiality. "Be sure to set some portion of your goals around what is gained if you *all* succeed—together."[20]

Edison's approach to team dialogue fostered a growth mindset. His emphasis on team learning as part of the collaboration process underscored the value of pursuing conversations whose outcome could benefit the joint success of the entire group. As Keeley, Carlson, and Copenhaver have done in their organizations, ensure your team is engaging in casual discussions that allow new ideas to surface in a meaningful and constructive way.

## Encourage Experimentation as a Vehicle to Identify Context for Your Challenge

Experimentation served as a key step to coalesce options being debated by Edison's teams. *Edison viewed experimentation as a hands-on discovery process that bridged the thinking that emerged from team dialogue with actual doing.* Not only did experiments offer Edison and his collaborators a springboard for new and unexpected insights to emerge, *they launched the process through which the team would generate a complete reframing of the problem.* Edison rarely locked down on one absolute "problem statement" until after his teams had conducted a raft of experiments. Instead of pursuing just one course of thinking based on one core scenario, Edison preferred to have multiple scenarios in play at the same time.

The only way to keep ahead of the procession is to experiment. If you don't, the other fellow will. When there's no
experimenting there's no progress. Stop experimenting and
you go backward.

—*Thomas Edison*

As a spur to these experimentation efforts, Edison relished
developing what I term *unreasonable hypotheses*. Although
Edison adhered to the scientific method in his work, he
considered himself an inventor rather than a scientist. Seeing
himself as an inventor gave him the freedom to develop
creative hypotheses with unconventional twists, twists that
allowed him to consider options that other scientists of his day
would likely ignore. Edison's willingness to test ideas that
appeared unreasonable distinguished the work of his laboratory, elevating it to the point of legend.

That's just where your trouble has been. You have tried only
reasonable things. Reasonable things never work. Thank God
you can't think up any more reasonable things, so you'll have
to begin thinking up unreasonable things to try, and now
you'll hit upon the solution in no time.

—*Thomas Edison*

For example, Edison used unreasonable hypotheses to
shake loose new thinking about the nature of incandescence
as he began his lighting experiments in 1878. These hypotheses breached the conventions that had been followed by
teams of scientists exploring incandescence decades earlier.
From his reading, Edison had noted the failure of more than a
dozen previous teams to create a long-burning incandescent
power source using compounds such as carbon and platinum.
Wondering why this might be, Edison had paid a visit to
colleague William Wallace, whose well-equipped laboratory

specialized in arc lighting, the technology used to illuminate outdoor spaces in the 1870s. Powered by electrochemical batteries that yielded a weak current, arc lights featured a very broad illuminating surface, much like a Hollywood spotlight does today.

While walking through Wallace's lab intent on "finding the means of heating an element to glowing without destroying it"[21]—a phrase that served as a working version of Edison's problem statement—Edison suddenly realized that the solution to incandescence lay in creating different conditions for the flow of the electrical current itself. Rather than a weak resistance current and a large illuminating surface, the combination characteristic of arc lights, Edison seized upon the notion of experimenting with a high-resistance current and a small illuminating surface. In effect, Edison hypothesized that a solution for incandescence lay in creating the inverse conditions to virtually everything that had previously been tested.

I have struck a big bonanza.

— *Thomas Edison in a wire to scientist and colleague*
*William Wallace*

Returning with feverish excitement to his Menlo Park lab, Edison set about creating unreasonable hypotheses whose roots reflected the *opposite conditions* to the ones he saw in Wallace's arc lights. Working with the hand-selected team of Menlo Park colleagues you read about in Chapter 3, Edison began building new context around his understanding of incandescence. Rather than seeking to solve the big question, *"What will burn the longest?"* as prior scientists had, Edison realized he needed to solve, *"How do substances burn?"* Rather than asking the same questions that had been considered unsuccessfully by other scientific teams, Edison asked new questions. By developing unreasonable hypotheses from these questions, he accessed new, unexplored context regarding "burning."

Working with Edison's breakthrough hypothesis that a high-resistance current and a slender burning surface were needed to create incandescence, his team began exploring what kinds of substances—and in what types of containments—such a combination could be tolerated. Selecting more than 100 different compounds in what to modern eyes looks like a wild-eyed endeavor, Edison's team searched for what would ultimately become known as the filament. They experimented with boar bristles, thread, human hair, feathers, tar, metals, bark, hemp, and dozens of other substances. Instead of seeking which substances would burn the longest, Edison and his collaborators identified *what kind of burning* was needed to create a successful incandescing surface.

The team's bizarre selection of compounds yielded a realization that their solution lay in a substance that burned steadily across an entire surface all at once rather than a substance that burned slowly from one end to another, as many previous scientists had aimed to achieve. In their broad swath of experiments, Edison and his teams ultimately hit upon a novel solution—bamboo fiber impregnated with carbon—as the ideal filament compound.

By asking big, different questions and generating unreasonable hypotheses around them, Edison recontextualized and reframed the problem of incandescence itself. For Edison, this combination of questioning, hypothesizing, and experimenting offers the fundamental triumvirate of how new context is discovered. *Rather than locking down on an old question or a problem statement that resembled what others had already explored, Edison's unreasonable hypotheses and creative experimentation allowed him to newly define the problem at hand.*

Many teams today lock down on their problem statement too early. They think they know what they are solving, but they haven't really explored the context of the problem deeply enough yet. Experimenting and asking new questions is a good way to avoid locking down too soon.

—*Richard Perrin, author,*
**Real World Project Management**

Jonah Lehrer, author of *Imagine: How Creativity Works*, describes the process Edison used to develop new context as mental restructuring.[22] He notes that often, "a problem is only solved after someone asks a completely new kind of question." The presence of multiple types of expertise is crucial for such new kinds of questions to emerge, and Edison's use of diverse team structure provides a perfect environment for mental restructuring to occur.

By undertaking this mental restructuring process within your small team, you can newly frame the problem being addressed and generate an entirely new context in which solutions can be explored. Your team can replicate the power of Edison's process by asking new and different questions than your predecessors have asked, developing unreasonable hypotheses, and using experimentation to explore new territory. By following this approach, you increase the likelihood that your insights will bring you to an entirely new context for framing solutions to the problem itself.

### Toyota's Big Question

Much as Edison's big question, "How do substances burn?" radically shaped the hypotheses for his incandescence experiments, the big question asked by a team of engineers at Toyota completely redirected their hypotheses about how an energy-efficient car could be designed.

In the early 1990s, a team at Toyota began an exploration driven by this radical question: "How can we build a car that gets over 47 miles per gallon?" After developing numerous hypotheses and conducting detailed experiments flowing from this query, three primary scenarios emerged. One scenario engaged an unreasonable hypothesis, which ultimately triumphed: if an automobile can achieve over 47 miles per gallon, then it is propelled by two integrated fuel sources—gasoline and battery-powered electricity—in one engine.

The result? An entirely new context for thinking about automobiles. After years of additional experiments and prototyping, the team launched the Toyota Prius in Japan in 1997, pioneering an entirely new segment of automobiles: hybrid vehicles. The Prius revolutionized how customers and automakers came to view fuel economy in cars. From the time the Prius reached US shores in 2000 through 2010, the Prius was consistently rated number 1 by the US Environmental Protection Agency (EPA) for fuel efficiency. More than 2.8 million Prius vehicles have now been sold worldwide.[23]

## Embracing Live, Real-Time Experimentation

Our modern-day mental models often classify experimentation as something that happens only in a laboratory. We mistakenly think that a place with beakers, test tubes, and petri dishes offers a better experimental environment than cubicles, water coolers, and Aeron chairs. More often than not, we ascribe the process of experimenting to some other place—but not here.

> He taught me to experiment, and properly.
>
> —*Reginald Fessenden, Edison employee and chemist*

W. L. Gore is a company that believes in the power of experimentation to yield new context. It is common practice for associates to ask big questions and devise radical hypotheses. The company has found deep value in allowing employees to explore new product ideas using experiments as a foundation. W. L. Gore so deeply values experimentation that it has created a rough framework guiding teams on how to conduct experiments, develop questions that will steer the experiment toward unmet customer needs, bring a group together to conduct the experiment, as well as communicate the results.[24]

Insights generated from an experiment that involved coating guitar strings with the company's patented compound for waterproofing fabric yielded new context for how W. L. Gore thought about its customers, as well as its markets. Dave Myers, a W. L. Gore engineer primarily engaged in developing cardiac implants, put the company's famed waterproofing compound on his mountain bike cables as a grit-repellent coating. Pleased with the results, he thought it might also work as a coating for guitar strings, which lose tonal quality as skin oils build up on the fine metal surface, shifting the strings' vibration pattern. Myers decided to explore his idea further via internal experiments. Although Gore had no products in the music industry at the time, Myers pulled together a team of colleagues that spent spare working hours on the coating concept, cobbling together funds for their experiments. Myers's team hit the jackpot when the guitar strings they were testing held their tone three times longer than the industry standard. Today, Gore's Elixir guitar strings outsell competitors by two to one.[25] Praised by musicians as a string that not only deflects moisture from their fingers while playing but creates longer-lasting resonance within the string itself, the Elixir brand has won numerous awards from both inside and outside the music industry. For W. L. Gore, the value of allowing employees to experiment with new questions that in turn create new usage contexts for its technology has yielded revenue-generating results.

> We never get it right the first time. Experiments allow us to iterate and be more productive in our thinking each time.
>
> —*Dr. Curt Carlson, CEO of SRI*

## Embracing Digital Experimentation

Digital tools also offer your team an array of options for experimentation in Phase 2. In a twist that Edison would relish, collaboration teams from many organizations are turning their questions and hypotheses outward to the public rather than simply considering them solely within their team. Using platforms like Facebook and Twitter to tap input from massive online communities, teams can receive results from their queries in a matter of hours or days rather than weeks or months. Crowdsourcing offers another format for conducting experiments digitally. Although crowdsourcing and the broader topic of using social networks for digital experiments will be taken up at greater length in Phase 4, in Phase 2, your team needs to evaluate the pros and cons of using digital methods for the types of questions you have in mind. The ready availability of software for gathering and analyzing input from large numbers of respondents can make the opportunity to gain insight from individuals beyond the boundaries of your team an attractive one.

By making experiments a standard form of group learning, Edison positioned experimentation itself as a shared experience for every worker in the lab. The ongoing process of conducting experiments coupled with the open sharing of experimental results created a deeply collegial environment. *By valuing experimentation, Edison instilled in his workforce a proactive posture of questioning and risking.* Experimentation supported Edison's notion that there is rarely just one right answer to any given challenge, but rather multiple possible answers. Experiments not only served as a means of reskilling Edison's workers to be more insightful and observant but reinforced Edison's belief that the creation of context happens as a continuum. It is not a discrete, stop-start process. Context emerges from a dedication to asking new questions, developing unreasonable hypotheses, and experimenting.

## The Power of Experimentation

In a letter penned to investor Daniel Craig in December 1870, Edison wrote, "No experiments are useless." Believing that even our failures represent a form of learning, Edison viewed experimentation as a discovery process holding wide reaching impact. Famous for his persistence in considering every conceivable combination of options within his experiments, Edison remained undaunted even when the number of outcomes that did not fulfill his hypotheses reached the thousands.

Craig Wortmann, adjunct professor of entre-
preneurship at the Chicago Booth School of Business,
suggests that the errors and pitfalls experienced when
experiments fail creates adaptability and flexibility of
thinking. "Getting to Plan B is one way to look at
failure."[26] When your hypotheses are not borne out,
don't give up. Review your initial assumptions or
develop another big framing question. Use analogical
thinking to spur new ideas. But whatever you do,
don't discard your findings and don't stop experimenting. Every outlying result holds the seeds to a
solution whose question you just haven't asked yet.

What is your big question? How are you shaping unreasonable hypotheses around it? What new context are your
experiments leading you to create? How do your efforts
reflect a continuum of interactions between questioning,
experimenting, and context development?

## Prototyping Requires Reflection and Evaluation of Assumptions

Prototyping brings us to a third tool Edison found valuable in
Group meld. Prototypes became a vehicle for making con-
crete in three dimensions the outcomes yielded by Edison's
experiments. In developing prototypes, Edison continued his
engagement of the discovery learning process for every team
member, with some individuals serving the role of prototypers and others serving to test the prototypes. Given an
opportunity to touch, feel, and even verbally describe the
prototypes that emerged from their experiments, Edison
nourished the creating brain of each member. Engaging in

prototype development also uniquely fed iterative team discussions, as the entire team reflected on what was working and what might not be.

Wortmann notes that prototypes serve a unique bridging role between context that is complete, and context that is partially emerging. Like a Japanese garden unfolding to a visitor, prototyping unveils an idea in gradual stages over time. We absorb the ideas behind an evolving prototype like walking the winding pathways of a garden dotted with strategically placed clusters of trees and flowers. Just as we might gradually take in details of the garden, the act of prototyping slows down the leaps of abstraction our mind often desires to make, focusing it instead on patterns within the broader workings of the prototype itself. *Prototypes help us connect our thinking to a physical expression of reality.*

> In the design of a classic Japanese garden, bridges are intentionally angled so that they slow you down just enough as you walk, allowing you to observe from a new perspective within the complexity of the garden itself.
>
> **—Craig Wortmann, *adjunct professor of entrepreneurship,* Chicago Booth School of Business**

Although prototyping proved crucial to all of Edison's inventions, one of his most remarkable prototypes emerged via the construction of the Black Maria, the world's first movie studio, shown in Figure 4.5. A large, rough-and-ready shack made of tar paper and wood, the studio sat on a rotating swivel base toward the front entrance of the West Orange campus. With the use of long poles, large sections of the roof could be opened and closed from the interior, allowing in differing levels of light during "shoots" Edison produced with motion picture cameras housed in the studio. Constructed in 1892 at a cost of $637.67—or about $15,000 today—the

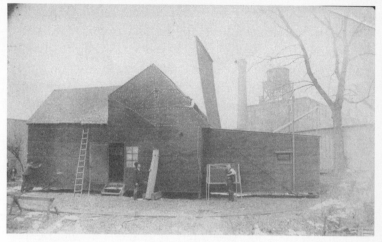

**Figure 4.5 The Black Maria, Edison's First
Movie Studio**
*Source:* National Park Service, Edison National Historic Site.

prototype lasted for nearly 10 years and was used extensively
by Edison to film his early movies prior to his purchase in
1901 of a glass-enclosed rooftop movie studio in Brooklyn.
The Black Maria not only engaged Edison and his motion
picture team in a breakthrough understanding of *how to make
movies* but created a new context for what moviemaking
entailed from the vantage point of both the actors who starred
in his films and the team members who produced them.

## Rapid Prototyping

Edison believed that prototypes did not have to be perfect;
they could be rough and directional. Leveraging a process
now known as rapid prototyping, Edison would often have
an engineer or prototype specialist mock up a team's ideas
in the machine shop at Menlo Park, offering a quick look
at how a solution might appear in three dimensions. Today,

rapid prototyping can even mean constructing a concept in minutes from simple office supplies like paper, tape, paper clips, markers, and rulers. Or it can entail constructing a prototype from spare wood and metal parts in machine shops like the one at the Ford Engineering Design Center at Northwestern University's McCormick School of Engineering. Its rapid prototyping facility allows teams to concoct working prototypes in hours rather than days, much as Edison's engineers did.[27]

New high-tech forms of prototyping have also emerged in recent years, with "three-dimensional (3D) printing" serving as a favorite at the Mayo Clinic, a world-famous hospital and research complex in Rochester, Minnesota. Kevin Bennet heads up Mayo's division of engineering, the small group tasked with developing breakthrough new surgical instruments and measuring devices for physicians throughout the Mayo system. Bennet and his team frequently rely on physical prototypes developed through 3D printing, a new technology that takes images drawn in two dimensions and translates them into 3D objects developed to scale. By scanning a drawing into the software system that drives the 3D printing process, ink jets "spray" bits of liquid polymer (plastic) to create the 3D prototype. Bennet says, "We can program a simple drawing into the software system at 5 PM before we leave the office, and come back at 8 AM the next morning—and voila! There's our prototype."[28] Bennet and his team use the resulting 3D objects as a basis for creating a working representation of the item from finished materials.

David Kelley, founder and chairman of design firm IDEO, stresses the value of watching the progression of prototypes over time as a method for capturing the evolving context of a team's thinking. Prototypes capture both the options that have worked and those that have not. Embodying the different contexts in which a team is considering its solutions, prototypes become what IDEO calls project artifacts, physical items that underpin the evolution of the team's thought process. At IDEO, project artifacts actually reside in the work space of the team that creates them. They represent a living, organic expression of the team's efforts and are not considered secondary or separate from the team's collaborative endeavors.

> An absolute secret weapon throughout all of this is to translate insights into stories.
>
> —*Daryl Travis, CEO of Brandtrust, author of* **Emotional Branding**

## *Narrative Prototypes*

In a world increasingly connected by virtual networks and portable smart devices, many teams are turning to narrative prototypes to complement, or even replace, physically constructed ones. Narrative prototypes, which we might more commonly refer to as stories, offer a particularly compelling solution to virtual teams who do not operate FTF. Also valuable to true collaboration teams seeking solutions in a software-driven or a service-driven context, where working prototypes can prove costly, stories can serve as a prototype of choice. By capturing visual impact through video, narrative prototypes offer solution scenarios presented through the spoken word. A portal into the creating brain, vivid storytelling triggers neural connections between the process of discovery learning and deeply shared human experiences. Tim Brown, CEO of IDEO, comments on the rising power of narrative prototypes today:[29]

> As we extend out into these different forms of design— whether it be software, whether it be service . . . we're having to explore new types of prototyping. We're having to

explore narrative prototyping, the prototyping through storytelling using various techniques—whether it be film or whether it be online techniques. We're having to create virtual prototypes as well as hardware prototypes where we're using all kinds of narrative techniques for exploring ideas really early on.

Part of the mystique Edison created around his experimentation efforts was his ability to craft a narrative around what he and his teams were undertaking. Through vivid stories, he reached out to broad audiences including investors, journalists, politicians, and other scientists, powerfully weaving together information in charismatic style as he sought support for his ideas.

What stories is your team capturing about its prospective solutions? How you can you use narrative prototyping as part of your presentation process when bringing your ideas to other groups or leaders?

## Live and Computer Simulations

A hybrid form of narrative prototype, simulations offer a unique technology-driven solution for today's teams. Sometimes the context or the solution frame being considered for a true collaboration initiative is too complex to fully translate into physical form. It may involve buildings and community spaces that would prove cost prohibitive or unsafe to re-create. Recognizing this, the Mayo Clinic has begun developing a spectrum of simulation formats as a complement to its clinical work, featuring simulated encounters between doctors and first responders in disaster situations. Run by the Mayo Clinic Multidisciplinary Simulation Center in Rochester, Minnesota, simulations help collaboration teams translate the specific types of skills and procedures a physician may need in diverse disaster situations. Most medical professionals are not trained as first responders. In a disaster, they must operate within a context dramatically different from their day-to-day practice. Dr. Ashok Patel of the Mayo School of Graduate Medical Education notes, "Simulation prototypes help deliver an awareness of Edison's belief that when people come together with the right intentions and under the right circumstances, they can multiply their individual strengths in an expanded framework of positive, creative energy."[30] Mayo's simulation prototypes offer an array of contexts spanning both clinical and community environments. Although more costly than other forms of prototyping, Mayo finds its simulation investment benefits many internal teams serving hundreds of practitioners and service personnel, all drawing discovery learning from the examples depicted in its simulations.

Birthed through experimentation and team discussion, which Edison found so crucial, your team's prototypes will not only serve as a way to visualize your solutions and ideas but offer a footprint marking the ongoing progression of your team's thinking. Like a walk in the Japanese garden described earlier, prototyping will slow down your thought process just enough to examine the assumptions that underlie your work as it unfolds. Consider using multiple forms of prototyping as you progress, offering your team different angles and per-spectives as you generate a new context for possible solutions.

## Accelerate True Collaboration by Crafting Physical Space to Support It

Do you remember the holodeck on the famous *Star Trek* television series? A physical space where crew members of the USS *Enterprise* often went to relax, each holodeck visitor needed only a brief phrase to command the ship's computer to conjure fantastical spaces meeting their every desire. Whether it was a favorite beach on planet Earth or even a past memory, upon the crew member's command, the holodeck immediately transformed a barren room into the context desired.

Although we have yet to develop technology allowing us to re-create worlds as instantly as the holodeck could on the *Enterprise*, industrial science tells us that the physical context in which we operate has a huge impact on the efficiency—and energy—with which we work. Recent research from noted architectural firm Gensler found that only half of US workers feel their work environment empowers them to innovate.[31] And studies from leading office design company Steelcase reveals that 70 percent of workers today waste up to 15 minutes just looking for a collaborative space to meet, with 24 percent wasting up to 30 minutes.[32] Rather than fostering a spirit of collaboration and making it easier to meet in small teams, most work environments make it harder.

Part of this dampening effect stems from the prevalence of work space structures that dominated the Industrial Age. To maximize worker efficiency, companies created linear rows of desks and offices positioned to reduce the amount of time required for one person to find another. In recent decades, these linear layouts evolved to become cubicles, or cubes, offering small partitioned walls between desks lined up in huge, open floor plans shaped like rectangles. Packing scores of people into small stretches of carpeted real estate, the few available corner offices and window offices came to hold particular prestige, largely the domain of powerful managers.

However, in the Innovation Age, these linear, legacy spaces often fail to support the more networked, horizontal flows of information required by collaboration teams. As Ms. Anat Lechner, a professor of business management at the Stern School of Business at New York University, describes it, today's workers require "I space," "you and I space," and "we space" to work most effectively.

Employees need to have areas for concentrated work (such as unassigned individual workstations), emergent social exchange (free-flowing hallways), learning (rooms equipped with technology and tools), and collaboration (group spaces for co-creation). The key is to make sure the different types of spaces are integrated with each other and open to all, so people can freely choose where to be based on what they're doing.[33]

Diverse work spaces served as a signature component of Edison's Menlo Park and West Orange laboratories. Every employee had ready access to "I space," "you and I space," and "we space." These came in the form of specialized rooms for team experimentation, empty rooms for solitude, libraries for quiet reading and study, and machine shops for collaborative efforts such as prototype creation. Edison's campus-style environment allowed diverse physical spaces to lie within just yards of each other. Encouraging what today are known as spontaneous dyads—unplanned conversations between employees as they walk from place to place—Edison's campuses also nourished the collegiality that he so deeply prized. With few restrictions, collaboration teams could hunker down and experiment using any area they desired. *Edison's collaboration culture was nourished by diverse work spaces addressing a broad array of team-based initiatives.*

A key point of emphasis within its global leadership training programs, the Dale Carnegie organization zeros in on the role of environment as a key to shifting the context for employee engagement. "A change in environment leads to a change in expectations,"[34] Greg Cox of Dale Carnegie notes "By shifting the physical space in which people operate, their perceptions of what they can accomplish also shifts."

A deep believer in the power of collaborative work space to collide unexpected ideas together, Steve Jobs, while at Pixar, positioned the animation studio in a location that forced employees to visit the building's main atrium on a frequent basis rather than stay in their own familiar work areas: "Mailboxes were shifted to the lobby; meeting rooms were moved to the center of the building, followed by the cafeteria, coffee bar, gift shop and bathrooms."[35] The revised flow of traffic through the building helped employees who might not otherwise bump into each other. Pixar's emphasis on collaborative encounters in these open spaces was reinforced by the ready availability of collaborative "we spaces" within the animation studio and elsewhere within the Pixar complex.

Challenging the Industrial Age notion that ideas for space modification always have to come from leaders or others in charge, in *Make Space*, by Scott Doorley and Scott Witthoft of the Institute of Design at Stanford—commonly known as the d.school—the designers describe more than 50 ways that existing physical space can be restructured to accommodate collaboration and innovation goals. Doorley and Witthoft believe crafting physical space for a team's sessions can be a powerful, creative, do-it-yourself effort within reach of an individual team and does not always have to lie under the thumb of a manager.

Most work spaces were designed according to an industrial labor model, from a time when our work was tethered to big machines and our status was rooted in the size of our office space. . . . Collaboration and creation aren't bound to [a] designated area; they evolve throughout a space, absorbing different people, places, and perspectives. . . . Reconfiguring the physical [environment] is a powerful signal that participation is truly welcome.[36]

Increasingly, companies not known for their collaboration focus are harnessing physical space as a means to support the kinds of initiatives Edison had in mind in Phase 2. Spurred by efforts originating in Microsoft Finland, Microsoft Europe has recently instituted an award-winning collaborative space concept called the New World of Work, which allows employees to engage in five different work areas:

1. *The Beach:* Featuring small tables and comfortable chairs, music, and soft lighting, this space is where most employees come to work individually or in pairs.

2. *Bistro/Cafeteria:* An eating space with tables, where most meetings take place.

3. *Nature Room:* A room full of plants, generally used for individual or pair work.

4. *Marketplace:* A fluid area, where people come either to work alone, to meet in large groups, or to look for others.

5. *The Library:* A setting reserved for undisturbed work, where employees must maintain silence and are not permitted to interrupt anyone.

Anthony Gyursanszky, vice president of innovation for Microsoft Finland, comments:[37]

> To drive the best ideas and attract the best employees, we needed to transform our workspace to be more collaborative, supporting the ways we want our teams to connect today. Breaking out of a more traditional office design allows us to facilitate more creative collaborations and deeper relationships between people. We're seeing a greater diversity of work styles our teams can engage in now versus how we've operated in the past.

Phase 2 represents the most extensive of the phases within Edison's true collaboration framework. Unlike most other collaborative structures, Edison's process prepares each team member for the collaboration process through individual creativity-driving skills, which maximize their contributions to the team. By understanding the mental model that each person brings to Phase 2, the full impact of diversity emphasized in Phase 1 can blossom. Guided by casual team discussion, experimentation, development of new context for the team's solutions, prototype creation, and a collaboration-friendly work space, your true collaboration initiative can experience the multiplicative power of minds working together toward a shared goal. Recognizing that not every unreasonable hypothesis you generate will yield the fruits you anticipate, ensure that your team is documenting its narrative prototypes alongside its three-dimensional ones. Be sure to record the big questions that have begun driving new thinking around context for the problem you are solving, plus any analogies that you've found to be particularly fruitful. By recognizing that the development of context is a continuum rather than a static process, the insights you've developed in Phase 2 will gain added momentum as you progress into Phase 3 (see Figure 4.6).

## TRUE COLLABORATION TOOLKIT: HANDS-ON EXERCISES—PHASE 2

Here are several exercises to strengthen the concepts you've learned from the Solo meld and Group meld facets of Phase 2—Context.

### Make Space for Your Team's Project Work

Most office environments today pull us away from the kinds of hands-on collaborative experiences Edison valued. Why not build a work space for your team—together? The

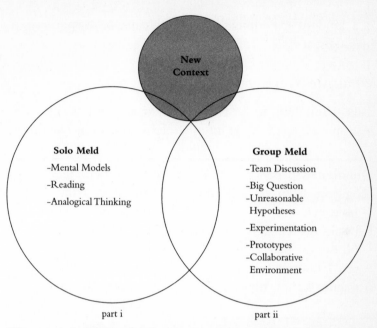

**Figure 4.6 Phase 2: Context—from Thomas Edison's Four Phases of True Collaboration**

*Note:* New context emerges when individuals meld their best thinking and experiment with multiple solutions rather than locking down on one too early.

MIT-Lemelson Center's 2011 annual study evaluating the state of innovation revealed that "less than half of respondents have done things like used a drill or hand-held power tool, or made something out of raw materials in the past year."[38] Combine a playful, shared experience for your team with an opportunity to create a new space for your work efforts. Use hand or power tools, paint, posters, duct tape, and fabric to build a creative, collaborative work space. Could you knock out a small wall in an unused section of your work area? Transform a series of cubes into a tent-like space? Consider it a kind of experiment. Be creative in your approach to making space!

## What Are You Reading?

Take 10 minutes to list the primary ways you draw in information each week. Your list might look something like this:

---

| | |
|---|---|
| Online newspapers | Books a friend lent me |
| Blog posts from my 3 favorite bloggers | Gourmet cooking magazine |
| E-books on Kindle, Nook, or iPad | A top 10 business best seller |
| A top 10 fiction best seller | A mystery novel |
| A science fiction novel | Outdoor gardening magazines |

---

Drawing from this list or developing a completely new one, write down five other reading sources—books, blogs, or magazines—that will intentionally shift the context of what you're reading. Consider a historical biography of an inspirational figure from world history, science fiction, a play, or a collection of poems. Pick up a book written by a famous musician or sports star. Commit to focus your reading on a new set of sources for the next 90 days and record your insights in a notebook. Plus, see if your reading yields any new analogies for your Group meld!

## Attend a Unique Out-of-Industry Special Event or Trade Show

Like Edison's visit to William Wallace's lab, consider how you can interact with spaces outside your immediate work environment to help you ask new questions or shape unreasonable hypotheses. A colleague of mine, Bill Gale, recently was named Inventor of the Year by a large global company that operates in a highly competitive technical environment. Bill has been able to maintain an edge in his collaboration and innovation efforts by intentionally attending conferences outside his industry—and beyond his expertise. Rather than attending all the same big conferences his colleagues do, he purposely seeks out conferences where he will know no one. This allows him to Solo meld, preparing his mind through exposure to new networks of people with an entirely different thought frame and mental model than his. What conferences or other special events could you attend to shift the context of your thinking? What are some of the music, design, art, or automotive events you've always wanted to attend?

# CHAPTER 5

# Phase 3

*Coherence—Building Coherent Teams*

**D**avid Bohm, a Hungarian immigrant who contributed his deep knowledge of theoretical physics to the Manhattan Project and later served as a professor at the University of California, penned a series of intriguing essays recently bound into an anthology titled *On Dialogue*. Among the pithy thoughts Bohm pursues in these essays is coherence and its role as a formative team dynamic. Viewing coherence as an experience that arises from "sharing a common content,"[1] Bohm emphasizes that coherence can be created even if not all parties on a team agree. He describes it as an organic rather than a static force: "It's a harmony of the individual and the collective, in which the whole constantly moves toward coherence."

Bohm recognized that coherence can be difficult to achieve even in small groups due to the preconceived roles its members desire to play. "Some people want to assert themselves. . . . Some people adopt the dominant role, some adopt the role of the weak, powerless person who can be dominated." For Bohm, coherence is optimized when there is a balance in the contributions of the team members rather than dominance by one. The dynamic interplay between team members engaging deeply at some times yet probing or remaining silent at other times offers a unique signature for how coherence operates. For coherence to thrive, he states, there is "a subtle situation in between, where you are not jumping in too fast, nor holding back too much."

Although we don't often use the term *coherence* when thinking about a team, coherence will become a central part of your attentions in Phase 3. Now that your true collaboration team has made progress in Phase 2 through Solo meld and Group meld, you may have begun experiencing conflict. Disagreements may have arisen. Some team members might be pulling and tugging at each other. Even though you still can all remain colleagues, it doesn't mean that it's easy to stay together.

Edison viewed coherence as the central, binding force uniting true collaboration teams in Phase 3. Like a kind of gravity that permeates the entire group, coherence connects team members with an invisible grasp that allows the team to keep functioning even if there are disruptions. Edison recognized coherence as a force that united his teams in a common purpose, driving each member forward with a sense of resolve and persistence in face of setbacks.

> We sometimes learn a lot from our failures if we have put into the effort the best thought and work we are capable of.
>
> **—Thomas Edison**

In Bohm's description of coherence as a dynamic process of "not jumping in too fast, nor holding back too much," we find an important role played by catalysts in Phase 3. Often without prior intent, some team members will find themselves in new roles in this phase—catalytic roles that they had not anticipated. Some will serve as change agents, helping focus the team's sense of progress, whereas others will facilitate communication of the team's endeavors through powerful outreach efforts. The most important catalytic force in Phase 3, however, is inspiration, particularly inspirational leadership.

Whether serving as the day-to-day leader of a true collaboration initiative or operating as the main voice of the laboratory, Edison consistently inspired others through his relentless passion for excellence and his commitment to achieving the seemingly impossible. One wellspring for this inspiration lay in *the coupling of each project with an immediate action-based purpose as well as a broader, higher purpose*. In Phase 3, Edison laid the groundwork for team members not only to draw inspiration from the collective endeavors of the lab but also to find within themselves an answer to the question, "Why am I doing this?" Edison viewed inspiration as a kind of momentum, a force that drove coherence through "a common content," as Bohm would describe it. Team members came to realize they could fuel their efforts via inspiration from Edison, but they also had to find it within themselves to sustain creative momentum when Edison was absent.

In Phase 3, you'll learn how to develop coherence within your true collaboration team by weaving together inspiration, purpose, progress, and debate. Phase 3 will serve as the shift point for establishing a common purpose within your group— a higher meaning for your efforts, lying even beyond the team goals you began crystallizing in Phase 2. Coherence will enable your group to continue despite conflicts or frustrations that can make you feel like throwing in the towel.

Phase 3—Coherence, includes the following two true collaboration components:

- *Part i, Presence of inspirational and emergent leaders:* Inspiration pulls teams away from gnawing feelings of doubt as obstacles and conflicts arise. When inspiration or inspirational leadership is present, coherence arises through the engagement of purpose, elevating individual performance to new levels. Some inspirational leaders can be intentionally developed, and others will emerge unexpectedly.

- *Part ii, Communication of progress toward shared goals and purpose:* Team members learn to move forward constructively in the presence of internal debate or conflict. They learn to communicate progress, even if this comes in the form of sharing small wins. Shared goals and common purpose are communicated within the team as well as with external partners, aligning the team's expanding efforts in a coherent flow.

Let's begin by examining how inspirational leadership served as a factor in Edison's true collaboration success, as well as how he encouraged the emergence of inspirational leaders in his organization. Inspirational leaders can be developed from new and unexpected places on your team.

# PART I, PHASE 3: COHERENCE

One of the most powerful life experiences we can have as individuals is stepping out of the roles or situations we feel most comfortable in, and trying on a new role. Most of us feel hesitant to push the boundaries of what is possible for our own development. In Edison's organization, he continually pioneered new horizons for people to engage with, both in a technical sense as well as in a leadership capacity.

## Coherence Driven through Purpose and Inspiration

Years ago, I remember reading a gritty story about the Imperial Trans-Antarctic Expedition of 1914, a daring journey led by famous British explorer Ernest Shackleton on his ship, the *Endurance*. From the moment of the ship's arrival in Antarctica, Shackleton and nearly two dozen pioneering companions experienced one life-threatening cataclysm after another. Disaster first struck Shackleton's expedition when the *Endurance* successfully reached Antarctica but became trapped in ice "like an almond in toffee" miles from its intended docking point.[2] Its hull was crushed to smithereens over the course of several weeks. The loss of the *Endurance* to pounding ice flows meant the entire expeditionary party had to make camp while exposed to the windswept climes of the Antarctic, often sleeping under lifeboats from the ship to survive. Shackleton vowed publicly from the first moment of difficulty that every man who had ventured with him to Antarctica would return, a pledge made all the more dramatic by the permanent hobbling of the *Endurance*.

Feeling deeply responsible for the welfare of his entire party, Shackleton often personally shunned the comfort of special sleeping bags that had been provisioned for explorers originally slated to set out in dogsleds for the expedition. Desiring to create as much comfort for his teammates as possible, Shackleton also prepared hot tea and coffee over the fire most mornings, taking the last servings for himself.

As we clustered round the blubber stove, with the acrid smoke blowing in our faces, we were quite a cheerful company. . . . Life was not so bad. We ate our evening meal while the snow drifted down from the surface of the glacier and our chilled bodies grew warm.

—*Ernest Shackleton*

Over the course of time, vigorous debates concerning the best course of action broke out within the team, with particular rancor emerging in one instance early in the expedition after Shackleton's team had trudged miles in the wrong direction, seeking aid. But Shackleton's inspirational leadership enabled the team to continue operating as a coherent unit. Dedicating himself to a higher purpose—that every man who had accompanied him on the *Endurance* would survive—Shackleton maintained that returning to England could be accomplished, creating invisible bonds of hope between each team member during their months in the Antarctic. But daily, he dedicated his focus to keeping the team warm and fed. Ultimately, and with no lives lost, Shackleton's entire team returned to Britain, receiving a hero's welcome.

Although few true collaboration teams will face the life-or-death situation Shackleton's did, the expedition of 1914 offers us a backdrop for the same combination of qualities that infused inspiration and inspirational leadership into Edison's operations over a period of decades.

The magic of Edison's inspirational touch flowed in large part from his driving passion to serve humanity through his inventions, framing it this way: "My philosophy of life is work—bringing out the secrets of nature and applying them for the happiness of man. I know of no better service to render during the short time we are in this world." Similar to Shackleton prioritizing the welfare of his men before considering the riches his Antarctic explorations could garner him back in England, Edison's belief in service

155

to humanity outweighed his desire for fame. Edison said, "I never perfected an invention that I did not think about in terms of the service it might give others." Each of Edison's true collaboration projects were linked to a higher purpose, which he deeply internalized, modeling in his actions a dedication to "make real" the higher purpose he saw in each endeavor. Table 5.1 shows how Edison might have framed the broader purpose for some of his major true collaboration efforts.

Much as Steve Jobs lured John Scully from Pepsi to join him at Apple by saying, "Do you want to sell sugar water all your life, or do you want to come with me and change the world?" the magnetism of the vision and purpose behind Edison's efforts made workers feel they were a part of something bold and daring. The sweeping impact Edison

### Table 5.1  Edison Linked His Collaboration Work to a Higher Purpose

| True Collaboration Project | Higher Purpose |
| --- | --- |
| Edison Electric Pen and Press | Reduce the drudgery of copying documents by hand |
| Edison phonograph and record | Provide family entertainment and learning at home |
| Edison incandescent electric light | Provide safe power that can be used around the clock |
| Edison's system for electrical power | Provide light and power to entire communities safely and inexpensively |
| Edison's Kinetoscope and films | Provide education, plus family fun and entertainment |
| The Edison Storage Battery | Create a portable power source safe for anyone to handle |

believed could be achieved through his inventions made employees feel they could conquer the impossible.

> If you are working on something you really care about, you don't have to be pushed. The vision pulls you.
>
> —*Steve Jobs*

Inspiration and a sense of purpose moved through Edison's labs like a kind of osmosis, yielding an emotional connection between the daunting projects Edison conceived and the pioneering spirit they called forward in his workers. This common emotional fiber helped relieve the drag of seemingly endless late nights in Edison's lab as workers labored to deliver solutions.

Not always sitting at the top of the heap, there were times when Edison and his teams were viewed as the underdogs. With his reputation clouded by a series of failures known as Edison's Folly—stretching nearly a decade, from the early 1890s to the turn of the century—Edison had worked fruitlessly with an army of teams to deliver new technology for iron ore mining and grinding. Seeking to create new ore processing capability for the burgeoning steel industry, Edison spent weeks at a time in Ogden, New Jersey—later renamed Edison—building gigantic rock crushing machines which constantly required troubleshooting and repair. After a string of dead ends coupled with a major drop in the price of ore as large new ore fields were discovered, Edison was being called a back number by his peers, a once famous guy now all washed up.

Desiring to inspire a renewed sense of hope and purpose among his employees following this very public failure, Edison set out at the turn of the century to create a storage battery containing no lead or liquid chemicals, a feat that went against all the known chemistry of the day. Edison galvanized his battery team to hunt for new combinations of materials that could store electricity, an effort virtually 180 degrees opposite to the laboratory's competency for *distributing* electricity via the gridded network Edison's own teams had invented in 1882. Edison's ability to drive coherence through inspiration and purpose after long bouts of failure is revealed in this comment from a team member, who had endured months of setbacks and disappointments toiling on the positive node of the battery:

> I guess that question of conductivity of the positive pocket brought lots of gray hairs to his head. I never dreamed a man could have such patience and perseverance. Any other man than Edison would have given the whole thing up a thousand times, but not he! Things looked awfully blue to the whole bunch of us many a time, but he was always hopeful. I remember one time things looked so dark to me that I had just about made up my mind to throw up my job, but some good turn came just then and didn't. Now I'm glad I held on, for we've got a great future.[3]

Edison's collaboration team ultimately hit success in 1903, yielding an alkaline storage battery made of thin sandwiches of nickel and iron stacked in tall columns the size of a large thermos jug. Edison commented, "All the fellows said it could not be done, but I've solved the problem." Figure 5.1 shows Edison holding an alkaline storage battery, which was light enough for an individual to carry.

Inspirational leaders—in good times and in bad—vividly paint the best picture of the current situation while also drawing a compelling vision of the future, one that pulls people forward. As Greg Cox of the Dale Carnegie organization notes, "An inspirational leader anchors you at the starting point and at the ending point. The distance between those points feels long, it feels far. It feels impossible."[4] Much like the proverbial "reality distortion field" favored by Steve

**Figure 5.1 Edison Holding His Storage Battery**
*Source:* National Park Service, Edison National Historic Site.

Jobs when calmly asking the impossible, Edison held a deep conviction that the shared efforts of his team could push knowledge to new and unknown heights, bringing purpose to what seemed unobtainable.

The sense of purpose behind each of Edison's true collaboration efforts helped his teams maintain coherence despite grueling challenges and setbacks. Does your team hold something deeply and authentically about its project? Is there a broader meaning that lies behind your endeavors that will allow you to sustain your passions and energy, even when you encounter roadblocks? Is there a person—or a shared philosophy—that drives inspiration for your true collaboration effort, especially when it seems impossible that you will reach a solution? Compare notes on answers to these questions between members of your team and see where you agree and where your answers may differ.

## Drawing Out the Best in Each Team Member Inspires the Entire Team

In addition to the power of an inspirational leader to drive momentum and purpose, a second factor present in Edison's true collaboration efforts served as the subject of a recent *Harvard Business Review* article by Claudio Fernandez-Araoz, Boris Groysberg, and Nitin Nohria: *the presence of an individual who desires to see others on the team succeed can serve as a catalyst for inspiring the entire team.* Different from the absolute inspirational power of a single charismatic leader, this form of inspiration comes from what could be called a shoulder-to-shoulder connection within a team. Shoulder-to-shoulder connections yield inspiration through daily activities that require team members to roll up their sleeves together. When team members work side by side, there is a recognition that individuals know and understand the real challenges in play within an initiative, rather than merely having a conceptual grasp of them. Having a grassroots view of what's happening on a project allows team members to shape new meaning and inspiration for one another as the team progresses in its endeavors over time.

While conducting research around the characteristics most needed in executives who would be serving in diverse roles in emerging markets, Fernandez-Araoz, Groysberg, and Nohria observed that companies were grappling to gain a deeper definition for qualities such as "ability to address high levels of ambiguity" and "ease in handling the unfamiliar." Selecting candidates for collaborative assignments in emerging economies by calling upon fast-track superstars, change agents, and high-potential employees had not yielded success.[5]

However, the authors' research revealed that one crucial quality—*the desire to have a positive impact on others*—emerged as a key predictor for whether an individual could serve as a catalyst in building collaborative teams. Executives deriving deep satisfaction from seeing others succeed were most able to inspire unity and common purpose in leading diverse groups even in another culture, propelling those groups to accomplish something powerful together.

In examining the array of factors that yielded greatest leverage for one individual to impact his or her team, the authors identified the scale shown in Table 5.2. Starting with factors holding the least impact at the top of the table and moving down toward the greatest, findings revealed that what an individual knows is less likely to rally the best performance from other team members, versus what an individual can do to drive insight and understanding from other members. But the most powerful leverage point of all lay in

**Table 5.2  Factors Influencing Impact of an Individual on a Team**

| Leverage Factor | Impact Contributed by the Individual |
| --- | --- |
| Knowledge | What an individual knows |
| Skills | What an individual can do |
| Addressing conflict | Balancing competing viewpoints |
| Engagement | Driving insight and understanding |
| Motivation | Desiring to have positive impact on others' success |

the presence of an individual who served as a catalyst desiring to positively affect the success of every other team member.

The researchers found that with the presence of a catalyst who helped draw out what success meant to each team member, the team itself became better able to determine what the entire team was striving to accomplish. By holding a vision for the success of each individual, these catalysts were ultimately able to inspire the best performance from the entire team, creating a vision of *mutual success*.

Although Edison did not fashion individual career strategies for his employees, he generated a unique inspirational power on his teams through a willingness to work shoulder-to-shoulder with anyone in his employ. Whereas other industrial magnates of his era sought to remain more separate from their workers, Edison stretched the vision of what an individual could accomplish through self-improvement and the power of collaboration to help drive that self-improvement. Always willing to roll up his sleeves, Edison had an uncanny ability to zero in on what an individual team member needed to do to address a specific problem, pushing the thinking of each person to the next level. As a business owner who also understood the inner workings of his operations, Edison served as a catalyst who recognized what was needed to achieve team success and held a vision for that success.

It's not the money they're after, it's their chance to succeed.

—*Thomas Edison*

Jim Ziganto, former corporate vice president of human resources for Carlex Glass, America, notes that individuals who can see success for each team member are a key to the inspiration and motivation that drive coherence. "Collaborative assignments help keep the best, most motivated people working for you. By engaging one or two folks that see a big vision for the team and its members, they can serve as catalysts to stretch what the team believes is possible. You'll drive better motivation levels overall, keep the team on track, and improve the performance of each member."[6]

But inspiring others is not a quality that many senior leaders today seek to develop in their workers. Even Ricardo Semler, head of Semco's extensive industrial and real estate operations in Brazil, believes it's not always possible for the passions of an individual—even a charismatic leader—to inspire others. "It's unfair to expect all employees to feel passionate about their work. Some will, some won't."[7] But what Semler does aim to establish within his portfolio of companies is a concept he calls a minimum common denominator, a coherent thread that ties all of Semco's teams together: *individually contributing to the success of your entire team.*[8] Whether an individual believes he or she can be an ongoing source of inspiration for others, Semler's aim is to develop this quintessential yet often elusive quality of desiring success for the team itself. This goes to the heart of true collaboration.

> We are all leaders and followers, aiming for success—together.
>
> —*Paul Farmer, director of innovation,*
> *Veridian Credit Union*

Larry Keeley of the Doblin Group holds yet a different view. Emphasizing the importance of a practice known as human effectiveness, Keeley finds that inspiring the maximum potential from each individual on a team comes through the elimination of limiting beliefs. Increasingly popular as a tool to achieve high-impact results from diverse groups when timetables are short, human effectiveness practices help teams "find the greatness" in each member. "The aim is to work at your brilliant best rather than your tepid best. Most people dislike teams because they so often devolve into groupthink—which only leads you to bland, vanilla stuff.

Don't try to homogenize everything—look for the ideas that challenge and motivate each member. Find out how you can be collectively great."[9] The Illinois Institute of Technology's top-ranking Institute of Design builds principles of human effectiveness into many of its courses, rooting the notion of collective greatness into the mental model of every graduate student.

Regardless of whether you feel you personally possess the qualities of an inspirational leader, you can serve as a catalyst who contributes deeply to the success of your team by seeking to aid the success of each member. Consider how viewing yourself as a catalyst for your team can strengthen your growth mindset. Rather than simply focusing on your own role and your own outcomes, think about ways you are uniquely able to spur the best performance from other members of your team.

## Spurring Inspirational Leaders to Emerge: Go Beyond the Comfort Zone

It's not always possible to know which members of a team will step forward to inspire their colleagues—or when. This uncertainty represents a particular challenge for virtual teams, where shoulder-to-shoulder engagement can be extremely difficult, if not impossible, to achieve. It is also a challenge for leaders who need to ensure that those who are brave enough to step forward as inspirational catalysts are not set up to fail. Edison offers us an approach that can help fill the void that often exists around inspiration and inspirational leadership on today's teams.

Although Edison realized that his ability to drive coherence and "share a common content" would come through personally inspiring others, he also realized that inspiration was not something he could teach. Instead of describing to

164

workers what it meant to inspire others, *he created leadership opportunities to seed the principles of inspiration through direct experience*. Not fully knowing where his decisions might lead, Edison often plucked promising employees from the lab to take on project leadership or project facilitation roles, intentionally stretching their abilities by giving them assignments that lay beyond anything they had ever previously endeavored. In Phase 1 as we examined the importance of diversity on teams, for example, Edison drew upon the talents of electrician Reginald Fessenden for projects that ranged from working on new insulation materials to heading up the chemistry laboratory at West Orange. Edison found that laying out big challenges for individuals in turn prompted these individuals to inspire others to work jointly with them on these new projects, pushing his selected cadets beyond the comfort zone of what they might normally volunteer to do. Stretch assignments served as a form of reskilling.

Although Edison had no certainty that the individuals he chose to groom in this fashion would succeed, he did guarantee them one thing: their experience would not involve losing face in front of their peers. No matter the outcome, Edison viewed the taking on of a project leadership role as a form of discovery learning, an offshoot of the growth mindset he sought to model. Shown in Table 5.3 is a list of several employees who emerged as inspirational leaders and catalysts in Edison's laboratories based on his unique approach to offering stretch assignments. The background and expertise of these individuals varies widely.

Edison's pattern for unexpectedly assigning people to fulfill new roles rings a familiar note for Greg Cox, who frames Edison's actions within the precepts of Dale Carnegie's approach to leadership: "Leadership means taking people where they would not willingly go on their own."[10] Cultural theorist and author Margaret Wheatley would also describe

## Table 5.3 Inspirational Leaders Who Emerged as Catalysts through Unique Assignments from Edison

| Inspirational Leaders | Expertise |
| --- | --- |
| Charles Batchelor | Master experimenter, general manager |
| Francis Upton | Mathematics, physics, acoustics |
| William Andrews | Electrical wiring, electrical systems |
| William Hammer | Lighting, power distribution, radium |
| Wilson Howell | Phonograph design, recorded sound |
| John Lawson | Chemistry |
| Reginald Fessenden | Electrical wiring, chemistry, R&D manager |
| William Kennedy Laurie Dickson | Photography, moving pictures |
| Arthur Kennelly | Electrical engineering |
| Francis Jehl | Lab assistant, experimenter |

Edison's approach to developing cadres of inspirational leaders as a means to tap a powerful place of meaning and contribution within an individual. Wheatley says inspirational leaders "offer us the possibility of becoming something different and greater than anything we had been."[11] Edison's desire to facilitate greater collaboration and inspiration in the lab yielded "connections to create new and surprising capacity."

Robert Schmidt, chief executive officer (CEO) of Systems Engineering & Manufacturing, Inc. (SE&M), headquartered in Forest, Virginia, has adopted a means to develop inspirational catalysts in his organization in a way very similar way to Edison's. A seasoned veteran of the metals fabricating industry, he worked in large national manufacturing operations for more than 20 years. Bob established SE&M more than 10 years ago after a large employer he was working for

**Figure 5.2 Edison with West Orange
Phonograph Team, 1888**

*Note*: Edison's small phonograph collaboration team generated big results,
yielding a perfected machine in 1888. Pictured here is Edison at center
with the sales and marketing rep for Britain, George Gouraud (seated at
right), William Kennedy Laurie Dickson (standing at left), and master
experimenter Charles Batchelor (standing, second from left) along
with other team members.
*Source:* National Park Service, Edison National Historic Site.

went bankrupt. Schmidt recalls the exhilaration he felt when
he decided to form a new company, drawing upon the
workforce of the bankrupt operation. He says, "I just looked
around and said, 'I want you and you and you and you.'"[12]
Schmidt recognized the unsung potential of these individuals
and sought a unique means to tap it within the new company.
Schmidt instituted a process he calls tag, after the childhood
game. "My employees know that, on any given day, I can

walk into the office, point my finger and say, 'Tag, you're it!' When someone gets 'tagged' it means I've identified them for a new project—one which they probably will have no idea how to begin. It stretches them and makes them think."

Schmidt emphasizes this approach has enabled him to attract and keep high-quality talent. "People know they will get unique opportunities working for me that they would never get anywhere else." SE&M, an operation with 50 full-time employees, has doubled in size in the past five years, booking its best year ever in 2011.

Like Edison in his ability to place people in positive, unexpected opportunities, Schmidt, through his game of tag, pushes his people beyond the expected, allowing employees to uncover a place of power and contribution that inspires the individual and those around them.

> Every change is fostered by a change in self-perception. . . . We ourselves engage in change only as we discover that we might be more of who we are by becoming something different.
>
> —*Margaret Wheatley*, **A Simpler Way**

In your true collaboration effort, have you been asked to take on a stretch assignment? Can you see the possibility for shifting the mental model you have of yourself in this process? Is there a new, surprising quality that you can uncover through your participation in your true collaboration effort? If you are in a position of leadership and could play tag with another person on your team, what unexpected assignment would you give them?

Recognizing the role of inspiration as a pivotal component for creating coherence, let's turn to the second facet of Phase 3, which emphasizes how to navigate debate and communicate the work of the team in a way that signals progress to both internal and external partners.

# PART II, PHASE 3: COHERENCE

Among the most challenging aspects of any collaboration lies in the reality that debates and disagreements come with the territory. It is rare for a truly productive, effective collaboration to flow without some form of conflict. Creating a coherent team requires that we take a focused look at how to successfully navigate situations where team members—internal or external—disagree.

## Debate Can Strengthen Common Purpose

Although we may wish to believe that success in a collaborative effort is correlated with perfect clarity from the outset, the most positive team results emerge when debate about shared objectives and shared purpose is encouraged rather than suppressed. As innovation author Steven Johnson writes, "We value good ideas because they tend to have a high signal-to-noise ratio. But that doesn't mean you want to cultivate those ideas in noise-free environments, because noise-free environments end up being too sterile and predictable in their output."[13] The best innovation and collaboration solutions are derived in environments that are not perfectly harmonious. Johnson says, they "are always a little contaminated."

In wake of the global reset, increasing overlap between innovation, strategy, and value creation bring collaborative activity into heightened focus. Individuals serving in capacities connected with growth-propelling functions will interact more and more. That means differences in perspective will butt against each other with greater regularity. As revealed in Phase 1, the very fact that Edison constructed his true collaboration teams using diversity of expertise as an underlying principle means that your own team is likely to experience conflict.

In its highest form, true collaboration doesn't zap all discontent within a team. In fact, by allowing debate to take place, groups can reaffirm their common purpose and even uncover new ideas or directions via the team dialogue that results when disagreements arise. Edison said, "I believe in criticism because it brings out all the cold facts about a thing, and promotes discussion, which is always beneficial." By recognizing debate as a healthy part of your true collaboration process, you can begin to prepare yourself for the inevitable wrangling that emerges when diverse viewpoints collide. Practicing the principles of coherence in Phase 3 allows you to gain insight on methods that will help ensure that heated discussions move you forward rather than ripping your team apart.

First, when considering what's *worth* debating, here are three guidelines recommended by strategists Saj-nicole A. Joni and Damon Beyer in their published research on group conflict:

1. Focus on what is possible rather than what has already happened, guiding the discussion toward future events rather than historical events.

2. Identify what is compelling about the benefits of a given course of action.

3. Don't argue about facts or engage in debate when there is no clear-cut answer or when uncertainty is present.

Joni and Beyer emphasize that debating within these parameters expands the shared understanding of the team and its purpose rather than yielding finger-pointing.[14] It keeps the team focused on a growth mindset rather than devolving into a discussion of tasks. Focused debate can become a method for renewing the team's commitment to the shared goals established in Phase 2 and its sense of purpose as it works through the early stages of Phase 3. Although these debates may ultimately reshape the team's purpose or goals, it is healthier for the team to accomplish this openly rather than stuffing differences under the surface.

## *Avoiding Defensive Routines*

In managing debate within your team, it's important to recognize whether you as well as others in the group are being productive in your team encounters, or actually standing at the brink of what learning expert Peter Senge describes as "defensive routines"[15]—potentially divisive head-to-head confrontations. Senge's research, conducted with Chris Argyris of the Harvard Business School, reveals that teams can break down when individuals resort to long-rooted defensive patterns. Argyris notes, "School trains us never to admit that we do not know the answer, and [many organizations] reinforce that lesson by rewarding the people who excel in advocating their own views, not inquiring into complex issues. Even if we feel uncertain or ignorant, we learn to protect ourselves from the pain of appearing uncertain or ignorant." Without the ability to address conflict constructively, "the capacity for team learning is unreliable," and our mental models become hobbled by an inability to integrate the insights that debate can offer.

Senge and Argyris suggest the following five areas represent our biggest defensive responses:

1. Deliberately opposing another person's ideas as a show of power

2. Agreeing to a request with no intention of fulfilling it

3. Saying "yes" simply to avoid a confrontation or a deeper discussion

4. Sheltering ourselves from real engagement by changing the subject

5. Criticizing others before we have a chance to recognize our own shortcomings

Do any of these defensive behaviors sound familiar? All of us have been engaged in some form of these defensive routines whether on a collaboration team or as part of a broader work-related effort. The danger of these defensive responses lies not only in their potential to stall your team's progress but in the blocked energy that results when a group begins to swirl around and around in its defensive postures. Connections to the common vision of the true collaboration effort, as well as its shared goals, lie in jeopardy when defensive routines take over.

You and your team members can respond to defensive routines in several ways. Appreciative inquiry offers one approach that has yielded positive results for groups at British Airways, Merck, Verizon, and GE-Capital, among many others. Appreciative inquiry focuses the attention of the team on "its most positive potential—its positive core."[16] Rather than beginning with faults, appreciative inquiry uses open-ended questions to address four core aspects of the team's endeavors. Known as 4D, these include discovery, dreams, design, and destiny.

Senge and Argyris suggest other key steps for teams to begin tackling the swirling effects of defensiveness during team dialogue:

- Identify the core source of fear and diminish the emotional threats surrounding it.

- Offer "permission to speak freely" while ensuring confidentiality.

- Tell the truth as objectively as possible, revealing the unmet expectation or the gap between current reality and the intended position of the team.

- Ask open-ended questions, such as, "What leads you to have this view?" or "Where do our efforts differ from your expectations?"

- Offer transparency by identifying other challenges that the group has previously addressed successfully.[17]

Adhering to these approaches as part of your team dialogue is particularly crucial for virtual teams who don't meet face to face with frequency. Distance can breed misunderstandings, which are often much tougher to hammer out on Skype or via telepresence than they are in person.

In addition, differences in how various cultures handle conflict can come into play when members of your team are drawn from diverse corners of the globe. Erin Meyer, an adjunct professor in the Organizational Behavior Department at INSEAD and a specialist in the field of multicultural leadership, suggests these additional steps when concerns about misunderstandings that may originate from differences in culture arisewith:[18]

- Many Asian cultures prefer to make agreements outside of a team setting, with team meetings representing only the formal okay to proceed with something that has already been agreed to via side conversations. If you believe this is in play, make one-on-one phone calls to any individual who may be reluctant to make a commitment in a team setting.

- Instead of personally challenging one another's opinions in full view of the group, have team members send in their ideas or grievances to a nominated third party before a scheduled team meeting, anonymously. This way participants can confront areas of disagreement without confronting the person directly associated with a particular conflict. Use of a skilled coach can help the team prevent excessive rancor in airing points of disagreement.

Are defensive routines causing your group's progress to stall? Consider employing one or more of the remedies recommended for breaking the grip of defensive routines, taking particular care if you are working with a multicultural team.

## Collaboration Is Not a Democracy

Once all viewpoints about a conflict have been aired, the reality is that someone either from within the team or beyond it will need to make a decision on how to proceed. Jim Whitehurst, president and chief executive of Red Hat, provider of Linux and other open source technology, comments: "We let debate happen, and you let it kind of burn its way out, with people offering their opinions on both sides of an issue. And then you say: 'We've listened to all of this. We've taken it into consideration and here's what we're going to do.' Even the most ardent people opposing whatever decision is ultimately made will at least think: 'I had my say. You heard me, and you told me why you made the decision.' It does not have to be a democracy."[19]

Verne Harnish, author of *Mastering the Rockefeller Habits*, agrees that meritocracy rather than democracy best forwards the work of true collaboration teams. "Collaboration is not democracy. It's not about voting and winning. In collaboration, there is a sense of community contribution. It's about getting more brains on the problem. Even after collaborative discussion, the path forward can still be one person's decision."[20]

In Edison's lab, Edison himself was often the keeper of crucial final decisions, although he gave team leaders considerable latitude in keeping the work of an individual project moving forward. Although debate certainly existed, it tended to be less defensive in nature and focused more on shifts in processes for gathering new insights or concerns about quality and customer deadlines rather than battling for turf. The collegial culture of the laboratory was dedicated to pushing the frontiers of new thinking and new technology in an open environment that valued diverse debate and team discussion. This environment became sustainable in large measure due to the fact that Edison made himself vulnerable to questions from his colleagues by openly sharing his own experimental results, including outcomes that fell short of expectations.

Ensure that your team has a go-to resource for aid in addressing conflict situations. This resource can be an internal team member but can also be a trusted champion of your work who lies beyond the team. If you need to call on such a resource, gain agreement up front that any decision on how to proceed will be made by this trusted party rather than a democratic vote within the team.

## Edison Grappled with Defensive Routines in Relationships with Some Suppliers

Although individuals in Edison's laboratory and manufacturing operations rarely engaged in head-to-head conflict, Edison did run into defensive routines in his personal relationships with vendors and outside partners. These periodic breakdowns negatively impacted his business by creating disruptions in materials contracts and even manufacturing agreements. One such defensive routine led to the dissolution not only of a business partnership but a personal friendship between Edison and longtime colleague Ezra Gilliland.

Extending back to Edison's days as a young inventor in Cincinnati, Gilliland had served as a resource for manufacturing Edison's Electric Pen and Press, as well as aiding in the production of several of Edison's telegraph improvements and his telephone transmitter. Gilliland had also introduced Edison to his second wife, Mina Miller, following the death of his first wife, Mary.

Although the two men had remained in contact for some time, Edison formally reunited in the 1880s with Gilliland, while Ezra was serving as head of Alexander Graham Bell's research and development operations. Gilliland ultimately left Bell's organization—Bell and Tainter—to work with Edison on improving his phonograph technology, as well as to expand phonograph sales.

In late 1887, Gilliland became a high-level sales agent for Edison, months later securing an agreement with millionaire glass industrialist Jesse Lippincott to purchase various phonograph rights from Edison. Although Edison's phonograph operations benefitted greatly from the deal, it turned out that Gilliland had also cut a side deal with Lippincott, securing for himself a healthy finder's fee. Furious that Gilliland had siphoned away funds without his knowledge, Edison sued Gilliland, forever ending their friendship. The emotional pitch that surrounded the matter never enabled Edison and Gilliland to remedy their disagreements.

Edison did not follow the principles of coherence in this challenge, nor did he recognize the defensive routines in play. His entanglement with Gilliland stemmed from differences in the understanding between the two men about the boundaries between their business and personal relationship. Edison believed he was senior to Gilliland and that because the phonograph was his intellectual property, Gilliland's role was secondary. However, Gilliland believed he held equal stature to Edison in cutting the business deal with Lippincott.

Gilliland also felt he held special status with Edison, as Ezra and his wife were personal friends with Edison and his wife Mina, even sharing vacation property with them in Fort Myers, Florida. The fallout from this misunderstanding could probably have been averted if Edison had been more transparent with Gilliland about where the two men needed to draw a line between their business and personal relationship. The intermingling of their work and personal lives created entanglements that led to a failure in their collaboration.

---

**Myths and Perceptions: Thomas Edison and Nicola Tesla**

Although much attention has been given to the existence of a high-profile conflict between Edison and Nicola Tesla, a brilliant Croatian-born engineer who worked for Edison in one of his small New York laboratories, "the personal relationship between Edison and Tesla remains largely a mystery," notes Dr. Paul Israel, a leading Edison expert at Rutgers University.[21] Tesla did not report directly to Edison during his employment, and the two barely knew each other.

But in a flap that coincided with Tesla's departure from Edison's employ, Tesla believed Edison had shorted him some money. Although historical research has since proved this not to be the case, "the popular mythology is that Edison was trying to thwart Tesla by trying to oppose alternating current. But you'd be hard pressed to find Tesla's name in the press." Israel states the

*(continued)*

*(continued)*

yellow journalism around the subject "was more about George Westinghouse versus Edison."

Israel also comments that Tesla, years later, praised Edison in an article for an engineering journal but later joined other inventors in "harshly criticizing him" in 1929, when Edison received all the publicity surrounding the 50th anniversary of the electric light. Media hype over the supposed falling out between the two men has created a lasting impression, albeit a false one, highlighting the fact that the media and other external influencers can have a major impact on how debate and conflict are perceived.

The example of Edison's conflicts with Gilliland offers an extreme view of what can arise when defensive routines are allowed to build unchecked. Examine your team's activities and be candid in assessing whether there may be defensive routines in play. Allowing defensive routines to operate freely dissolves shared purpose, reducing the power of the team to fulfill its goals in a coherent way.

The conversations that build community are those where people speak with authenticity and vulnerability about themselves, one another, and about the problems they're faced with.

—*Robert Hargrove*,
**Mastering the Art of Creative Collaboration**

## Monitor the Use of Collaborative Language to Gauge Potential for Conflict

If Gilliland and Edison had been able to speak more openly about their respective views of what collaboration looked like in their business relationship, they might not have experienced such a dramatic falling out. Today, several early warning tools exist for reducing the likelihood that internal team conflict will advance to the level of all-out warfare.

One such warning tool lies in a deeper understanding of team-oriented language. When individuals on a team begin using self-referencing language more frequently than team-referencing language, it can mean the group is entering a danger zone where defensive routines can be activated and coherence weakened.

Adapted from *Team Talk* by Anne Donnellon, Table 5.4 offers a valuable monitor for determining whether your team in Phase 3 is functioning as a truly collaborative group or if it is a team in name only (that is, a nominal team). Through

**Table 5.4 Listen for the Language That Signals the Presence of True Collaboration**[22]

| Nominal Team | Collaborative Team |
| --- | --- |
| Individual identifies primarily with his or her functional group. | Individual identifies primarily with the work team. |
| Individual makes key decisions independent of the work team. | Individual engages work team in key decisions they make. |
| Individual affiliates closely with title, tenure, or salary rank when speaking. | Individual does not operate based expressly on title, tenure, or salary. |
| Individual remains at a distance from others on the team by using formal language and pat phrases. | Individual uses casual language or respectful nicknames while still maintaining respect and dignity. |
| Individual manages conflict through dictates, ultimatums, or avoidance. | Individual manages conflict by confronting directly yet constructively. |

tracking the presence of self-referencing language versus team-referencing language, you can avoid the eruption of defensive routines. Consider what is true about each of your collaboration team members based on the elements shown in Table 5.4.

As you weigh the contributions of individual team members, if more of your responses fall on the right side of the chart, your true collaboration team is building toward higher and higher levels of coherence and collegiality. If you note the presence of distancing language, formalities, ultimatums or the use of power plays by most group members, your team is in jeopardy of losing momentum toward its shared goals. Unless action is taken to realign the motivations of members who perceive your group as a nominal team, defensive routines can derail your progress. As cautioned by 3M Post-it Note inventor Art Fry in Phase 1, you may ultimately have to get rid of the "slow molecules" on your team.

> Try honestly to see things from the other person's point of view.
>
> **—Dale Carnegie, Principle #17,**
> **How to Win Friends and Influence People**

Jay Scherer of BPI Group North America comments that when a mismatch exists between the self-orientation of a group member and his or her inability to connect with the broader mission of the collaboration team, there is often a tension between the collaborative group's role and other constituencies the individual feels require his or her loyalty. Scherer urges the use of coaching tools as well as the inquiring and reflecting posture advocated in the mental models conversation in Phase 2. Whether conducted via a leader-to-team-member connection or via a team-member-to-team-member approach, Scherer suggests holding a coaching conversation that includes the following components:

- Identify where the perceived competition for the individual's loyalty lies.

- Determine what, in the eyes of the team member, shared success would look like.

- Listen and seek to influence from a base of credibility, respect, and humility.

- Identify where you may be able to advocate for the individual's views.

- Recognize where ambiguity may exist within the individual's viewpoint and define steps to help reduce it.

- Return to the discovery learning goals of the team and its relationship to the goals of the individual, emphasizing where shared learning offers key benefits.

Scherer also notes that a failure to see common learning outcomes often serves as a source of disengagement by team members. "Learning objectives are development goals that build capability to achieve higher levels of performance. They must be developed with an eye to shared success and driven primarily by the individual with support from others. Although it can be a tough road, teams must learn to navigate the conflict that can exist between individual goals and collaboration goals."[23]

## Coherent Teams Draw Upon Expertise and Focus on Progress and Small Wins

In addition to the value of productively addressing conflict within a true collaboration team, *coherence is aided by creating a climate of progress.* In research conducted by Harvard Business School professors Teresa M. Amabile and Steven J. Kramer, progress was identified as a crucial factor in maintaining cohesiveness and engagement in a team's shared initiatives.[24] Linking progress to the team's larger purpose as well as the meaning of its work on a day-to-day basis proved pivotal to maintaining the coherence of the group's efforts over time. Importantly, Amabile and Kramer indicate that progress can be perceived as small wins; it does not always have to come as sweeping victories:[25]

> Of all the things that can boost emotions, motivation, and perceptions . . . the single most important is making progress in meaningful work. And the more frequently people experience that sense of progress, the more likely they are to be creatively productive in the long run. Whether they are trying to solve a major scientific mystery or simply produce a high-quality product or service, everyday progress—even a small win—can make all the difference in how they feel and perform.

Coherent groups find a way to draw the small wins out of perceived setbacks. They create a climate of progress even when the team's bigger goals feel out of reach or are not being achieved as originally planned.

> I like to begin at the large end of things; life is too short to begin at the small end.
>
> **—Thomas Edison**

Amabile and Kramer also found that the person to whom a team turns when desiring to communicate progress is generally the individual who holds the greatest expertise, generates the greatest trust, or operates as the inspirational leader for the team. Although in Edison's era, the mantle of communicating team progress often fell to Edison himself, he also engaged other inspirational leaders he'd nurtured within the lab to take on this role. Francis Upton, a mathematician and acoustics expert, was one such leader. This excerpt, taken from an April 1879 letter from Upton to his father, frames a climate of progress for the lightbulb within the broader context of the lab's challenges to perfect this new technology:[26]

> There is still hope that this summer will see a public exhibition of the electric light. There are thousands of difficulties to be overcome yet before it can be given to the public and Mr. Edison will overcome them if any does. I have not in the least lost my faith in him for I see how wonderful the powers he has are, for invention. He holds himself ready to make anything that he may be asked to make if it is not against any law of nature.

The optimistic tone in Upton's letter reveals a second important factor that Amabile and Kramer discovered is crucial for setting a climate of progress: "framing recent progress in positive terms."[27] Amabile and Kramer note that all communications about progress must be threaded with a sense of optimism; otherwise, there is no perception of forward movement. Optimism links the team's collaborative efforts to its broader shared goals. Without a kernel of optimism, the team can be perceived to be drifting backward, in turn leading to a disengagement from its goals.

> My message to you is to be courageous. . . . Have faith. Go forward.
>
> —*Thomas Edison*

In what ways is progress acknowledged on your team? How can you begin intentionally cultivating a climate of progress? What small wins has your team experienced? How is optimism reflected in your communications about the team's forward movement? Consider how you can begin looking at your efforts "from the large end of things," as Edison did.

## The Impact of External Partners on True Collaboration

Reflecting the convergence of innovation, strategy, and value creation that Dr. C. K. Prahalad noted would be part of the global reset, collaboration teams are increasingly drawing on diverse internal resources within an organization itself, as well as accessing collaborative resources from external partners. As your team progresses further into Phase 3, you may determine that you need to either restructure your team or add new expertise to help bring the initial solutions you've identified through experimentation and prototyping in Phase 2 to a more advanced stage. Edison, for example, found that he needed to engage external partners to expand his expertise in specific production capabilities, as well as develop new materials for his teams' collaborative efforts in electric lighting, electrical power, and motion pictures. These external partners did not all come onto the scene immediately; they were accessed after Edison's teams had already begun their work.

Although your true collaboration efforts up to this stage may have been operating primarily with internal resources, it is likely that some form of external partnering will be required for you to advance to the next level of development for your project. Given the growing preference for virtual teaming and the ready availability of globally networked technology platforms to aid in virtual communication, it may be that your organization even pushes you toward a hybrid team structure that blends internal and external resources.

Although hybrid teams can be effective, they place increased emphasis on the presence of diverse expertise and collegiality, as noted in Phase 1, and on developing shared goals, valuing experimentation, and engaging in casual team discussion, as highlighted in Phase 2. Hybrid teams also require skills for navigating debate and conflict, which you read about earlier in Phase 3. If external partners are added, or if your team structure is otherwise modified, sustaining team coherence will require an honest examination of the team's ability to seamlessly integrate input from new resources; it could even require a reskilling of team members.

Bohm's definition of coherence from the perspective of a single operating team offers us valuable insight here. Bohm describes a single team as a kind of microculture. This microculture generates its own environment and, in effect, its own operating system. For Bohm, coherent teams are "the germ of the microcosm of the larger culture."[28]

Rather than reflecting a tiny drop in the ocean, Bohm believes a single team, over time, can actually reframe the entire workings of a larger body. Although this type of transformation requires multiple mechanisms, some of which will be explored in Phase 4, by creating new groups and by people communicating the topics they perceive to be of greatest value, Bohm emphasizes individual teams hold the power to ultimately impact the way collaborative activities take place in larger organizations. Bohm's comments about the nature of an individual collaboration team and the impact of its microculture holds particular relevance for how we think about advancing the collaboration efforts of a single mixed group of internal and external partners in Phase 3.

Jim Ziganto of Carlex Glass, America comments that increasingly, collaboration teams represent a mix of "consultants, contractors, and a direct workforce. When collaboration resources are brought onto a client's team from a supplier, they are likely to go through a formal onboarding process that includes training on technical subjects, an understanding of the company's brands, and a thorough grounding in its vision-mission-values."[29] Ziganto indicates that any time external resources are brought onto an existing true collaboration team, or when the team's structure is otherwise modified, the new members must go back through the process of establishing shared goals and creating a platform for team dialogue with the existing members—just as if they had been present in Phases 1 and 2.

Likewise, Rishad Tobaccowala of VivaKi sees the lines blurring between what kinds of resources are considered external and what are considered internal. He comments, "What's starting to happen is companies are beginning with the best of breed within their organizations, then they add a cadre of people which become semi-permanent outsourced resources. This can include technological resources, art directors, web designers, or product developers with specific expertise. Companies are linking traditional ways of collaborating with a greater reliance on technology. This shift creates entirely new economies of scale around collaboration."[30]

If your collaboration becomes a hybrid combining internal and external resources in the way Ziganto and Tobaccowala describe, here are three approaches to bear in mind as you seek to find an operating pattern that delivers your desired outcomes. Recognizing that mixing internal and external resources will follow no single set pattern, each of these three approaches reflects a different kind of team microculture. Consider how the nature of the team microculture present in each approach bears potential ripple effects on the larger organization. After examining these three options, we'll look at how Edison navigated his collaborations with external partners.

## Create Internal Collaboration Teams with Extensive External Partnering

Collaboration activity at Whirlpool offers us a window into how the workings of internal teams seeking to become more engaged with external partners can have a ripple effect on the broader culture of an organization. Ranked number six on *Fast Company*'s 2011 list of the World's Most Innovative Companies in Consumer Products and number one on *Fortune*'s 2011 list of the World's Most Admired Companies in the Home Equipment, Furnishings industry sector, Whirlpool is currently incorporating several different types of collaboration structures as it seeks to more rapidly drive innovation and value creation across its massive global operations.[31]

Moises Norena, global director of innovation at Whirlpool Corporation, guides the development of small collaboration teams for diverse internal product development efforts as well as initiatives for gathering insights from customers. "These collaborations do not fully constitute open innovation, but have incorporated new kinds of internal and external exchanges within our overall innovation process. They represent a kind of discovery learning that helps us see the customer from a different perspective, and progressively expand how we think about collaboration."[32] Here are three different thrusts that bring internal Whirlpool teams into deeper collaboration with external resources:

1. Collaborating with consumers to refine product design options that better meet changing lifestyles

2. Collaborating with suppliers to reframe Whirlpool's existing assumptions about customer usage patterns

3. Collaborating with local companies in international geographies to expand an understanding of evolving lifestyles and habits

Norena comments, "These structures help us find solutions that we wouldn't be able to see on our own. They give us access to data on market size, trends, quality, and technical solutions that we wouldn't typically get otherwise."[33]

Although Whirlpool's collaboration formats are still driven by small internal teams, they represent a shift from the more transaction-based relationships of the past, creating engaged dialogue with external partners. With this shift, Whirlpool Corporation has found that reskilling its employees has been necessary. Collaboration has become a hybrid process that connects internal leaders and technical champions in ways that have never existed before. Norena reveals, "We were concerned that we wouldn't have enough internal resources to meet the demands of these kinds of collaborations. We could bring in consultants to do it, but that would be too expensive."

To tackle the reskilling challenges that surfaced as internal teams deepened engagement levels with external partners, Norena devised a network structure known within Whirlpool as the i-NETWORK, a virtual network that connects internal groups of innovators. Called i-NET for short, the structure offers participants two different paths. The first path, the leader work stream, helps train decision makers and inspirational leaders on how to operate in a flatter, more collaborative team structure rather than a more hierarchical one, just as Edison advocated. The second path, the practitioner work stream, offers guidance on how to facilitate the more technical aspects of a project, how to use virtual tools to gather and synthesize data, and how to operate as a technical expert within the context of a collaboration team rather than a functional department. Although Norena recognizes that Whirlpool's learning about collaboration is still evolving, i-NET continues to gain momentum within the organization.

Consider using Whirlpool's deepened engagement with external partners as one template for your own team's efforts.

As Norena is doing via the i-NET, consider how your team members may need to be reskilled in areas requiring more advanced use of virtual technologies, data gathering, and data synthesis to sustain coherence. If you choose this path, the microculture of your team could push the broader culture of your organization to connect innovators and collaborators together, like Whirlpool is doing. Recognize that the microculture of your team can ripple out in ways that affect the broader culture.

### Value Exchange Crucial to True Collaboration

In the Innovation Age, determining how internal and external partners give and receive value is increasingly crucial. Rather than being viewed as purely transactional, parties engaging in true collaboration now need to feel that shared learning and shared purpose are fundamentally part of the collaboration effort itself. Here are some ways a collaborative project can either offer benefit to outside providers or seek value from resources external to your team.

#### Key Areas of Value Exchange in True Collaboration

- Opportunities to experiment with a new technology
- Opportunities to build new data streams
- Development of intellectual property
- Access to a new target audience

*(continued)*

*(continued)*

- Access to a pool of workers with a unique specialty or experience base
- Opening a new geographic region
- Connection to new networks of subject matter experts
- Access to global marketing, technology, or other operational resources
- Deeper understanding of customer behavior
- Insights into a new product or service platform

How does your true collaboration team view its relationship with outside partners? Do you engage external partners in an ongoing stream of communications around your project, or do you connect in more discrete transactions? Are there new ways value could be exchanged that would aid your true collaboration project? What shared purpose or discovery learning could these new exchanges yield?

## Open Innovation Structures

A second template your team can consider if it elects to adopt the use of external resources is a model called Connect+Develop, pioneered by global consumer products company Procter & Gamble (P&G). CEO A. G. Lafley in 2003 elected to completely alter the structure of the organization, which was seeing increasing competition in every one of its 12 core categories. Recognizing that the knowledge assets of P&G represented only a small percentage of the total knowledge assets available globally in each of these categories, Lafley elected to shift P&G's culture from one that was driven by closed, internal teams to one that operated on creating flows of information from the inside out, as well as the outside in.

Lafley boldly shifted P&G's entire culture from a 100 percent internal product development approach to one that now derives more than 30 percent of its revenue from product development efforts drawn from the company's external partners. Today, nearly a decade after the launch of Connect+Develop, P&G CEO Bob McDonald notes, "Over 80% of our innovations have some kind of external partner. We even have joint development laboratories with our suppliers."[34]

The open innovation structure that propels Connect+ Develop allows, with very few restrictions, individual small teams to tap specific expertise that lies outside the walls of P&G. Connect+Develop has driven the creation of an entire innovation ecosystem within the company that is highly reliant on collaborative structures. Braden Kelley, author of *Stoking Your Innovation Bonfire*, describes in a recent white paper how P&G also has been required to reskill its internal teams to navigate this highly collaborative approach. Rather than merely handing off their initiatives to external parties like an outsourced project typically would be, internal P&G teams actively manage their Connect+Develop efforts.

P&G thinks of its internal resources as the castle keep, and develops local resources that it can turn to as needed. It has a tiered system of partners based on cost, location, and capabilities. The company also maintains its own collection of 85 networks . . . focused on creating ecosystems locally in different geographies around the world—which it can then mine and look for solutions.[35]

Kelley also comments that collaboration teams within P&G are charged with "the integration of external projects" as well as developing "soft skills [such as data management, communication, and team motivation] to foster a collaborative approach." The company clusters these skills under an employee success driver known as agility.

Although your team may consider Connect+Develop an extreme example of how true collaboration can operate, this structure reminds us that small collaborative teams are increasingly accessing sprawling networks that link to the outside world. The microculture of a Connect+Develop team requires that its members be agile so that they can access networks and leverage them to fullest advantage. Although further thoughts on this will be offered in Phase 4, consider what types of reskilling you might require if your collaboration project needed to handle more incoming data from outside parties or become more agile, as P&G's teams have.

## The Silver Bullet Resource

A third type of structural approach you can consider if you need to add external resources to your team is a solution used by Dr. Curt Carlson, CEO of the Stanford Research Institute (SRI). Desiring to keep his operations focused solely on scientific research and the commercial application of breakthrough discoveries, SRI has not attempted to internally cultivate the hybrid collaboration skills and organizational competencies required to actually launch new products. Instead, Carlson has created the concept of an "entrepreneur in residence." For collaboration projects that have progressed to Phase 3 and appear to hold promising commercial potential, Carlson conducts a directed search to find an individual who can join an existing internal collaboration team and colocate within his firm to prepare the initiative for a funded launch. Because internal teams share in the financial reward of their projects at SRI, bringing in an external person to take an initiative into the launch phase does not cause ripples in the organization. A kind of silver bullet approach, SRI's teams can focus on keeping their efforts from Phases 1 through 3 strictly internal and then bring onboard a single external resource as they head into Phase 4.

In Edison's time, his laboratory and manufacturing operations developed strong external relationships with providers who recognized Edison's high quality standards and the breakthrough nature of his innovation and collaboration efforts. Central to Edison's desire to work with external parties was a willingness to engage in a discovery learning process while also yielding a tangible desired outcome. Edison sought a growth mindset in his suppliers just as he did in his employees, favoring partners who could work closely with him in the development of new materials or in the creation of new manufacturing techniques that accelerated his progress.

In Edison's era, concepts like colocation and codevelopment as we know them today were virtually nonexistent. Indeed, Edison, as the father of research and development, felt the pull of others who wanted to work with him more so than the reverse. However, Edison created a depth of dialogue with his external partners atypical for his era, and he was highly selective in his choices. Table 5.5 offers a sampling of the firms Edison engaged to supplement his true collaboration efforts. You may recognize them, as each one still exists in some form today.

Consider where your current collaboration efforts engage the use of external resources. How do the roles of these external bodies connect with your team's shared goals? With your team's higher purpose? Is value being created that will

**Table 5.5 Edison Carefully Chose External Partners for True Collaboration Projects**

| Company | Collaboration Contribution |
|---|---|
| J. P. Morgan | Large-scale financing |
| Spencer Trask | Angel financing |
| Ansonia Copper & Brass | High purity levels in copper, copper wire, and brass |
| The Babcock & Wilcox Company | Construction resources for new factories |
| Eimer & Amend | Manufacturing supplies and resources |
| Corning Glass | Glass for use in lightbulbs |
| Eastman Kodak Company | Imprinting images on celluloid, rolled film |

positively impact the longer-term efforts of your group? Think about how learning is being communicated among external resources and your team. Step through all the same components you've read thus far in Phase 3: the role of inspirational leadership, management of conflict and debate, minimization of defensive routines, and emphasis on progress and small wins. Be sure you are building in these same components with any external groups or providers who become central to your team's true collaboration effort. Reference the illustration in Figure 5.3 as a visual reminder of the core components you need to engage in Phase 3.

# TRUE COLLABORATION TOOLKIT: HANDS-ON EXERCISES—PHASE 3

Use these exercises to strengthen your skills within Phase 3, building on what you learned in Phase 2 and preparing you to advance to Phase 4.

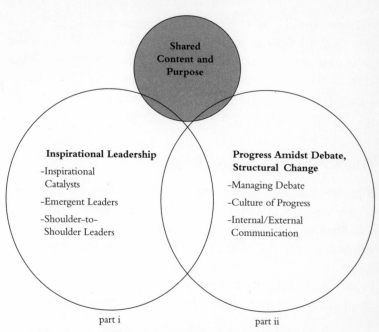

**Figure 5.3 Phase 3: Coherence—from Thomas Edison's Four Phases of True Collaboration**

*Note*: Unite your team around the content you hold in common, yielding progress and inspiration around your shared purpose.

## Create an Inspirational Message

Imagine that you are placed on a small diverse team that has been charged with a high-profile project addressing a topic you know well—an area within your expertise. The project is modeled around true collaboration principles. The catch? The group has been hobbled by the departure of an individual perceived to be the inspirational leader of the team. Although no one has stated it explicitly, the group views you as the replacement for this individual and expects you to fill those shoes.

How would you respond? What could you do to inspire hope and confidence within the team? How could you unite your new team members around a common purpose? What kind of language would you use? How could you begin laying the foundation for other inspirational leaders to emerge on the team so that it's not all up to you?

## Practice Your Defensive Routines

Imagine that you're receiving a presentation from a colleague who has put a great deal of time and effort into taking you through the results his or her collaboration team has generated over the past three months. You are responsible for funding 75 percent of the project. The results you've heard from the presentation are positive in large part, but you believe one area of the team's efforts are significantly off track.

What kinds of questions could you ask to prevent a knee-jerk negative reaction from the team? What questions could you offer to get a conversation going about ways to redirect the team's efforts in areas where you believe no further value can be gained? What coaching techniques could you use? What kind of defensive reaction from the group might you anticipate, and how could you practice ahead of time to address these?

## Who Inspires You?

World history and business history are filled with leaders who have inspired others to achieve their highest and best results. From the following list, select three names of those leaders who most inspire you. What are the inspirational leadership qualities you see in each person? Why do these three leaders especially resonate with you? Are there elements within their unique inspirational style that you could develop within yourself? What are they?

| | |
|---|---|
| Winston Churchill | Queen Elizabeth I |
| Benjamin Franklin | Abraham Lincoln |
| Thomas Jefferson | Steve Jobs |
| Eleanor Roosevelt | Martin Luther King, Jr. |
| Mahatma Gandhi | Richard Branson |
| Julius Caesar | Margaret Thatcher |

# CHAPTER 6

## Phase 4

*Complexity—Forming Smart Layers and Developing Collective Intelligence*

**E**very 60 seconds, 30 hours of video are uploaded to YouTube. Within the space of 1 minute, Facebook logs an average of 6 million unique page views. In just 18 months, the Apple iPhone skyrocketed to a record 50 million users, making it one of the most popular digital tools on the planet. In the words of Harun Asad, former chief strategy and innovation officer at Lodestar, navigating the zettabytes of data available to a single individual—let alone a collaboration team—"feels like being hit by an avalanche."[1]

*Good to Great* author Jim Collins, who has long advocated that leaders succeed by "getting the right people in the right seats on the bus," now believes that organizations must also consider ways to get millions of people on the bus.[2] How can we harness true collaboration with millions of people? What does the dizzying scale of the collaboration opportunities afforded by smart devices and virtual technologies mean for your team?

# PHASE 4

In Phases 1 and 2, focus has been placed on helping you optimize the structure of your small team and its creative problem-solving capabilities. Phase 3 advanced the importance of skills such as driving inspiration, navigating conflict, and communicating progress around your team's efforts with internal and external partners.

But in Phase 4, it's now crucial to understand how your team can bring speed and scale to bear in its work. Given that the Innovation Age will span only roughly 20 more years and that many organizations will turn to "worldsourcing" to tap the millions of young people projected to flood into the global workforce within the next 10 years, speed and scale will prove increasingly crucial to the competitiveness of your collaboration efforts—and your organization.[3] This means that tackling the complex systems governing social networks and magnetizing the vast potential of major demographic groups such as Gen Y will be mandatory. Phase 4 is designed to offer you *tools for attacking diverse types of complexity your team will face as it aims to bring speed and scale to the collaboration process.*

> For the Pearl Street station was the greatest adventure of my life. It was akin to venturing on an uncharted sea.
>
> —*Thomas Edison*

Although we cannot draw a straight line between the complexities of Edison's era and the complexity of our own, even with breakthrough technologies like the Internet, tablet computers, smartphones, Internet browsers, GPS, cloud computing, space travel, and search engines, the Innovation Age has not surpassed the number of disruptive innovations generated in what is sometimes termed the Golden Age of American invention, roughly spanning four decades from 1880 to 1920. Edison expert and noted resource on the history of technology, Dr. Paul Israel, states, "Although the

## Table 6.1 Disruptive Technologies Emerging from the Golden Age of American Invention

| | |
|---|---|
| Telephone | Radio |
| Incandescent electric light | Airplane |
| Electrical power distribution | Plastic |
| Motion picture entertainment | Polymer chemistry |
| Alkaline storage battery | Steel |
| Recorded sound | Automobile |
| Assembly line | Refrigeration |

speed of our communications today has dramatically increased and it feels like things are happening fast, digital technologies have built upon advances that began 30 years ago. The speed of infrastructure shifts from the post–Civil War period to World War I—which roughly corresponds to Thomas Edison's lifetime—saw even more significant shifts in an even greater number of industries."[4] Table 6.1 shows a few examples of disruptive technologies emerging from this Golden Age of Invention.

The magnitude of infrastructure shifts experienced in the decades leading up to and immediately following the turn of the twentieth century offers us perspective on the complexity Edison was facing in his own businesses—ironically, some of it driven by his own innovation activities.

Examining the sophistication and pace of the collaboration efforts Edison undertook over his decades-long career allows us to draw upon the daring scope of his success even now. Here are three themes that consistently emerged as Edison grappled with complexity:

- Creating streamlined yet robust inputs that reduce the total number of moving parts in a system while still achieving robust output

- Driving interactions of talent that create a multiplier effect, yielding unexpected new skill combinations that could not have been perceived at the start
- Using networks of resources to tackle a new or emerging problem with intensity, generating a creative and adaptive response

Phase 4 fashions these themes into what I call smart layers. Nimble structures that link to the groundwork you've already laid in the first three phases of true collaboration, smart layers drive specific digital and face-to-face (FTF) capabilities your team will need as it shapes new solutions going forward. Smart layers ensure that the role of discovery learning is not lost in the raw "doing"—namely the implementation—of your initiative. Smart layers will also serve as a reskilling mechanism that can make collaboration an attractive magnet for training Gen Y workers and other talent within your team.

A second facet of Phase 4 embraces the complexity of documenting your efforts in a way that leaves a footprint for others to follow. We can actually look back to Edison's own collaboration efforts today because he consistently documented his work, *contributing to the collective intelligence of all the teams that would follow.* He viewed collaboration as a knowledge asset within its own right, a way of operating that could be repeated again and again to generate value from any discovery learning initiative. Your team's footprint can capture the heart of your findings in a way that offers new knowledge for the next wave of teams that follow in your wake.

The two primary components of true collaboration in Phase 4 are:

- *Part i, Organize for complexity through the development of smart layers:* Build smart layers into your team rather than hierarchies. Learn how to recognize the circumstances that drive complexity. Capitalize on social networks and other networked resources to anticipate shifting conditions rather than merely responding to them. Recognize collaboration as a superskill that connects to a crucial array of secondary skills you can leverage—and master—as part of a team reskilling process.

- *Part ii, Footprint your team's collective intelligence:* Consider your project a knowledge asset, a kind of collective intelligence that contributes to a broader sphere of understanding that lies beyond your team. Document your team's journey in a "footprint" that creates a unique legacy for your efforts, paving a path of learning and purpose for teams that will follow yours.

Let's begin by briefly considering how complex systems work. Then we'll examine three ways your true collaboration team can effectively grapple with complexity.

# PART I, PHASE 4: COMPLEX SYSTEMS AND SMART LAYERS

Over the past 20 years, scientists have probed the roots of complexity, aiming to unearth clues on how nature's extraordinarily diverse and complex networks of plants and animals have operated sustainably for centuries. Studying the exquisite efficiency and flow within natural complex systems reveals an unseen yet intricate web of connections. Complex systems operate in nature before our very eyes, in places ranging from ant colonies to coral reefs and bee hives to the human cell. In mapping the exquisite inner workings of these natural complex systems, we have gained new insights for how to organize people and information more effectively.

John Holland, a professor at the University of Michigan and author of *Hidden Order: How Adaptation Builds Complexity*, actually develops mathematical models to simulate how complex systems operate. Insights from Holland's work reveal how complex systems adapt to shifts from new external stimuli, particularly new threats or new phenomena that the system has not ever experienced before.

Focusing on what are termed complex adaptive systems, or CAS for short, the work of Holland and others help us understand the underlying adaptive mechanisms we can inject into manmade complex systems to make them function and respond more effectively—and more rapidly. For example, we can see in manmade CAS such as the stock market, the international banking system, hedge funds, air traffic control systems, or the World Wide Web a tendency to jam up when the system encounters inputs it doesn't recognize. These snags often come in the form of sneak attacks, such as rogue trades, counterfeiting, or hacking—low-frequency but high-impact occurrences. As we humans collectively progress into greater reliance on digital technologies as a means of interacting with our environment, our ability to navigate the growing number of complex systems around us will become a major factor in our success.

Three core characteristics govern every complex system, whether natural or manmade:[5]

1. *Multiplicity:* the number of potentially interacting elements in a system

2. *Interdependence:* the level of connection among the elements in the system

3. *Diversity:* the degree of uniqueness or heterogeneity in the elements in the system

Although you may not ever have thought of it this way, your true collaboration team actually operates as a complex system. The diverse forms of expertise woven into your team back in Phase 1 have actually helped set the stage for this. Even the team discussions and exchanges your team holds, or its connections to outside parties, place it within a larger network of interactions, some of which can be anticipated or planned and others that cannot be. By intentionally focusing your attention on the number of actors in your team's initiatives, how these actors interconnect, and the level of diversity among the actors, your team can begin looking at its own activity through the lens of a complex system rather than a discrete task-based one. As complexity expert Dr. Jean Egmon of Northwestern University notes, "Collaboration acknowledges the existence of complexity rather than running from it. Collaboration actually *requires* complexity."[6] Armed with this perspective, you can begin leveraging new ways to handle complexity more effectively rather than allowing it to catch you by surprise, like the "avalanche" Harun Asad described earlier.

Edison recognized that complexity was a factor ever present in his teams as well as his broader business operations. But rather than addressing complexity by building static hierarchies or roles that served only one function, he created smart layers instead. These smart layers were built on principles that allowed for greater connections between the actors in his workforce, melding new forms of learning with the diverse operational needs required to complete his wide-reaching efforts. Edison's smart layers could flex and shift as resource needs changed or when unexpected external influences arose. They did not conform to the boxes on an organizational chart, limiting him to discrete areas of action or knowledge.

The job of a great collaboration team is to embrace the complexities without trivializing them.

—*Larry Keeley, CEO of the Doblin Group*

Here are three types of smart layers Edison used to address complexity, each of which has been contemporized to serve an expanded purpose in our digital era.

## Create the Fewest Moving Parts Possible in Your Team's Efforts

It's likely that a large percentage of the incoming information your team receives stems from the plethora of formal procedures required to simply conduct your project work. Recognizing that teams in the Innovation Age are being required to manage increasing flows of information at an ever-accelerating rate, the Boston Consulting Group (BCG) developed an "index of complicatedness"[7] based on a study of more than 100 US and European companies. The index showed that "over the past 15 years, the amount of procedures, vertical layers, interface structures, coordination bodies, and decision approvals needed" for teams to fulfill their objectives has increased anywhere from 50 percent to 350 percent. This means that the tangle of activity teams must address today has increased 35-fold since 1955.

All these complicated layers and procedures come with a major downside. BCG estimates that within the 20 percent of organizations in the study that were the most complicated, "managers spend 40 percent of their time writing reports and 30 to 60 percent in coordination meetings." That doesn't leave much time for understanding how to collaborate or how to build effective collaboration teams.

The study also revealed that employees in the most deeply layered firms exert a lot of effort chasing requirements that don't bring value to their collaboration projects. Employees who experience this kind of runaround "are three times as likely to be disengaged" as employees required to navigate fewer layers. Offering an extreme example of the impact of this type of disengagement, KPMG currently experiences nearly 20 percent turnover in its global workforce every year, with "hierarchies" being one of the top three reasons people leave the organization.[8]

Runarounds and excessive management layers are not unique to the business community. Plaguing governments and nonprofit groups as well, the topic of excessive complexity in national governments surfaced as a major hot button at the 2012 World Economic Forum (WEF). Bain & Company consultant Chris Zook, a strategy specialist attending WEF, wrote in a blog post for the *Harvard Business Review* that the few governmental departments and nonprofit groups experiencing revenue growth were seeing advantages "due to an ability to keep things simpler and more transparent."[9] By streamlining processes that enabled constituents to obtain a desired outcome by undertaking fewer steps and experiencing fewer layers, the groups that were growing delivered value with less effort and at less overall cost.

Although Edison did not advocate the dumbing down of genuinely complex problems, he did believe in creating systems with the fewest moving parts possible. Just as he favored nimble teams as a starting point for his collaborations in Phase 1, he valued fewer coordination steps and fewer rules in order to pare back the stream of unnecessary inputs that could hinder rapid development of a solution. In response to a reporter touring the West Orange laboratory who remarked at the prolific output of the lab with seemingly few formal procedures, Edison remarked, "Hell, there are no rules here—we're trying to accomplish something."

Comments from Stephen B. Mambert, a senior finance executive who worked in several of Edison's operations, also reveal the streamlined, nonhierarchical nature of Edison's organizations. Edison designed flat structures that allowed his enterprises and his teams to mobilize rapidly:[10]

> The Edison Organization is headed by a man who, without doubt, is the most democratic man the world has ever known, which leads to the fact that we are privileged to work in an organization where every function is free to communicate with, request service of, and make suggestions of a supervisory nature to, every other function in the organization.

For Edison, the speed yielded by having less internal complexity and fewer layers was not only about getting more done in less time but about relieving customers from experiencing unnecessary complexity. Edison desired to have a sense of simplicity pervade not only his internal operations but his customers' experiences as well. Although his teams spent months perfecting the inner workings of the incandescent electric light, Edison sought to ensure that the lightbulb itself would not be complicated for customers to use. Once purchased, all a lightbulb required was to be screwed into a wall fixture and activated with the push of a button. (The light switches we recognize today were preceded by two on/off buttons placed vertically on a small panel.) Similarly, the Edison Storage Battery represented a complex, multiyear breakthrough in the chemistry of metals, but it required no special handling or equipment for customers to install.

> Can we take what used to take 10 clicks for someone to get the information they need and reduce it to three?
>
> —*Mark Zuckerberg, CEO of Facebook*

If your team is operating within an organization with excessive hierarchies, *build a smart layer that adopts a posture of streamlining, transparency, and simplicity.* Work with your internal team leader or another champion who holds influence to clear away internal roadblocks that add unnecessary time and complexity to your efforts or require you to penetrate lots of management layers. Adopt streamlining as a kind of mantra for the microculture of your team. Reflect your desire to minimize the number of moving parts in your own output as well—fewer memos, no unnecessary meetings, focused conversations, pithy instructions. Create operational simplicity everywhere possible.

In addition, consider making a visual map that identifies where bottlenecks lie in your current endeavors. Estimate the number of steps it's going to take for you to reach a key objective with these bottlenecks in mind. Identify how many steps lie ahead. Give ratings to the steps that yield the most value, ranging from 1 to 5, with 5 signifying high delivered value. Consider how you can create the shortest distance between the highest-value steps, aiming to eliminate those that rate lower. See if fewer streamlined yet robust steps can be taken to accomplish the outcome you desire.

A smart layer focused on the creation of the fewest internal moving parts was recently adopted by Tom Barwin, former village manager of Oak Park, Illinois, a community in greater Chicago. While spearheading a complex, multiyear initiative involving an energy aggregation program for the 53,000 residents of Oak Park—the first of its kind in the state— Barwin rallied his small team around a theme of simplicity and transparency. With a staff of fewer than 10 employees and operating within the bureaucratic hierarchy that accompanies most local government, Barwin centered each facet of his initiative on key, focused thrusts. "We started by engaging large external partners in the core idea of energy aggregation.

These partners helped us understand how we could bundle different types of renewable energy together in ways that reduced our costs."[11] From there, Barwin conducted open forums with residents to determine which renewable energy themes resonated most strongly with constituents and related those themes to cost factors. "In everything we did, we focused on just a few key leverage points that created momentum. We looked at these as streamlined layers building one upon the other." Ultimately, Barwin and his collaboration team harnessed the resources of nearly 500 volunteers who aided in communicating details of the energy aggregation plan, which was voted upon and accepted by the community in early 2012. Barwin's intentional desire to create a streamlined process with as few moving parts as possible at the very outset offers an example of how to build a smart layer within a complex system while still yielding robust output.

## Leverage Collaboration as a Distinctive Superskill within Your Team's Culture

For the last several decades, leaders have sought a singularly elusive Holy Grail: to create a culture of innovation in their organizations. With the rise of the Internet and the viral adoption of digital technology, it seemed at last that this Holy Grail was within reach.

There is little question that innovation has come to the forefront of business discussion today. But have we made progress in making a culture of innovation a workplace reality? A May 2012 *Wall Street Journal* article revealed that in 2011, the word *innovation* was used more than 33,525 times in annual reports.[12] More than 250 books were published within the first five months of 2012 featuring the word *innovator* in the title, and a whopping 43 percent of the firms surveyed as part of the *Wall Street Journal* segment indicated their company had a chief innovation officer or its equivalent. But despite this feverish intent to find the innovation Holy Grail—and plenty of solid advice on how to obtain it—few organizations actually can sustain the leadership and internal structures required to complete the entire innovation journey.

Is it possible we're looking in the wrong place? If anyone could claim success in generating a culture of innovation, it is Thomas Edison. And yet, Edison's four phases reveal that true collaboration provided the crucial backbone supporting his extraordinary innovation prowess. Perhaps it is a *culture of collaboration* that we should be seeking as the Holy Grail.

One difficulty leaders have had supporting collaboration as a core thrust in their organizations lies in the network of soft skills that effective collaboration requires. These networked skills are sometimes challenging to define and even more challenging to measure. However, if in the post-reset landscape we are all heading toward collaboration as a common denominator for the merging of innovation, strategy, and value creation, we should be paying more attention to this network of soft skills. Edison clearly saw value in reskilling his workforce around true collaboration as a central cultural practice, emphasizing inspiration, leadership, communication, questioning, and a host of other capacities that did not specifically relate to functional expertise.

A recent study conducted by John Zenger, Joseph Folkman, and Scott Edinger may offer clues on how to make collaboration's network of soft skills a more attractive and tangible investment for leaders today. After examining data from more than 30,000 executives tracking factors that correlated to workplace success *as well as revenue enhancement*, the researchers identified interlocking relationships between 16 core skill sets. Executives possessing just 1 of these 16 skills as their primary skill—defined as something they excelled at doing—also possessed a network of secondary capabilities that supported this primary skill. The correlation between a single primary skill and multiple secondary skills was extremely high. Furthermore, each time a new primary skill was added by an executive, an additional cluster of secondary skills became linked to it. The researchers describe this unique clustering phenomenon as the interaction effect.[13]

For example, individuals with a primary strength in building stronger relationships revealed an interaction effect with secondary strengths in both self-development and an ability to communicate powerfully and broadly. For those executives whose primary strength lay in solving problems and analyzing issues, the interaction effect for them included secondary strengths in technical expertise and development of strategic perspective.[14] Edison's own technical expertise in chemistry, referenced in Figure 6.1, gave him a unique strategic perspective on solving problems related to electricity and mechanical systems. The full array of all 16 core skills identified in the study is shown in Table 6.2.

But one primary skill—collaborates and fosters teamwork (item 13)—stood out as a unique superskill within the master list. *This primary skill alone embraced seven other secondary skills*, placing it among the top two most influential core skills in the entire research study. Collaborates and fosters teamwork as a primary skill clustered with these seven crucial secondary skills:

1. Develops others
2. Inspires and motivates others
3. Displays honesty and integrity
4. Communicates powerfully and broadly
5. Establishes stretch goals

**6.** Develops strategic perspective

**7.** Builds strong relationships

Do these seven secondary skills sound familiar? Hopefully they do, as they all operate in some facet of Edison's true collaboration process within Phases 1, 2, and 3, including inspiring others, communicating through team discussion, motivating others to go beyond what they believe is possible for themselves, speaking authentically even amidst conflict, strategically developing new context, and building strong internal and external relationships with others.

The power of these findings revealing collaboration as a superskill lies not only in that Zenger, Folkman, and

**Table 6.2 The Interaction Effect: Complementary Skill Sets That Drive Success**

| Core Skill Sets | Area of Emphasis |
| --- | --- |
| 1. Displays honesty and integrity | Character |
| 2. Exhibits technical expertise | Operational capability |
| 3. Solves problems and analyzes issues | Operational capability |
| 4. Innovates | Personal capability |
| 5. Practices self-development | Personal capability |
| 6. Takes initiative | Results orientation |
| 7. Focuses on results | Results orientation |
| 8. Establishes stretch goals | Results orientation |
| 9. Communicates powerfully and broadly | Interpersonal |
| 10. Inspires and motivates others | Interpersonal |
| 11. Builds strong relationships | Interpersonal |
| 12. Develops others | Interpersonal |
| 13. Collaborates and fosters teamwork | Interpersonal |
| 14. Develops strategic perspective | Leadership |
| 15. Champions change | Leadership |
| 16. Connects groups to the outside world | Leadership |

**Figure 6.1 Edison Held Deep Technical Expertise in Chemistry**

*Source:* National Park Service, Edison National Historic Site.

Edinger's research bears out what Edison intuitively knew, but in the realization that these seven skills together position collaboration as a capacity essential for every discovery learning team and every organization. As a superskill, collaboration offers revenue-driving benefits and holds the power to operate as an amplifying force both within teams and across them.

In Phase 3, you read several ways to think about the microculture of your team and how you could structure it in relationship to outside groups or partners. Now, think about how collaboration can be viewed as a superskill networked across this same team. Being able to discretely name all seven components within this superskill allows you to begin threading each of them through the microculture of your team in a way that complements all your learning from the prior three phases. Consider how you can position the seven capacities within the collaboration superskill as a smart layer that rests squarely within the microculture of your small group. Which of the seven superskill capabilities do you possess? Which others are present on your team? How can you expand the presence of these seven interlocking skills among those within your external network or partner base? Can you use these seven capabilities to help gauge the fit and chemistry you seek in new resources for your efforts? Build discovery learning objectives as well as your performance objectives around your smart layer. You can even consider forming communication or strategic objectives that emphasize the collaboration superskill.

By positioning the collaboration superskill as a smart layer in Phase 4, you will begin generating new forms of power and connective influence. According to Yves Morieux, an organizational design specialist with BCG's Paris operations, in a technology-driven era like ours, "New sources of power can be created around expertise-building and knowledge transmission."[15] Morieux finds teams that serve to connect expertise *and* bear new knowledge so other groups can generate transformational power that shifts cultural norms. Even when working within a larger hierarchical structure, teams with connective influence begin morphing the structures around them and accelerate the process of transforming how activities occur in their sphere.

Just as David Bohm, the theoretical physicist who emphasized the importance of coherence discussed in Phase 3, described the microculture of a team as a kernel of influence impacting the broader organization, consider how collaboration as a superskill can become the driver for your team to connect new knowledge and expertise beyond the borders of your group. Your superskill smart layer can serve as a new kind of integrative currency that expands its reach.

Edison fundamentally viewed collaboration as a connecting force, a transformational force that facilitated and made possible the development of new knowledge assets. As Dr. Israel comments, "Edison wanted people to take charge of things to accomplish a goal rather than to just be in charge of others. In Edison's operations, individuals facilitated processes across diverse realms of his operations. Edison valued the facilitation process more so than the pure directing or controlling of others."[16] As a smart layer, the collaboration superskill enables your team to become a facilitation force in addition to its work in "learning" and "doing." This facilitation function becomes even more crucial as you read further in Phase 4, where the role of social networks and the development of collective intelligence around your team's efforts are discussed.

If you are a leader in your organization, the seven collaboration superskills represent a smart layer you'll want to build into all your collaboration teams. You may even choose to make the collaboration superskills a part of everyone's performance development process. Regardless of how you elect to position them, the seven collaboration superskills need to be part of your workforce strategies, encouraging the formation of powerful true collaboration teams that can, in turn, begin transforming your culture.

> I've become more intrigued with people who have multiple skill sets. If they are a mechanical engineer and an electrical engineer plus they have other secondary skills, that's a big win. That means I can have one person do what three people could do before. I can do more things on multiple levels, and that helps me tackle complex challenges.

> —*Ted Grabau, vice president of global technology, Emerson*

## Leverage Social Networks and Digital Platforms to Anticipate New Patterns and Create Value

Despite Edison's success in spawning such a diverse array of industries and technologies, he sometimes missed cues that would have allowed him to hold a deeper, more lasting leadership position in many of them. For example, after pioneering the electrical power industry in 1882, Edison began designing and building power stations with customized capabilities for small and midsize communities. However, he did not anticipate that so many of the funding responsibilities would fall on his shoulders rather than the shoulders of the communities themselves. Ultimately, Edison did not act swiftly enough to bring in additional funding to keep his cash flow at a manageable level, and this reduced the speed with which he could construct new power stations. The slowing of Edison's efforts enabled others to gain a foothold in the growing market for electrical power.

Similarly, although Edison's cylindrical record became the preferred standard for the recording industry, he missed the shift from cylindrical to flat records in the early 1900s and never gained a leadership position in flat disc recordings. Had Edison been more closely attuned to shifts in how customers viewed musical entertainment and known in more depth what his overseas competitors were endeavoring, he might have developed a flat record sooner, enabling him to dominate this new segment.

In both these examples—tapping additional financing sources and collecting better market intelligence—had social networks been available in his era, Edison could have benefited from their use as part of his Phase 4 process. If the technology had existed for Edison to build a social network smart layer into his true collaboration approach, he might have generated more funding resources for his utility business. And he might have been the king of disc records! Despite the brilliance of his innovation and collaboration efforts in recorded sound, document duplication, electrical power, motion pictures, lighting, and portable power, Edison's frequent failure to anticipate and create new responses to markets he himself had created led to competitive challenges that dogged him throughout his career.

Building a smart layer that embraces digital technologies, smart devices, and an engagement with social networks into the functioning of your team, you can navigate complexity in ways Edison could not. Although Edison was masterful at communicating probing questions to his entire workforce and rapidly engaging their best thinking in this process, he was not always able to translate the outcomes into new marketplace activities. The brilliance of Edison's research and development capability, coupled with his prowess in translating basic research into profitable commercial applications, continually placed Edison at the leading edge of technology. However, once launched, the fruits of his collaboration and innovation efforts sometimes ran into competitive scrapes. Many of these could have been prevented if Edison had possessed access to the types of digital smart layer your team can build.

There are two key reasons why developing a smart layer that connects your team to social networks and digital platforms is crucial for your collaboration efforts. First, long, formal planning cycles are fading. In *The Future of Management*, strategy guru and innovation author Gary Hamel states that today, "Elaborate planning and control rituals can lull executives into believing the environment is more predictable than it is."[17] The post-reset blurring of boundaries between markets and customer groups, and even the total disappearance of familiar business models, has made it more difficult to distinguish "between value-destroying irregularities and value-creating ones."

The trademark pattern for handling planning decisions in the late Industrial Age has been typified by a command-and-control posture, where one leader positioned at a high level in an organization made crucial judgments. Complexity experts Gokce Sargut and Rita Gunther McGrath note it's now very difficult "if not impossible for an individual decision maker to see an entire complex system. . . . It's hard to observe and comprehend a highly diverse array of relationships from any one location. . . . Most executives believe they can take in and make sense of more information than research suggests they actually can. As a result, they often act prematurely, making major decisions without fully comprehending the likely consequences."[18] The notion of one vantage point, one perspective, and one decision maker has contributed to a silo mentality in many organizations still bearing the hierarchical imprints of the late Industrial era. Companies with heavy management layers often lack the flexibility to respond to complex systems increasingly present in the global economy, hanging on to outdated mental models that have not kept pace with new definitions of progress in the Innovation Age—whether they be structural, technological, or both.

Nobel Prize–winning economist Daniel Kahneman, in *Thinking, Fast and Slow*, describes the notion of "cognitive blindness"—totally missing things that are right in front of us because the brain is not sorting for the right signals. The avalanche of data from our smartphones, smart devices, online reading, and yes, social networks, can prompt us to sort for what is familiar, *focusing only on the types of things we already understand*. Unless we begin consciously sorting for new information—data or patterns that are less familiar—we can miss important input that is not part of that sorting process. Just as Edison insisted on generating unreasonable hypotheses and considering outlying options as part of his experiments, we need to develop new mental and digital routines around social networks and other digital platforms that prompt us to probe and question more broadly, moving beyond boundaries we recognize.

> You don't make decisions about things you don't understand. Leaders and teams must be continually adapting and changing, seeking deeper understanding of complex issues.
>
> *—Art Fry, 3M Institute fellow and inventor of the Post-it Note*

Building a smart layer into your true collaboration team themed around social networks and networked platforms can help you prevent cognitive blindness, and avoid relying on planning structures that may no longer be nimble enough to adjust to rapidly changing business conditions or customer demands.

A second key reason why developing a smart layer that connects your team to social networks and digital technology platforms is that old mental models cause us to miss market shifts and new customer usage patterns. The recent, dramatic implosions of once-leading companies Kodak and Research in Motion (RIM; maker of the iconic BlackBerry) were propelled by a refusal among leaders at both firms to believe that their markets and customers were changing in ways that did not look familiar. Rather than adopting an "anticipate and create" mindset, Kodak and RIM discouraged the use of sensing mechanisms to rapidly track market changes, including customer usage patterns and competitive thrusts from Apple and Motorola.

As a result, Kodak got sideswiped twice, first in a shift away from analog cameras to the digital camera (a breakthrough platform that Kodak had actually invented in the 1990s) and a second time when mobile phones began featuring miniaturized, high-quality cameras embedded directly into the phone itself. As for RIM, although it initially enjoyed broad adoption of its smartphones among business executives, its closed operating system never gained traction with software engineers or app developers, which prevented it from moving beyond its primary business customer base. RIM changed its mind too late to make its phones more broadly appealing in face of intense competition from Apple and Android operating systems. On top of these challenges, both companies faced disruptive shifts in technology platforms for exchanging photos online and sharing content across diverse formats such as gaming and videos via social networks like Facebook, catching both firms flat-footed.

Both Kodak and RIM missed big opportunities to use collaboration as a force to drive speed and scale behind their once robust innovation capabilities. Their internal teams did not use networked smart layers to navigate complex competitive activity, nor did they anticipate and create new patterns within their customer groups. Think of how each of these once-leading companies could have designed new markets if they had only been less slavish to definitions for the Industrial Age boundaries of their respective industries. Could these two companies have avoided the missteps that ultimately spelled their demise by embedding digital smart layers in their teams years ago? Could Kodak have pioneered flickr.com, or Instagram? Could RIM have become a force in mobile apps?

Although the odds might be long, I believe they could have. As Yves Morieux of BCG and Edison both knew, small groups hold transformative power, which often lies untapped. Harnessing this power can ultimately shift the culture of an organization. Providing a networked, digital smart layer to your teams offers a key method for accelerating their collaborative power, speed, and scale.

When a smart layer is linked to social networks and other networked platforms, it provides your team with three capabilities that are crucial for keeping pace with market and customer complexity:

1. *Sense:* Monitor new trends and detect newly emerging patterns.

2. *Anticipate:* Adjust the focus of team experiments or collaborative outreach activities to tap social networks or engage in metalogue.

3. *Create:* Use the information you gain to actually lay the groundwork for something new, affecting value creation options for your team.

By building in a digital smart layer to your true collaboration team, you can begin navigating new patterns in the environment, detecting new customer usage preferences, spying gaps in the jobs customers want done, and determining how your products or services can more powerfully fulfill those jobs. As you will read shortly, you can even run high-stakes scenarios to determine what outlying possibilities might catch your team unprepared.

Your digital smart layer offers diverse applications and can be leveraged to accelerate your work in other phases, particularly experimentation, prototyping, or simulation efforts in Phase 2. You can also use digital smart layers to develop a footprint for your project, capturing customer interviews or even video footage as part of your collective intelligence endeavors, which are discussed later in Phase 4.

Regardless of the specific approach you take, building a digital smart layer into your collaboration team gives you access to networks ranging from one to millions of collaborators. *It is intended to help you see collaboration as a continuum of exchanges rather than a static clustering of facts, expanding your ability to productively mine information from these exchanges.* Smart layers enable you to navigate the post-reset convergence of innovation, value creation, and strategy.

Figure 6.2 will help you get started in forming the best type of digital smart layer for your needs. The figure is laid out in four zones, with the relative skill level required to engage in the sensing/anticipating technologies shown along the vertical axis and the relative level of complexity of the tasks you are seeking to accomplish represented along the horizontal axis. By arraying options in this fashion, you can begin matching the complexity of the questions you wish to address in your true collaboration effort with an appropriate social network or virtual platform application.

As a final note, many of the tools you see in Figure 6.2 are geared for use by individuals as well as groups, although they do not all lend themselves equally to both. The figure overall is intended to be directional and does not attempt to reveal

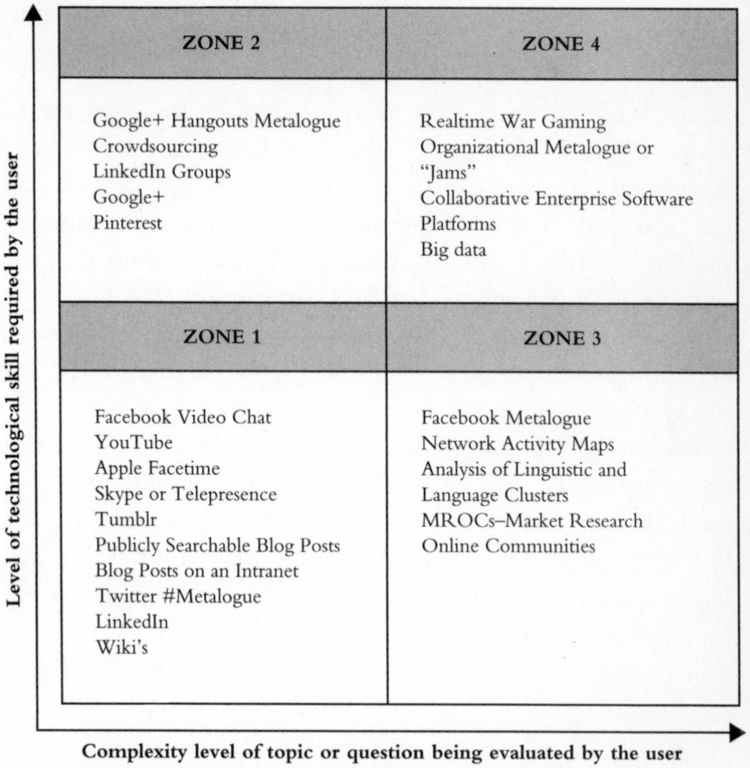

| ZONE 2 | ZONE 4 |
|---|---|
| Google+ Hangouts Metalogue<br>Crowdsourcing<br>LinkedIn Groups<br>Google+<br>Pinterest | Realtime War Gaming<br>Organizational Metalogue or<br>"Jams"<br>Collaborative Enterprise Software<br>Platforms<br>Big data |
| **ZONE 1** | **ZONE 3** |
| Facebook Video Chat<br>YouTube<br>Apple Facetime<br>Skype or Telepresence<br>Tumblr<br>Publicly Searchable Blog Posts<br>Blog Posts on an Intranet<br>Twitter #Metalogue<br>LinkedIn<br>Wiki's | Facebook Metalogue<br>Network Activity Maps<br>Analysis of Linguistic and<br>Language Clusters<br>MROCs–Market Research<br>Online Communities |

*Level of technological skill required by the user* (vertical axis)

*Complexity level of topic or question being evaluated by the user* (horizontal axis)

**Figure 6.2 Social Networks, Digital Technology Platforms, and Complexity: Anticipate and Create**

every option or every scenario your team may encounter. The figure can also show you how the zones shift as you develop more complex questions and endeavor more complex challenges.

The following section provides a background description of all four digital smart layer zones shown in Figure 6.2, along with comments about a few key tools applicable to each zone. Remember, the zones are intended to help you use collaboration to anticipate, and create what's next.

## Zone 1: Simple Questions or Experiments/Simple Technical Applications

Zone 1 offers the biggest array of choices for your digital smart layer. It consists of the low-hanging fruit options composed of low-cost or no-cost technologies. You can position queries in this zone through easy-to-access platforms such as Twitter, LinkedIn, blog searches, or YouTube surfing. Zone 1 provides a baseline for gaining initial traction around any new ideas or questions you may be toying with and noting where these may already be resonating in the marketplace.

Remember to check out internal resources within your organization as well as part of Zone 1, including blogs available via your intranet or comparable in-house network. For example, IBM alone has more than 17,000 internal bloggers that offer insight into specific topics.[19] Like a big pulsing digital brain, the knowledge assets generated by your own internal colleagues can be an initial target for your digital smart layer.

## Zone 2: Simple Questions or Experiments/More Complex Technology Applications

Moving higher along the spectrum of skill and effort required for digital anticipating/creating mechanisms, your smart layer can leverage tools that either cut a big swath across an audience, like crowdsourcing does, or tap specific expert clusters via LinkedIn Groups or Google+. Pinterest also offers a unique visual method for communicating ideas and watching trends develop. If you're seeking a live video-based experience with prospective collaborators, Google+ Hangouts allows up to 10 people to hold a video conversation, but additional people can participate if you choose to publicly broadcast your session via its Hangouts on Air function. For example, President Obama held a public Google+ Hangouts session in January 2012 following his State of the Union speech to tap into trends in feedback stemming from young voters. (The president's session is available for viewing on YouTube at www.youtube.com/watch?v=eeTj5qMGTAI.)

If you have a general hypothesis you're toying with or a theme you wish to explore, crowdsourcing offers a tool for drawing input from large numbers of internal or external collaborators. Recognize, however, that crowdsourcing feedback often comes in broad strokes that require additional analysis and complex data mining, as well as weeks or even months to gather. For example, Pia Erkinheimo, former director of innovation crowdsourcing at Nokia's world headquarters in Finland, indicates Nokia has run more than a half dozen internal and external crowdsourcing programs over the past three years, drawing from employee ideas as well as input from consumers, lead users, developers, and universities. Its ambitious IdeasProject crowdsourcing initiative was opened to the public at the South By Southwest (SXSW) Festival in the United States in March 2011; during a nine-month period, it gathered 7,500 ideas, 14,000 community members, 6,000 comments, and 37 million page views.[20] Input for the SXSW initiative was based on 12 questions, called "challenges," themed around new uses for mobile platforms, asking collaborators to comment. Nokia has also leveraged crowdsourcing to solicit ideas from top developers to generate apps, offering lucrative cash incentives.

Overall, although crowdsourcing can engage huge numbers of collaborators around general questions, be sure that your team allocates time to drill into the results and has access to analytical tools for visualizing and clustering the data into meaningful pods.

### Zone 3: More Complex Questions or Experiments/ Simple Technology Applications

Zone 3 allows your digital smart layer to combine relatively easy-to-use social network or digital platforms with more complex question sets your collaboration team may have devised. This zone offers excellent applications once you have a specific array of refined questions to pose to prospective collaborators or when you wish to search for specific combinations of concepts or attributes. Zone 3 is also helpful when you're seeking to gain focused feedback from a particular target audience or usage group.

Among other tools, Zone 3 embraces applications that will help you search for the frequency of specific word clusters that relate to your true collaboration endeavor. This type of tool helps you see who else is thinking along the same conceptual lines you are, grouping together conversations or queries that are similar to yours. Richard Guha, president of North America for Synerscope, calls this type of activity *virtual listening*.[21] The value of Zone 3 tools was underscored during the writing of this book. Within 18 months, four Zone 3 firms offering software geared to cluster natural language phrases via simple online queries were acquired. These include:

- Wisewindow.com acquired by KPMG
- BuzzMetrics acquired by Nielsen

PHASE 4

- Radian6 acquired by SalesForce.com
- Cymfony acquired by Visible Technologies

In addition to analyzing unique word strings, Zone 3 can help you search for specific users who can help you test or experiment with some of the prospective solutions you've developed in Phase 2. Market research online communities (MROCs) represent one fascinating application. An MROC functions like a pop-up community of users who will pursue specific questions and specific tasks you assign. They generally consist of 50 to 200 prescreened, hand-selected participants. Using smart devices and daily check-in periods, you can monitor how your questions are faring within the group. Carol Phillips, founder of market research consultancy Brand Amplitude, comments, "Several companies license software by the week, allowing outside teams to run and manage a pop-up session. Participants that your team has selected to be part of the pop-up operate in a virtual space and can upload pictures or videos of whatever they're doing as part of your exercise."[22] MROCs are gaining popularity as inexpensive testing forums for new ideas that require hands-on engagement. They also offer the opportunity to monitor progress in real time.

Another digital tool in Zone 3 relates to visually mapping networks of users and mining this information for data or insights relevant to your queries. Similar to the kind of mapping you can do of your own contact network via InMaps on LinkedInLabs.com, many organizations are purchasing software programs that allow them to identify who the heavy users are of their own intranet or other networked digital platforms within their organization. Visually analyzing the intensity and quality of these linkages enables leaders to see who is connecting with others outside their immediate sphere of knowledge or expertise. 3M leverages this type of network tool, for example, in determining who is reaching out beyond their own departments to request white papers and expertise from other groups. Visually mapping networks of employee groups, users, or customers helps you determine who the influencers in the group are, allowing you to target them with questions for your collaboration efforts.

Growing in popularity as a complement to more time-consuming and costly traditional market research methods, Zone 3 offers your team new tools that can help speed and scale customer engagement and product testing approaches.

## Zone 3 Helps Drive More Diverse Solutions

To accelerate the capture of unarticulated needs ripe for innovation or intellectual property potential, Maria Thompson, director of innovation strategy for Motorola Solutions, leverages Zone 3 resources to mine unarticulated customer needs originating from common "repetitive tasks" or jobs that customers need done. Zone 3 aids her internal collaboration team in uncovering trends and issues across diverse customer demographic segments, comparing and contrasting them to trends in emerging technologies. Thompson comments, "Often the best input comes from people who aren't so close to the problem, or the question you're posing. Leveraging digital tools in Zone 3 allows us to seek information in unique ways, tap new usage sources, and generate solutions that are more diverse

than what we could have devised without them."
Thompson also notes that digital smart layers are
particularly important for organizations which have
international scope, or do business in even a few
countries beyond their own home borders.[23]

## Zone 4: More Complex Questions or Experiments/ Complex Technology Applications

Zone 4 is the place within your digital smart layer where
complex questions and complex technologies meet. Zone 4
embraces collaboration forums involving massive amounts of
data that generally require huge computing power. This zone
is best accessed when you want a broad array of collaborators
to respond either in real time or within a set period of time to
one very specific question, or a small cluster of questions of
deep interest to a particular community. These sessions can
require extensive preparation and can be costly to administer
and analyze. However, the output is often laser-focused,
offering a big "return on network" for your effort.

As virtual teams rise in popularity, sophisticated collaboration platforms that engage diverse constituents simultaneously in an online environment are becoming increasingly
crucial. Virtual collaboration platforms such as Brightidea's
enterprise software, for example, help a single organization
span diverse geographies and multiple realms of expertise.
Using Brightidea to collaborate around very targeted, very
specific questions—called challenges—participants connect
for a condensed, preset time period defined by the user
community. Brightidea's software organizes massive information sets around each challenge, including quantitative
data, trend data, blogs, images, user posts, and user comments,

allowing review by every participant within the designated community either in real time or at staggered intervals. Challenges are broadcast by a single designated collaboration champion to a large community of users who are pre-authorized to review data streams generated by the community—or to access stored data for use in the sessions themselves. To incentivize community members to engage their best thinking, participants receive virtual compensation for their comments, usually in the form of points, much like a Klout rating.

Matthew Greeley, cofounder and CEO of Brightidea, comments, "We help bring deeper social connections to collaboration by customizing the virtual environment as much as possible. Each collaboration community is given a name that means something to the organization and the users."[24] At Hewlett-Packard, for example, the Brightidea community is called the Garage, reflecting the entrepreneurial heritage of the company. Brightidea's online collaboration platform has been used by small teams to gather input on major product development questions, as well as to power more broadly based initiatives such as Ecomagination at GE and challenge projects at Motorola, Kraft, and Bosch.

Beyond the direct advantage of using a digital smart layer to gather insights for your collaboration team, your use of social networks and technology across all the zones serves as a huge drawing card for Gen Y. As Rishad Tobaccowala of VivaKi notes, "Gen Y realizes learning is going to be a big part of their entire careers. So if you can offer learning by collaborating with both internal and external people, it fundamentally makes your organization more attractive, and it makes employees feel more valuable. Any time you can make individuals feel more valuable, they will bring more passion to your cause, and stay more engaged."[25]

## Zone 4 Enables Rapid Development of Multiple Scenarios

At Ford, Zone 4 has been used for the online equivalent of war gaming. When determining whether to accept or decline government bailout money in the fall of 2008, Ford launched Project Quark, a massive internal collaboration process that operated simultaneously in Dearborn, Michigan, and Ford's regional headquarters in Asia and Europe. Project Quark also linked small teams from Ford's internal legal department, as well as its government liaison personnel, finance groups, human resources, and production units. Running real-time scenarios that "included the collapse of Chrysler, the failure of GM, and a decision by Toyota Motor Corp. or Honda Motor Co. to close one or more of their US factories,"[26] Ford vice president of global purchasing Tony Brown kept CEO Alan Mulally apprised of Project Quark's team progress. Ultimately, the Zone 4 smart layer in this massive true collaboration effort helped Ford devise a plan allowing the company to operate without bailout aid from the US government.

Ford used Zone 4 to ask complex questions about scenarios and options relating to its future, drawing upon an equally complex network of digital resources to accomplish its objectives. This type of war gaming represents the ultimate level of sophistication that a small team—or group of small teams—can experience. It taps essential components learned in every

*(continued)*

(*continued*)

phase of Edison's true collaboration process: intense team communication, diversity of expertise, inspirational leadership, navigation of conflict, and recognition that the group's collective intelligence multiplies the thinking of any one individual.

As you consider how to build your social network or digital technology smart layer, consider the expertise required in each of the four zones, recognizing how the sophistication level of your own communication patterns needs to rise as you progress from Zone 1 to Zone 4. Consider how your team can exercise its acumen in each zone, progressively moving from one to the next.

## A Note on Metalogue

Before we move on to Part ii of Phase 4, Footprinting Captures Collective Intelligence, I'd like to comment on the role of metalogue as a uniquely powerful facet of your digital smart layer. Unlike any other tool available to your collaboration team, metalogue operates in all four zones shown in Figure 6.2.

In Chapter 2, I described metalogue as a method of inquiry for exploring diverse conversations and the context around those conversations. Within the realm of true collaboration, metalogue becomes a progressive stream of virtual discussions that are sometimes broad and sometimes deep. A metalogue, for example, can radiate outwardly from one individual to many individuals or from one team to many individuals, teams, or communities. Metalogue is not a random clustering of conversations; it must be spurred by a particular query or small set of queries that are of interest to a broad array of people. A metalogue is always designed with intention and thematic focus.

In its broadest possible application, metalogue holds potential to impact entire societies, not just one team. Consider how the Arab Spring uprising of March 2011 represented a metalogue that first arose between a small body of individuals desiring to air their political views. The queries and insights of a few key organizers caught fire with a huge body of others, ultimately leading to physical gatherings protesting government policies across several Middle Eastern nations. In this sense, metalogue "from one to many" can have a massive impact across an entire nation. Ultimately, *we can begin viewing metalogue as a kind of core capability that the growing global presence of networks will increasingly spur us to develop over time.* As the technologies linking individuals together become more and more advanced, metalogue will play an even greater role in how we communicate within organizations and within society.

Although I believe metalogue will increasingly serve a positive role in creating cultural and social change out into the future, I will focus here on how metalogue operates as part of a commercial objective, such as developing new products or services, or increasing emergency preparedness rather than political upheaval. Metalogue remains an important concept for your team to understand because, unlike any other facet of your digital smart layer in Phase 4, *tools to generate metalogue exist in every zone.*

Your true collaboration team can choose to engage in metalogue at any point in its project trajectory. However, recognize that each zone offers *differing levels of intimacy* with the collaborators you choose to engage in your outreach

233

queries. Figure 6.3 offers a guide for visualizing these intimacy levels.

- *Metalogue in Zone 1—broad, not deep:* Using nothing more than text messages from a mobile phone, your team can engage in a simple Twitter metalogue using existing hashtags (#), such as #innovation, #collaboration, #trends, #sm (social media), or other tags you may be familiar with. Twitter also allows your team to designate a specific #word that enables any Twitter user to search on that hashtag and find your metalogue, readily tapping into the conversation flow. Twitter metalogues are free, and some metalogue organizers even put up websites so those who frequently engage in their question-and-answer sessions can have a core reference source. Several services are available to transcribe your metalogue and post it to the broader community.

- *Metalogue in Zone 2—broad, moderately deep:* Google+ Hangouts offers a visually based forum for metalogue. Entrepreneurs as well as television and cable program developers are starting to engage in metalogue with broad audiences this way, exploring purpose-driven themes such as hunger, diabetes, and obesity. A few free options exist for recording your Google+ Hangouts session so that your metalogue can be captured for others to view.

- *Metalogue in Zone 3—focused, moderately deep:* Facebook provides an excellent social networking platform for metalogue, capable of drawing thousands of prospective collaborators using visual as well as message-based exchanges, in addition to gaming, music, or images.

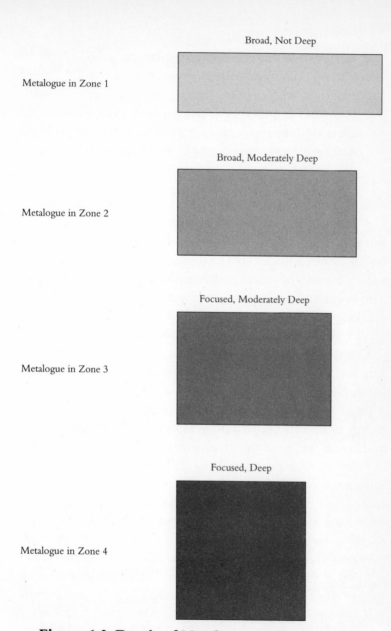

**Figure 6.3 Depth of Metalogue Varies by Zone**
*Note*: Match the intensity level of the metalogue you desire to the zone that best delivers that intensity.

- *Metalogue in Zone 4—focused, deep:* As noted earlier in Phase 4, enterprise software platforms such as Brightidea enable a single collaboration team to connect with thousands of others within a predesignated community, allowing metalogue to take place in real time within a diverse but predefined group of collaborators.

Ultimately, with continued advances in artificial intelligence and the availability of super-computing power in portable formats, metalogue will become a highly accessible form of collaborative dialogue. By recognizing that metalogue represents a big part of where collaboration activity is heading, you can begin reskilling your team now to master social networking capabilities and networked digital platforms. These tools will be needed to enable meaningful metalogue.

Overall, as you think about how your collaboration team can best organize to address complexity, recognize the role smart layers can play in helping you ramp up the speed and scale of your efforts. Commit as a team to ensuring that the inputs to everything you do are intentionally streamlined to add value without generating extra steps or unnecessary moving parts. Recognize how collaboration as a superskill affects the microculture of your team, expanding its ability to connect with and influence other teams, especially when additional resources may be needed. And finally, leverage social networks and digital platforms to maximize your power to collaborate with individuals and communities operating far beyond the physical boundaries of your group. Recognize that Phase 4 will help you tap new knowledge resources that can serve as creative, time-saving mechanisms for your experiments and partnered relationships, while also serving as a drawing card for participation on your team by Gen Y employees.

# PART II, PHASE 4: FOOTPRINTING CAPTURES COLLECTIVE INTELLIGENCE

As you progress through each of Edison's four phases of true collaboration, be mindful of the impact your work can have not only on your team, but on current or prospective customers—even an entire community or user group. The final component of Edison's true collaboration process offers you an opportunity to document the progress of your thinking, and record it in a meaningful way that can be accessed again and again.

## Footprinting Your Team's Collective Intelligence

Part of Edison's extraordinary power as a facilitator of innovation and collaboration was his ability to "zoom out" and see the big picture behind his project endeavors. Edison often held an understanding of what was needed to implement an initiative at both the tactical and strategic levels, while also seeing its broader contribution to human knowledge itself. Edison consistently viewed his work as connecting to a bigger world—"the mental world"—which today we would describe as collective intelligence.

> Well, there is another world . . . the mental world, which has its centre in the brain . . .
>
> —*Thomas Edison*

He realized this collective intelligence was enduring, that it was not subject to the constraints of time. Edison recognized that, in addition to his own desire to keep records of his activity for internal use, scores of others would hark back to the collaborative endeavors he and his teams had undertaken. Edison thus continually sought to make his work representative of the highest and best effort possible. He viewed the fruits of his collaborations as a form of collective intelligence that contributed to the advancement of humanity. The disruptive innovations delivered by his teams were magnified by the shared purpose they embodied, weaving the entirety of his work into streams of overlapping knowledge. Believing that such knowledge expanded and contributed to the work of others over time, Edison said, "Thinking is a cumulative process."

Documenting your team's efforts will place the knowledge you've gained within the collective intelligence of humankind. It will permanently link you and your team to the common purpose, the common vision you are seeking, or have sought, to create. By sharing the content you hold in common, your efforts become a reminder of the power that collaboration offers for achieving results that cannot be generated any other way. As you develop a record capturing your team's journey, consider it a "footprint" that will impact the road that others follow, linking it forever to the future—not just the past.

> One of the deepest desires underlying shared vision is the desire to be connected, to a larger purpose and to one another.
>
> **—*Peter Senge*, The Fifth Discipline**

Footprinting your work is not a rote endeavor, a mere must-do exercise requiring that you write everything down. Rather, footprinting yields a discovery process of its own. It creates new connections that actually transpire in real time while your observations are being recorded. *The footprinting process itself serves as a part of your team's discovery learning and is not distinct from it.* This facet of Phase 4—footprinting your team's collective intelligence—is dedicated to the capturing and recording of what your team has learned on its true collaboration journey.

Although Edison created masterful footprints of his endeavors, Larry Keeley of the Doblin Group believes *the establishment of collective intelligence today remains one of the biggest gaps plaguing the collaboration and innovation process globally*. Despite the plethora of technologies available to teams for creating project footprints of their work, "Team memory gets lost, and its loss negatively impacts the institutional memory of the organiza- tion. Collaboration teams can be so complicated and layered that the team itself builds its own process and keeps its own files rather than holding team files. Individual knowledge dom- inates. This problem is absolutely huge. It can take millions of dollars to track everything down once a team has dispersed, especially if there's intellectual property involved."[27]

Thinking is a cumulative process.

*—Thomas Edison*

Recognizing this same gap, Dr. Jean Egmon urges teams to develop a habit of documenting their thinking as they progress. "If you can build in the habit of stopping and sharing, reflecting on what you've learned for the good of the whole, that's really important. Through collective intelli- gence, the whole system gets smarter. The learning which is yielded makes the future inputs and outputs better. It's like a download of knowing. It's the encouraging and recording and sharing of content. In consciously weaving it all together, you create integration and synthesis from it."[28]

## Developing Different Types of Knowledge Assets

Robert Lowe, CEO of Wellspring Worldwide, emphasizes the importance of being able to footprint both the codified and the tacit knowledge that flow

*(continued)*

*(continued)*

from a team's collaborative efforts. *Codified knowledge* refers to the facts, data, or processes that may be unearthed or newly created by a team, whereas *tacit knowledge* refers to the less quantifiable yet hugely powerful contributions a team generates around context, passion, individual and shared experiences, and group dialogue.

After years of studying how collaborative teams successfully invent new intellectual property, Lowe's firm has developed an array of tools that help capture collective intelligence, embracing both tacit and codified knowledge. Describing his staff as specialists in what he terms *Knowledge Supply Chain management*, Robert says, "Looking at knowledge as a thought stream helps organizations go beyond the more rigid knowledge management approaches of the 1990s. We help customers track their knowledge assets in a way that flexes around the needs of the user—not the confines of a preset software platform."

One of Lowe's tools, called Flintbox, offers a method of documenting and then monetizing those parts of a team's total work output that can be codified and segmented into discrete segments, commercially extending them for use by other industries or user groups.[29] Using software to track the development of new knowledge also enables teams to see the progression of their thought process, offering deep insight into how the microculture of the team itself is operating.

How can you create a living, breathing, organic representation of your team's efforts? The aim of footprinting in
Phase 4 is not just to log a meaningful progression of your
project and its results but to create a record that allows the
heart and soul of your shared collaboration experience
to emerge. An expert in the development of intellectual
property, Robert Lowe notes, "Consciously footprinting
your efforts is a creative endeavor which must balance two
key factors—connections between those facets which can be
codified, such as factual project findings that can be readily
chunked into segments without a loss of understanding, and
facets that are tacit, project elements which may only exist
within a broader context and are so nuanced that they cannot
be easily captured or explained in simple terms."

As you begin considering what to document, here are key
questions to ask as you explore the footprinting process:

- *Phase 1—Capacity:* What factors led to the creation of
  our team? How did the team evolve from this initial
  point? Where did we encounter slow molecules that we
  had to change? What were some of the meaningful areas
  of diversity present on our team? How did we reduce
  social distance among team members?

- *Phase 2—Context:* How did we crystallize our initial
  goals? How did the team frame the problem it was
  tasked to solve? What big questions did we ask that led
  us to consider unreasonable hypotheses? What context
  did this lead us to create? How did our early prototypes,
  stories, or simulations spur the progress of our thinking?
  What did the collaborative environment we created
  look like?

- *Phase 3—Coherence:* How was inspiration transmitted
  through our team? What disagreements and conflicts

arose? What issues lay at the heart of these, and how did our team resolve them? What new awareness was yielded from these challenges? What was the shared purpose we agreed upon?

- *Phase 4—Complexity:* How did we engage smart layers in our efforts? What networked digital tools did we use? What were the key areas of complexity we observed over the course of our endeavors? How did our encounters with complexity yield changes in the way we viewed our work?

Edison perceived the recording of team actions and team progress as an integral part of discovery learning. For Edison, documentation served as a link to the cognitive stream of thinking that characterized true collaboration itself. Following are three steps that will allow you to capture both the head and the heart of your team efforts.

### Use Notebooks and the Written Word as a Backbone for Your Project Footprint

Over the course of his entire career, Edison used notebooks as a core documentation resource. Filling literally tens of thousands of pages from the 1860s until his death in 1931, Edison diligently maintained records of his insights as well as the nature and outcomes of his wide-ranging experiments. Intended to provide protection for his intellectual property, notebooks also yielded a ready reservoir of information that could be shared with colleagues. Paralleling virtual file sharing today, Edison and his teams frequently would share their notebooks "live" to delve into the details of an idea or a possible creative direction.

Rishad Tobaccowala of VivaKi underscores the need for written footprints in the Innovation Age, allowing information to be gathered from every team member, then shared—a process especially important for virtual groups. "You need proper note taking, leaving enough of a footprint so the underlying meaning is transmitted. Today it's possible to store multiple versions of a file. You can check in online to see who has made changes to the original version. This helps not only in documenting work, but in information sharing as well."[30]

A myriad of digital options exist for collaboration teams seeking to document their project efforts online. Following is a sample array of Internet-based services your team can access to post shared documents.

| | |
|---|---|
| Google Drive (formerly Google Docs) | Amazon Cloud Drive |
| Dropbox | Microsoft SkyDrive |
| Box | iCloud |
| Evernote | 37signals |

If you favor longhand writing for your notebook entries, consider Moleskine notebooks as *A Whole New Mind* author Daniel Pink does. Or, buy simple lined composition notebooks at any local convenience store to use as a repository for your insights.

## Track Ideas Using Drawings, Prototypes, and Infographics

Peppered within Edison's notebooks is a huge array of drawings—hand-rendered depictions of the fantastical workings of Edison's mind. Edison believed it was crucial to express his thinking not only in words but in pictures as well, a practice that allowed him to readily share concepts with others in the lab regardless of their expertise or discipline.

Sharing visual expressions of an idea expanded team thinking around what was being created or explored, allowing ideas to be viewed from multiple angles.

Edison was a tinkerer who relished taking things apart to see how they worked, and his drawings give the feeling that one could almost step inside his scrawled images and build something from them. Surviving sketches and working drawings offer a detailed look at the thought process Edison used, as well as the context he considered for his diverse inventions (Figures 6.4 and 6.5).

Through Edison's devotion to drawing his ideas on paper—and encouraging true collaboration team members to do the same—the creation of visual records became standard practice throughout the lab.

Today, in addition to the value of rendering drawings by hand as Edison did, your true collaboration teams can access electronic whiteboards, apps for the iPad, and inexpensive CAD/CAM options to visually capture their thinking. Teams can even use smart devices to take a picture of an idea that's been drawn in a team session and post it to an intranet site for further evaluation.

Infographics also offer a powerful way to create visual images capturing the work of your group. Several great online tutorials demonstrate how to generate compelling infographics; here are a few websites to help you get started:

- Wordle.net
- Statsilk.com
- Tableau.com
- Hohli.com
- Gapminder.org
- Creately.com

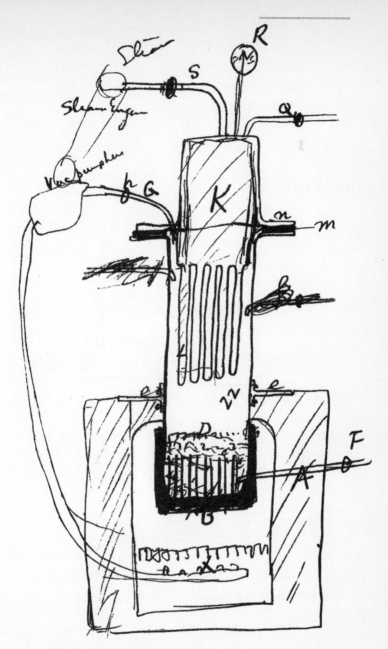

**Figure 6.4 Edison's Drawing of a Fuel Cell**

*Source:* Reproduced with permission by *The Thomas A. Edison Papers*, Rutgers University, Piscataway, New Jersey, http://edison.rutgers.edu.

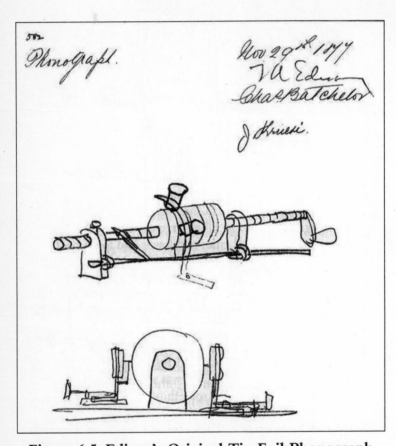

**Figure 6.5 Edison's Original Tin Foil Phonograph**

*Source:* Reproduced with permission by *The Thomas A. Edison Papers*, Rutgers University, Piscataway, New Jersey, http://edison.rutgers.edu.

When leaving a visual footprint, remember to include several of your three-dimensional prototypes as well. Project artifacts can rapidly show what could require thousands of words to describe on paper. Be sure to include narrative prototypes capturing stories from your project. Craig Wortmann, adjunct professor at the University of Chicago's Booth School of Business, comments, "Stories are provocative because they build context, they build emotion. . . . Stories connect the bits and bolts of our thinking, and therefore cut through complexity. They give shape and color to our experiences."[31]

By visually capturing the progression of your thinking through drawings and diverse prototypes, your team can tell its story in compelling terms. Be sure to include technical details but also select several stories that you believe are readily understandable by individuals not familiar with the technical underpinnings of your project or your industry. This ensures that you can fully describe the context of your work in a way that is meaningful to diverse audiences.

## Use Videos and Audio Files to Preserve Context and Emotion

Although Edison invented breakthrough technologies such as the phonograph, recorded sound, the motion picture camera, and moving pictures, unfortunately, he rarely used these as media to document his own work or the work of his labs. Edison's early focus in the movies, for example, sought to capture the activities of real life and real people. Called actualities, these brief films featured famous celebrities, news events, natural disasters, facets of war, new modes of travel, historic reenactments, and panoramic views of scenic vistas. Although Edison saw value in memorializing famous personalities of his time either on film or through capturing their voices in audio recordings, including rare segments of Mark Twain, President Teddy Roosevelt as a Rough Rider, and President William McKinley, he did not use sound or visual technologies to document his own internal operations.

Ironically, in our digital era, we can actually build on Edison's extraordinary technology triumphs in recorded sound and motion pictures as footprinting vehicles, using audio technologies plus smart devices to connect the complexities of context with emotion. Consider using videos and audio files either to capture longer stories or to reveal brief sequences that you have recorded with prospective customers. These can include segments from actual collaboration sessions you've run as part of your digital smart layer activity. Use videos and audio files as a way to engage streams of experience that mirror the emotion as well as the key insights your group wishes to convey.

Ensure that every team member participates in the footprinting process. Don't simply assign it to one person who serves as the team scribe. If you take that route, a big part of the shared experience that underlies the footprinting itself will be lost. Once you've assembled a footprint you believe captures the essence of your learning as a team, expose it to a few people whom you trust. Gather their feedback to see if there are any chunks of information that appear to be missing. Having a few outsiders offer an objective viewpoint will help your team shape its finished message in a way that is compelling while remaining true to the work and the purpose you've labored so hard to deliver. Use the visual illustration in Figure 6.6 to guide your efforts.

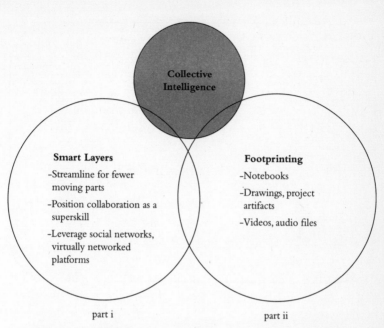

part i                                    part ii

**Figure 6.6  Phase 4—Complexity: From Thomas Edison's Four Phases of True Collaboration**

*Note:* Use smart layers to drive speed and scale for your true collaboration efforts, capturing collective intelligence and new knowledge assets as you progress.

# CHAPTER 7

## True Collaboration

### A Look into the Future

**A**s we progress through the Innovation Age over the next two decades, the underlying mechanisms of Edison's true collaboration process will surge as a crucial priority for every organization. In understanding how to shape collaboration capacity, develop new context, establish team coherence, and navigate ever-growing levels of complexity, a premium will be placed on workforce reskilling methods, and the ability to form smart layers.

Organizations that engage true collaboration as a backbone for their innovation, value creation, and hiring activity will remain competitive and nimble in the face of constantly shifting economic forces. In making their way to the trailing edge of the Innovation Age, leaders and employees alike must bring the following factors to the forefront of their thinking:

- *As the definition of progress changes with the ascendance of Generation Y, a premium will be placed on collaboration and discovery learning.* Gen Y's attraction to collaborative work environments and discovery learning will continue to hold magnetic power as this crucial cohort comes to dominate the US workforce by 2025. Because Gen Y defines progress as a creative continuum of learning and experimentation rather than reaching specific financial objectives or garnering a particular management title, opportunities to engage in purely task-driven activities will hold less value for this cadre of workers. With the merging of innovation, value creation, and strategy in the post-reset environment, collaboration will increasingly serve as a connective force in organizations and teams of every kind. Because true collaboration uniquely engages both a sense of shared experience and shared purpose, organizations must newly define how progress will be gauged, balancing "learning" and "doing" when framing individual and team performance goals.

- *Teams must organize for complexity, and reduce hierarchy.* Heavily layered, hierarchical structures will not survive the "anticipate and create" requirements of the post-reset era. Flatter, more pod-like teams that balance functional excellence with smart layers and collaboration superskills, particularly around communication, strategic thinking, and data synthesis, will become the new normal. Governments and educational institutions must be especially attuned to streamlining the number of moving parts in their operations to stay relevant and be perceived as value-creating structures. The presence of significant hierarchies in any organization means maintaining cost burdens that may ultimately become too heavy and create too much drag, diminishing relevance and adaptability in face of rapidly changing market dynamics.

- *Recognize collaboration as a transformative superskill.* Regardless of the industry segment or market grouping you compete in, collaboration will come to underpin virtually every business function, serving as a transformative force driving new forms of communication and metalogue. The arrival within the next decade of an additional billion working-age people on the planet will mandate that every worker possess the ability to manage streams of data from diverse sources—smart devices, video, and artificial intelligence—while also creating virtual and live connections. These connections must be meaningful, motivating, and aligned with a shared purpose.

- *Cultivate multiple forms of leadership within your ranks.* Inspirational leadership represents one of the most important yet least developed areas of management attention in organizations today. To maintain coherent collaboration teams over time, inspirational leadership will become a mandatory presence within every work culture. In particular, organizations must seek out—and groom—inspirational leaders capable of facilitating collaboration and value creation across teams bearing diverse skills and communication abilities. Offering stretch goals to younger workers will prove pivotal in creating space for additional inspirational leaders to emerge. Shoulder-to-shoulder leaders who can drive momentum for team efforts both internally and externally must also be equipped with the strategic thinking skills to guide business efforts with less hierarchical supervision.

- *Balance face-to-face interactions with the expanding role of metalogue.* Whether your core audience is composed of internal employees, external supplier groups, urban dwellers, or those in rural communities, using virtual environments to ask meaningful questions that draw upon the best thinking of large groups will become more common—and more necessary. As software platforms emerge to make metalogue increasingly affordable, the role of mass collaborations conducted around key themes will be aided by broader access to artificial intelligence, multiple forms of simulation, and other technologies that have yet to be developed. New job functions will emerge around driving metalogue and priming large groups to undertake it successfully. Teams and organizations must learn how to balance live, face-to-face interactions with the value of obtaining information virtually from dispersed groups of collaborators.

- *Competitiveness means continually creating new context.* Although innovation will remain an important success factor over the next two decades, collaborative problem solving and the development of new context for solutions will accelerate the speed of translating ideas into commercially viable products and services. Increased importance will rest on expanding collaboration teams that embrace diverse learning styles and expertise across multiple generations of employees. Synching simulation efforts, both live and virtual, with experimentation and prototyping processes as well as artificial intelligence will be key to maintaining cadres of knowledge workers who can ask new questions, anticipate change, and challenge existing norms.

- *Sustaining a culture of collaboration will become a new kind of knowledge asset.* Collaboration teams will form the nucleus of value-driving capabilities within an organization. The ability to collaborate both internally and externally will increasingly drive competitive advantage and marketplace visibility. Teams will be required not

253

only to manage increasingly complex webs of information but effectively translate and footprint processes being used within the team's microculture, nurturing the broader collaboration ecosystem. The collective intelligence of an organization will become a marketplace force magnetizing others to do business with its teams. Collaborative cultures will become a new form of knowledge asset in their own right, prompting the creation of new financial measurements such as "return on network."

If Edison were alive today, he would be employing his four phases of true collaboration to drive toward the highest expressions of collaborative experience, both engaging live interactions and harnessing the power of technology. He would no doubt remind us that, increasingly, *our success will lie in combining the mindset of the innovator with the toolkit of the collaborator.* He would urge us not to drift toward "the law of least effort," as Daniel Kahneman might phrase it.[1] Instead, Edison would challenge us to consider what is possible by maximizing the use of our creative and mental powers, collaborating to apply new knowledge through shared human experience.

Collaboration itself, including its very definition and boundaries, will continue to evolve over the next two decades. Edison leaves us a legacy we can return to over and over again as we newly shape a future that embraces the highest and best of our collaborative spirit.

*If we did all the things we are capable of doing, we would literally astound ourselves.*

—**Thomas Edison**

# Notes

## CHAPTER 1   WHAT IS TRUE COLLABORATION?

1. Margaret Geller, "Click . . . the Universe" (lecture, Chautauqua Institution, Chautauqua, NY, July 29, 2010).
2. "Employment: Can Private Industry Lift Countries Out of Poverty?" worldbank.org, accessed May 2012, http://youthink.worldbank.org/issues/employment/.
3. "The Next Billion," Nokia, accessed March 2012, http://conversations.nokia.com/2011/02/11/mobile-phones-the-next-billion/.
4. Rishad Tobaccowala (vice president of innovation, VivaKi), interview by Sarah Miller Caldicott, Chicago, IL, March 21, 2012.
5. Greg Cox (president and chief operating officer, Dale Carnegie - Chicago), interview by Sarah Miller Caldicott, Chicago, IL, March 23, 2012.
6. "Brandman University Research Study Shows Companies Can Better Embrace Virtual Work Force as a Competitive Advantage," Brandman University, accessed June 2011, http://www.brandman.edu/pressreleases/Pages/pressdetails.axp?PressName=052311.

7. Nina Fazio (former innovation project manager, Motorola), interview by Sarah Miller Caldicott, Chicago, IL, April 28, 2012.

8. Greg Cox, interview.

9. "Electrotechnology: A Light on the Past, Present and Future," distributed by Charles Edison Fund and John Keegan (Salt Lake City: National Energy Foundation, 1997).

10. Dr. Carol Dweck, "Mindset for Achievement," accessed April 2012, http://mindsetonline.com/howmindsetaffects/mindsetforachievement/index.html.

11. Dr. Paul Israel (director and general editor of *The A. Thomas Edison Papers*, Rutgers University), interview by Sarah Miller Caldicott, New Brunswick, NJ, March 5, 2012.

12. Jeremy Hsu, "Thomas Edison's Greatest Invention: Innovation Itself?" *Innovation News Daily*, accessed April 2012, http://huffingtonpost.com/2012/04/07/Thomas-edison-inventions-innovation-rivaly_n_1409957.html.

13. Hsu, "Thomas Edison's Greatest Invention."

14. Dr. Jean Egmon (executive director, Ford Center for Global Citizenship at Northwestern University and past director, Complexity in Action Network), interview by Sarah Miller Caldicott, Chicago, IL, March 13, 2012.

15. Herminia Ibarra and Morten T. Hansen, "Are You a Collaborative Leader?" *Harvard Business Review* (July–August 2011): 74.

16. Ibarra and Hansen, "Are You a Collaborative Leader?" 73.

17. Jay Scherer (managing partner, BPI Group North America), interview by Sarah Miller Caldicott, Chicago, IL, February 29, 2012.

18. Dirk Tussing and Kent Barnett, "The Value of Knowledge Assets" (Video, Chicagoland Learning Leaders, Chicago, IL, January 2010), http://www.learningexecutive.com/calendar/display_event.asp?id=397.

19. Scherer, interview.

# CHAPTER 2 WHY IS TRUE COLLABORATION SO CRUCIAL NOW?

1. C. K. Prahalad, "The New Age of Innovation" (lecture, World Innovation Forum, New York, NY, May 5, 2009), author's notes.

2. Ray Kurzweil, "Is the Singularity Near?" (speech, World Technology Summit, New York, NY, October 26, 2011); and Peter Diamandis, "Abundance Is Our Future" (speech, TED Conference at Long Beach, CA, February 29, 2012).

3. Steve Teig, "What If Everything Was Programmable?" (lecture and panel, 2012 Edison Awards, New York, NY, April 26, 2012).

4. Guy Blissett (distribution lead, IBM Wholesale), interview by Sarah Miller Caldicott, March 15, 2012.

5. Brian K. Walker, "Welcome to the Era of Agile Commerce," *eBusiness & Channel Strategy Professionals* (blog), Forrester Research, Inc., March 11, 2011, http://blogs.forrester.com/brian_walker/11-03-11-welcome_to_the_era_of_agile _commerce.

6. William H. Rogers, "Innovation Meets the Banking Industry" (speech, North Carolina Central University in Research Triangle Park, Raleigh-Durham, NC, April 10, 2012).

7. Robert Safian, "From the Editor: The Creative Economy," *Fast Company* (December 2011): 16.

8. "Intel Signs Black Eyed Peas' will.i.am to Boost Creativity," dailyfinance.com, accessed September 2011, www.dailyfinance.com/2011/01/25/intel-signs-black-eyed-peas-will-i-am-to-boost-creativity/.

9. McKinsey Global Institute, "Jobs and US Economic Recovery: A Panel Discussion," *McKinsey Quarterly*, accessed August 2011, www.mckinseyquarterly.com/Jobs_and_US_economic_ recovery_A_panel_discussion_2843.

10. Wayne A. Lindholm, "Innovation Simulation" (lecture, Business Innovation Conference, Wheaton, IL, October 5, 2009).

11. Lindholm, "Innovation Simulation."
12. "The Inventor's Finest Creation: Thomas Edison and the Making of a Myth," 1998, http://xroads.virginia.edu/~class/am485_98/brady/edison/edison.html.
13. "Our Values," IBM, accessed May 2012, www-03.ibm.com/employment/our_values.html.
14. Andy Dangerfield, "London Riots: Teenagers 'Lack Hope,'" *BBC News, London*, accessed April 2012, www.bbc.co.uk/news/uk-england-london-14462688.
15. Klaus Schwab, "The Great Transformation—Shaping New Models" (pre-agenda documents, World Economic Forum, released October 23, 2011 and accessed January 2012), www.weforum.org/content/great-transformation-shaping-new-models.
16. Kristin Burnham, "Gen Y Traits in the Workplace Unveiled," *CIO Magazine*, accessed January 2012, www.cio.com/article/697702/Gen_Y_Traits_in_the_Workplace_Unveiled.
17. Burnham, "Gen Y Traits."
18. Emily S. DeRocco, "Rebuilding U.S. Manufacturing," (speech, Iowa Association of Business and Industry Conference, Ames, Iowa, June 9, 2010).
19. Daniel Pargman, "The Great Reskilling," *Energy Bulletin*, accessed February 2012, www.energybulletin.net/51210.
20. Braden Kelley, "Harnessing the Global Talent Pool to Accelerate Innovation" (paper prepared for InnoCentive, February 15, 2012), 9.

## CHAPTER 3  PHASE 1

1. Steven Johnson, *Where Good Ideas Come From: The Natural History of Innovation* (New York: Riverhead Books, 2010), 47.
2. Frank Lewis Dyer and Thomas Commerford Martin, *Edison: His Life and Inventions* (Project Gutenberg Etext, February 1997), 250.

3. Michele Wehrwein Albion, editor *The Quotable Edison* (The University Press of Florida, 2011) 189.
4. Michael J. Mauboussin, "Embracing Complexity," *Harvard Business Review* (September 2011): 91.
5. Herminia Ibarra and Morten T. Hansen, "Are You a Collaborative Leader?" *Harvard Business Review* (July–August 2011): 72.
6. Mauboussin, "Embracing Complexity."
7. Ricardo Semler, *The Seven-Day Weekend: Changing the Way Work Works* (New York: Penguin, 2003, 2004), 64.
8. Bent Flyvbjerg and Alexander Budzier, "Why Your IT Project May Be Riskier Than You Think," *Harvard Business Review* (September 2011): 23–24.
9. Flyvbjerg and Budzier, "Why Your IT Project May Be Riskier Than You Think," 23–25.
10. Flyvbjerg and Budzier, "Why Your IT Project May Be Riskier Than You Think."
11. Thomas E. Jeffrey, *From Phonographs to U-Boats: Edison and His Insomnia Squad in Peace and War, 1911–1919* (New Jersey: The Thomas A. Edison Papers at Rutgers, The State University, endorsed by National Historical Publications and Records Commission, 2008), 31–32.
12. Michael J. Gelb and Sarah Miller Caldicott, *Innovate Like Edison: The Five-Step System for Breakthrough Business Success* (New York: Penguin, 2007), 33.
13. Anita Woolley and Thomas Malone, "Defend Your Research: What Makes a Team Smarter? More Women," *Harvard Business Review*, accessed June 2011, http://hbr.org/2011/06/defend-your-research-what-makes-a-team-smarter-more-women/ar/1.
14. Dyer and Martin, *Edison: His Life and Inventions*, 291.
15. Michael Schrage, "Why Zuckerberg Is (Almost) Right about Great Talent," *Harvard Business Review*, accessed June 2011, http://blogs.hbr.org/schrage/2011/06/why-zuckerberg-is-almost-right.html.

16. Alan Deutschman, "Inside the Mind of Jeff Bezos," *Fast Company*, accessed September 2011, www.fastcompany.com/magazine/85/bezos_2.html?page=0%2C0.
17. Semler, *Seven-Day Weekend*, 166.
18. Francis Jehl, *Menlo Park Reminiscences, Volume I* (Detroit: Henry Ford Museum & Greenfield Village, 1990), 416–419.
19. Anne Donnellon, *Team Talk: The Power of Language in Team Dynamics* (Boston: Harvard Business School Press, 1996), 26–38.
20. Mauboussin, "Embracing Complexity," 90.
21. Donnellon, *Team Talk*.
22. Gelb and Caldicott, *Innovate Like Edison*, 42.
23. Donnellon, *Team Talk*.
24. Gary Hamel, *The Future of Management* (Boston: Harvard Business School Press, 2007), 87.
25. Hamel, "Management," 97–100.
26. Anat Lechner, "Better Teamwork through Better Workplace Design," *Harvard Business Review*, accessed April 2012, http://blogs.hbr.org/cs/2012/04/better_teamwork_through_office.html.
27. "Brandman University Research Study Shows Companies Can Better Embrace Virtual Work Force as a Competitive Advantage," Brandman University, accessed June 2011, www.brandman.edu/pressreleases/Pages/pressdetails.axp?PressName=05321.
28. Rishad Tobaccowala, "Analog Feelings from a Carbon Form in a Digital World of Silicon Objects," Posterous.com, accessed January 2012, http://rishadt.posterous.com.
29. Mark Mortensen and Michael O'Leary, "Managing a Virtual Team," *Harvard Business Review*, accessed April 2012, http://blogs.hbr.org/cs/2012/04/how_to_manage_a_virtual_team.html.
30. Jason Sherman, (president, SHERMAN Communications and Marketing) interview by Sarah Miller Caldicott, Oak Park, IL, March 12, 2012.

31. Lynda Gratton and Tamara J. Erickson, "Eight Ways to Build Collaborative Teams," *Harvard Business Review* (November 2007): 36.
32. Larry Keeley (CEO, Doblin Group), interview by Sarah Miller Caldicott, Chicago, IL, February 28, 2012.
33. Keeley, interview.
34. Art Fry (3M fellow, inventor and technical scientist), interview by Sarah Miller Caldicott, March 14, 2012.

## CHAPTER 4   PHASE 2

1. "Tinfoil Phonograph," The Thomas Edison Papers, last updated 2/29/2012, Edison.rutgers.edu/tinfoil.htm.
2. Peter M. Senge, *The Fifth Discipline: The Art and Practice of the Learning Organization* (New York: Doubleday, 1990), 174–175.
3. Don Tapscott and Anthony D. Williams, *Wikinomics: How Mass Collaboration Changes Everything* (New York: Penguin, 2006), 55–56.
4. Senge, *Fifth Discipline*, 174.
5. Paul Israel, *Edison: A Life of Invention* (New York: John Wiley & Sons, Inc., 1998), 294.
6. Herminia Ibarra and Morten T. Hansen, "Are You a Collaborative Leader?" *Harvard Business Review* ( July–August 2011): 71.
7. Steven Johnson, *Where Good Ideas Come From: The Natural History of Innovation* (New York: Riverhead Books, 2010), 109–119.
8. Chuck Peters (CEO, The Gazette Company), interview by Sarah Miller Caldicott, Cedar Rapids, IA, February 21, 2012.
9. Malcolm Gladwell, *The Tipping Point: How Little Things Can Make a Big Difference* (New York: Little, Brown and Company, 2000), 141.
10. Senge, *Fifth Discipline*, 192.
11. Israel, *Edison: A Life of Invention*, 292–294.
12. Johnson, *Where Good Ideas Come From*, 61.

13. "Professor Robert Langer," Massachusetts Institute of Technology Department of Chemical Engineering, last updated July 12, 2012, http://web.mit.edu/langerlab/langer.html.

14. Dr. Robert Langer, (David H. Koch Institute Professor at MIT), interview with Sarah Miller Caldicott, June 29, 2006.

15. Johnson, *Where Good Ideas Come From*, 60.

16. Ted Grabau, (vice president for global technology, Emerson), interview with Sarah Miller Caldicott, March 5, 2012.

17. Dr. Curt Carlson (president, Stanford Research Institute), interview by Sarah Miller Caldicott, Mountain View, CA, October 10, 2010.

18. Larry Keeley (CEO, Doblin Group), interview by Sarah Miller Caldicott, Chicago, IL, February 28, 2012.

19. John Copenhaver, (director of disaster response and recovery services, WorleyParsons) interview with Sarah Miller Caldicott, February 28, 2012.

20. Copenhaver, February 2012.

21. Paul Israel and Robert Friedel, *Edison's Electric Light: Biography of an Invention* (New Brunswick: Rutgers University Press, 1986), 8.

22. Jonah Lehrer, "How to Be Creative," *Wall Street Journal*, accessed March 2012, http://online.wsj.com/article/SB1000 1424052970203370604577265632205015846.html.

23. "Worldwide Sales of Toyota Motor Hybrids Top 4M Units; Prius Family Accounts for Almost 72%," Green Car Congress, www.greencarcongress.com/2012/05/tmc-20120522.html.

24. Gary Hamel, *The Future of Management* (Boston: Harvard Business School Press, 2007), 90–96.

25. Gary Hamel, "Innovation Democracy: W.L. Gore's Original Management Model," Management Innovation Exchange, accessed May 2012, www.managementexchange.com/story/innovation-democracy-wl-gores-original-management-model.

26. Craig Wortmann, "The Power of Stories" (lecture, University of Chicago Booth School of Business, Chicago, IL, May 25, 2011).

27. "Northwestern Engineering," McCormick Northwestern Engineering, accessed April 2012, www.mccormick .northwestern.edu/about/facilities/ford_center.html.

28. Kevin Bennet (Chairman of the Division of Engineering, Mayo Clinic), interview by Sarah Miller Caldicott, Rochester, MN, January 4, 2012.

29. Brandon Schauer, "Interview with Tim Brown, CEO of IDEO," Adaptive Path, accessed May 2012, www.adaptivepath .com/ideas/e000700.

30. Dr. Ashokokumar M. Patel (Critical Care Medicine, Mayo School of Graduate Medical Education, Mayo Clinic), interview by Sarah Miller Caldicott, May 10, 2012.

31. Anat Lechner, "Better Teamwork through Better Workplace Design," *Harvard Business Review*, accessed April 2012, http:// blogs.hbr.org/cs/2012/04/better_teamwork_through_office .html.

32. Mark Adams, David Goodman, David Kelley, and Stephen Swicegood, "How the Workplace Can Improve Collaboration," Steelcase Workspace Futures, accessed May 2012, www.steelcase.com/en/products/category/integrated/collaborative/room-wizard/documents/threesixty%20 collaboration%20white%20paper%20v2.6.pdf.

33. Lechner, "Better Teamwork."

34. Greg Cox, "Engaging Your Workforce: Engaging People in Challenging Times" (lecture, Palmer House Hilton, Chicago, IL, May 20, 2011).

35. Michiko Kakutani, "How to Cultivate Eureka Moments," review of *Imagine: How Creativity Works*, by Jonah Lehrer, *New York Times*, April 2, 2012.

36. Scott Doorley and Scott Witthoft, *Make Space: How to Set the Stage for Creative Collaboration*. With a foreword by David Kelley (New York: Wiley, 2012).

37. Anthony Gyursanszky (vice president of innovation, Microsoft Finland), interview by Sarah Miller Caldicott, March 20, 2012.

38. Stan Schroeder, "Steve Jobs, Mark Zuckerberg on Greatest Innovators List," Mashable, accessed January 2012, http://mashable.com/2012/01/27/steve-jobs-mark-zuckerberg-innovators/.

## CHAPTER 5   PHASE 3

1. David Bohm, *On Dialogue*. Edited by Lee Nichol (New York: Routledge Classics, 2004), 30.
2. "Shackleton, Sir Ernest, 1874–1922," Cool Antarctica, accessed March 2012, www.coolantarctica.com/Antarctica%20fact%20file/History/Ernest%20Shackleton_Trans-Antarctic_expedition2.htm.
3. Frank Lewis Dyer and Thomas Commerford Martin, *Edison: His Life and Inventions*, (Project Gutenberg Etext, February 1997), 254.
4. Greg Cox (president and chief operating officer, Dale Carnegie —Chicago), interview by Sarah Miller Caldicott, Chicago, IL, March 23, 2012.
5. Claudio Fernandez-Araoz, Boris Groysberg and Nitin Nohria, "How to Hang On to Your High Potentials," *Harvard Business Review* (October 2011): 80–81.
6. James Ziganto (former corporate vice president of human resources, Carlex Glass, America), interview by Sarah Miller Caldicott, March 8, 2012.
7. Ricardo Semler, *The Seven-Day Weekend: Changing the Way Work Works* (New York: Penguin, 2003, 2004) 42.
8. Semler, *Seven-Day Weekend*.
9. Larry Keeley (CEO, Doblin Group), interview by Sarah Miller Caldicott, Chicago, IL, February 28, 2012.
10. Cox, interview.
11. Margaret J. Wheatley and Myron Kellner-Rogers, *A Simpler Way* (San Francisco: Berrett-Koehler, 1996), 53.
12. Robert W. Schmidt (CEO, Systems Engineering & Manufacturing, Inc.), interview by Sarah Miller Caldicott, Phoenix, AZ, March 2, 2012.

13. Steven Johnson, *Where Good Ideas Come From: The Natural History of Innovation* (New York: Riverhead Books, 2010), 142.

14. Saj-nicole A. Joni and Damon Beyer, "How to Pick a Good Fight," *Harvard Business Review* (December 2009): 48–57.

15. Peter M. Senge, *The Fifth Discipline: The Art and Practice of the Learning Organization* (New York: Doubleday, 1990), 237.

16. Michael J. Gelb and Sarah Miller Caldicott, *Innovate Like Edison: The Five-Step System for Breakthrough Business Success* (New York: Penguin, 2007), 157.

17. Senge, *Fifth Discipline*, 255–256.

18. Erin Meyer, "Managing Confrontation in Multicultural Teams," *Harvard Business Review*, accessed April 2012, http://blogs.hbr.org/cs/2012/04/how_to_manage_confrontation_in.html.

19. Adam Bryant, "The Memo List: Where Everyone Has an Opinion," *New York Times*, accessed May 2012, http://www.nytimes.com/2012/03/11/business/jim-whitehurst-of-red-hat-on-merits-of-an-open-culture.html?_r=2.

20. Verne Harnish (author, *Mastering the Rockefeller Habits*), interview by Sarah Miller Caldicott, March 22, 2012.

21. Jeremy Hsu, "Thomas Edison's Greatest Invention: Innovation Itself?" *Innovation News Daily*, accessed April 2012, http://huffingtonpost.com/2012/04/07/Thomas-edison-inventions-innovation-rivalry_n_1409957.html.

22. Anne Donnellon, *Team Talk: The Power of Language in Team Dynamics* (Boston: Harvard Business School Press, 1996) 34.

23. Jay Scherer (managing partner, BPI Group North America), interview by Sarah Miller Caldicott, Chicago, IL, February 29, 2012.

24. Teresa M. Amabile and Steven J. Kramer, "Start the New Year with Progress," *Harvard Business Review*, accessed January 2012, http://blogs.hbr.org/hbsfaculty/2011/12/start-the-new-year-with-progre.html.

25. Teresa M. Amabile and Steven J. Kramer, "The Power of Small Wins," *Harvard Business Review*, accessed May 2012, http://hbr.org/2011/05/the-power-of-small-wins/ar/1.

26. Francis Upton, letter of April 27, 1879. Paul B. Israel, Louis Carlat, David Hochfelder, and Keith A. Nier, editors, *The Papers of Thomas A. Edison* vol. 5, *Research to Development at Menlo Park* (Baltimore: The Johns Hopkins University Press, 2004), 187.

27. Amabile and Kramer, "Start the New Year with Progress."

28. Bohm, *On Dialogue*, 33.

29. Ziganto, interview.

30. Rishad Tobaccowala (vice president of innovation, VivaKi), interview by Sarah Miller Caldicott, Chicago, IL, March 21, 2012.

31. "Awards and Recognition," Whirlpool Corporation, accessed May 2012, www.whirlpoolcorp.com/about/awards_recognition.aspx.

32. Moises Norena (global director of innovation, Whirlpool), interview by Sarah Miller Caldicott, March 14, 2012.

33. Norena, interview.

34. "P&G Adapts R&D Model," warc.com, accessed February 2012, www.warc.com/LatestNews/News/PG_adapts_RD_model.news?ID=29389.

35. Braden Kelley, "Harnessing the Global Talent Pool to Accelerate Innovation" (paper prepared for InnoCentive, February 15, 2012), 9.

## CHAPTER 6   PHASE 4

1. Harun Asad (former chief strategy and innovation officer, Lodestar), interview by Sarah Miller Caldicott, April 16, 2012.

2. Verne Harnish (author, *Mastering the Rockefeller Habits*), interview by Sarah Miller Caldicott, March 22, 2012.

3. William J. Amelio, "Beyond Outsourcing to Worldsourcing," businessweek.com, accessed January 2010, http://www.businessweek.com/stories/2008-05-30/beyond-outsourcing-to-worldsourcingbusinessweek-business-news-stock-market-and-financial-advice.

4. Dr. Paul Israel (director and general editor of *The Thomas A. Edison Papers*, Rutgers University), interview by Sarah Miller Caldicott, New Brunswick, NJ, March 5, 2012.

5. Gokce Sargut and Rita Gunther McGrath, "Learning to Live with Complexity," *Harvard Business Review* (September 2011): 70.

6. Dr. Jean Egmon (executive director, Ford Center for Global Citizenship at Northwestern University and past director, Complexity in Action Network), interview by Sarah Miller Caldicott, Chicago, IL, March 13, 2012.

7. Yves Morieux, "Smart Rules: Six Ways to Get People to Solve Problems Without You," *Harvard Business Review* (September 2011): 80.

8. Emilie Doolittle, "How Fortune 100 Companies Are Flattening Hierarchies through Enterprise Social," accessed April 2012, www.tibbr.com/blog/topics/enterprise-2-0/why-are-leading-organizations-turning-to-a-flatter-organizational-hierarchy/.

9. Chris Zook, "Desperately Seeking Simplicity," *Harvard Business Review*, accessed March 2012, http://blogs.hbr.org/cs/2012/02/desperately_seeking_simplicity.html.

10. Thomas E. Jeffrey, *From Phonographs to U-Boats: Edison and His Insomnia Squad in Peace and War, 1911–1919* (New Jersey: The Thomas A. Edison Papers at Rutgers, The State University, endorsed by National Historical Publications and Records Commission, 2008), 67.

11. Tom Barwin (former village manager, Oak Park, Illinois), interview by Sarah Miller Caldicott, Oak Park, IL, March 15, 2012.

12. Leslie Kwoh, "You Call That Innovation?" *Wall Street Journal*, accessed May 2012, http://online.wsj.com/article/SB10001424052702304791704577418250902309914.html.

13. John H. Zenger, Joseph R. Folkman, and Scott K. Edinger, "Making Yourself Indispensable," *Harvard Business Review* (October 2011): 84–92.

14. Zenger, Folkman, and Edinger, "Indispensable," 87.

15. Yves Morieux, "Smart Rules: Six Ways to Get People to Solve Problems without You," *Harvard Business Review* (September 2011): 83.
16. Israel, interview.
17. Gary Hamel, *The Future of Management* (Boston: Harvard Business School Press, 2007), 152.
18. Sargut and McGrath, "Learning to Live with Complexity," 72.
19. Harun Asad, "The Role of Social Media in Innovation Strategy," SAP Community Network, accessed April 2012, http://scn.sap.com/people/harun.asad/blog.
20. Pia Erkinheimo and Karoliina Harjanne, "Idea Crowdsourcing at Nokia—12 Months Wiser" (paper published in Service Innovation Year Book 2012 by European Commission, DG Information Society and Media, Open Innovation Strategy and Policy Group, Q1, 2012).
21. Richard Guha (president of North America, Synerscope), interview by Sarah Miller Caldicott, June 16, 2012.
22. Carol Phillips (founder of market research consultancy, Brand Amplitude), interview by Sarah Miller Caldicott, Chicago, IL, April 16, 2012.
23. Maria Thompson (director of innovation strategy, Motorola Solutions), interview by Sarah Miller Caldicott, Chicago, IL, June 8, 2012.
24. Matthew Greeley (CEO and cofounder, Brightidea), interview by Sarah Miller Caldicott, April 13, 2012.
25. Rishad Tobaccowala (vice president of innovation, VivaKi), interview by Sarah Miller Caldicott, Chicago, IL, March 21, 2012.
26. Bryce G. Hoffman, "Inside Ford's Fight to Avoid Disaster," *Wall Street Journal*, accessed April 2012, http://online.wsj.com/article/SB10001424052970204781804577269410217101038.html.
27. Larry Keeley (CEO, Doblin Group), interview by Sarah Miller Caldicott, Chicago, IL, February 28, 2012.
28. Egmon, interview.

29. Robert Lowe (CEO, Wellspring Worldwide), interview by Sarah Miller Caldicott, Oak Park, IL, April 3, 2012.
30. Tobaccowala, interview.
31. Craig Wortmann, "The Power of Stories" (lecture, University of Chicago Booth School of Business, Chicago, IL, May 25, 2011).

# CHAPTER 7  TRUE COLLABORATION

1. Daniel Kahneman, *Thinking, Fast and Slow* (New York: Farrar, Straus and Giroux, 2011), 35.

# About the Author

A great-grandniece of Thomas Edison, Sarah Miller Caldicott has been engaged in creativity and innovation throughout her life. Inspired by a family lineage of inventors dating back five generations, Sarah spent the first 15 years of her 25-year career developing and managing new brands as an executive with Quaker Oats and the Helene Curtis subsidiary of Unilever. As a leader of global innovation teams, Sarah was responsible for revitalizing major brands in the US, Europe, and Asia.

Concerned that America now risks losing its edge as the Innovation Age accelerates, Sarah has spent years researching Edison's innovation methods with experts at Rutgers University. She coauthored the first book ever written on the subject of Edison's world-changing innovation process, entitled *Innovate Like Edison*, which has been translated into five languages and serves as a textbook in leading educational institutions. A selected presenter for the popular TEDx series, Sarah's thoughts on the kinds of projects Edison would be undertaking in the twenty-first century were recently captured in her e-book, *Inventing the Future: What Would Thomas Edison Be Doing Today?*

An award-winning innovation speaker, consultant, and author, Sarah advises leaders all over the world on how they can employ Edison's timeless Five Competencies of Innovation to drive growth in the global economy. Sarah and her work have been featured in the *New York Times*, *Forbes*, *Fortune Small Business*, *USA Today*, and *FastCompany*. Sarah has also appeared as an innovation expert on PBS television, CNBC, the Fox Business Network, and NPR. She is president of her own Chicago-based consultancy, The Power Patterns of Innovation, offering expert training and guidance on how to build innovation and collaboration capabilities in organizations of all sizes. Her clients have included Intel, John Deere, Emerson, the Mayo Clinic, and Microsoft among many others.

Sarah remains dedicated to translating Edison's world-changing methods for application in the digital era, offering executives at every level powerful new approaches for igniting and accelerating the innovation process.

Sarah holds a BA from Wellesley College, and an MBA from the Amos Tuck School of Business at Dartmouth. She resides in Chicago and has four boys.

Sarah can be reached via e-mail at info@powerpatterns .com, or at www.sarahcaldicott.com.

# Index

# INDEX

# INDEX

# INDEX

# INDEX

# INDEX

# INDEX

Unreasonable hypotheses, 121,
127–131, 134, 135, 146, 147,
219, 241
Upton, Francis, 166, 183

Value creation continuum
digital technologies and, 43–45
diversity of teams and, 63
employees, connecting to, 36, 37
true collaboration and, 11, 18, 19,
37, 38
Value exchange, 189, 190
Verizon, 172
Video and audio files, 247, 248
Village of Oak Park, 25, 208
Virtual listening, 226
Virtual teams
collaboration platforms, 229–232
communication issues and defensive
routines, 172, 173
distance, impact of, 4
external partners and, 184
face-to-face interaction, 86, 87
Group meld, 119, 120. *See also*
Group meld
leadership challenges, 164
narrative prototypes, use of,
139, 140
shared purpose, 87
use of, 4, 86–89
written documentation, importance
of, 242, 243
Visible Technologies, 227
VivaKi, 2, 34, 86, 186, 230, 242

W. L. Gore, 85, 132, 133
Wallace, William, 127, 128, 148
Wellspring Worldwide, 239, 240
West Orange laboratory
Black Maria (movie studio),
136, 137
chemical lab, 66, 165
collaboration at, 46, 47
collegiality at, 83, 84

context of projects, 96. *See also*
Context (Phase 2)
Edison with West Orange
phonograph team, *167*
Edison with West Orange team, *47*
establishment of, 14
ethnic and gender diversity of
workers, 69, 70
functions of, 14, 15
leadership at, 165, 166
library at, 15, 106, 107
lock-ins, 49
prototyping at, 15
small teams, use of, 72–75
team dialogue at, 122, 123
women employed at, 70
work space, 143
Westinghouse, George, 178
Wheatley, Margaret, 119, 165,
166, 168
*Where Good Ideas Come From* (Johnson),
58, 109, 116, 1225
Whirlpool Corporation, 187–189
Whitehurst, Jim, 174
*A Whole New Mind* (Pink), 243
Wilson, James Q., 111
Wisewindow.com, 226
Witthoft, Scott, 144
Women, employed by Edison, 70
Woolley, Anita, 70
Wordle.net, 244
World Economic Forum (WEF)
(2012), 52
WorleyParsons, 125
Wormholes, 91
Wortmann, Craig, 135, 136, 247

Yahoo!, 75, 76
YouTube, 42, 224

Zenger, John, 210, 212
Ziganto, Jim, 162, 163, 185, 186
Zook, Chris, 206
Zuckerberg, Mark, 41, 75, 76, 207